Working Knowledge

Working Knowledge

Work-Based Learning and Education Reform

Thomas R. Bailey
Katherine L. Hughes
David Thornton Moore

Routledge
Taylor & Francis Group

NEW YORK AND LONDON

Published in 2004 by
Routledge
270 Madison Ave,
New York NY 10016
www.routledge-ny.com

Published in Great Britain by
Routledge
2 Park Square, Milton Park,
Abingdon, Oxon, OX14 4RN
www.routledge.co.uk

Routledge is an imprint of the Taylor and Francis Group.

Transferred to Digital Printing 2009

Library of Congress Cataloging-In-Publication Data is available on file.

ISBN 0-415-94565-8 (hbk.)
ISBN 0-415-94566-6 (pbk)

Publisher's Note
The publisher has gone to great lengths to ensure the quality of this reprint but points out that some imperfections in the original may be apparent.

Contents

Acknowledgments

This book has been 20 years in the making. David Moore was the first of the three of us to conduct research on this topic. From 1978 to 1981, with funding from the National Institute of Education, he studied high school interns in 25 workplaces. In that research he began to develop the theoretical framework that we have used in this book. We also used some of the examples that he described in that project in our own discussions about the issues around work-based learning. Margaret Tipper, the chief research assistant in the original study, not only kept that work going logistically but contributed important ideas about the curriculum of experience.

Tom Bailey and Kathy Hughes were inspired initially by Stephen Hamilton's influential book *Apprenticeship for Adulthood* (1990), which argued for the educational benefits of the German apprenticeship system, including the work-based component, and offered a possible model for education reform in the U.S. But reading that book raised three questions: First, would it be possible to recruit enough employers to provide internships for a large enough number of students to make work-based learning a significant educational strategy? Second, what was the theoretical basis of the claimed educational benefits of work-based learning? And third, even though educators had much to say about pedagogy in the classroom, there was no developed on-the-job pedagogy. This book addresses those issues.

Our research went through many stages before its culmination. We began with a small project on apprenticeships for the Manpower Demonstration Research Corporation (MDRC). Rob Ivry provided important help on that project. We also explored the problem of employer recruitment in a conference organized by Tom Bailey for the Brookings Institute and funded by the German Marshall Fund. Henry Aaron of Brookings and Jeff King, then of the Fund, were both helpful in bringing that conference about. Margaret Vickers, David Stern, Robert Poczik, and Paul Osterman contributed papers for that conference and many of their insights influenced our thinking. In 1995 the National Center for Research in Vocational Education (NCRVE) funded a survey of employers participating in internship programs and a sample of comparison nonparticipating employers. That research was the basis for Chapter 4. During the course of that work, we had extensive conversations with David Stern and Cathy Stasz. The reader will see that we also made liberal use of conclusions and examples from Stasz's published research on work-based learning.

Also in 1995, the Institute on Education and the Economy received a grant from the Pew Charitable Trusts to continue our research through case studies of programs that included internships and through the observation and shadowing of interns on the job. This was the largest and most important grant among all of the sources of funds for this project. The data collected from these case studies and particularly the observations of interns form the foundation of the empirical work presented in Chapters 5–10 in this book and the basis for our most important contributions. Michael Timpane, President of Teachers College at the time, was helpful in securing the grant. Robert Schwartz, then at Pew, helped get the project started and Janet Kroll, also at Pew, worked with us later during the grant. Both made valuable substantive inputs. In 1997, we received a grant from the DeWitt Wallace–Reader's Digest Fund to do some supplemental analysis of the hypothesis that internships reinforce academic learning, which is the subject of Chapter 5 of this book. Our program officer there, Peter Kleinbard, provided important advice and support for our work on that topic.

Our thinking on work-based learning was also shaped by a faculty seminar that we organized at Teachers College during the 1997–98 school year. Participants in the faculty seminar, all of whom were very helpful to us, included Jo Anne Kleifgen, Henry Levin, Victoria Marsick, Terry Orr, Dolores Perin, Clifford Hill, Lisa Petrides, and Eric Larsen, all of Teachers College; as well as Cathy Farrell of LaGuardia Community College, Susan Poglinco of the Manpower Demonstration Research Corporation, and Janet Kroll of Pew. John Broughton participated in the seminar and also provided us with extensive background in psychological theory. Other colleagues and friends who have provided guidance and advice include Stephen Hamilton, Kevin Hollenbeck, Doug Magnuson, Gary Hesser, and Erwin Flaxman. John Wirt participated in some fieldwork and contributed to our exploration and analysis of the theoretical underpinnings of work-based learning. We want to thank all of these individuals for their insights and assistance.

We also taught a class on work-based learning in the fall of 1998. The discussion with the students in that class gave us a fresh perspective on these issues. Those students included Susan Arcamonte, Maria Barcellos, Erkanda Bujari, Charles Ogundimu, Heather Johnson, Jennifer Jones, Marie Keem, Chuchuang Lai, Doug Lynch, Nicole Marshall, Christine Rivera, Christopher Shamburg, and Jackson Wilson.

Throughout this process, we have benefited from the enthusiastic and very capable research assistance provided by many of our graduate students. These include Donna Merritt, Lea Williams, Tavis Barr, Briana Cons, and Latoya Conner. Susan Wieler, formerly a senior researcher at IEE, participated in the fieldwork at programs, and Annette Bernhardt, also a former senior researcher, helped us with the quantitative analysis presented in Chapter 4.

Lisa Rothman expertly managed the grants and demanding administrative tasks associated with this project. Many IEE staff members also helped with administrative and clerical tasks, including Kathleen Keane, Tia Dole, Jen D'Alvia, Gretchen Koball, Melinda Mechur Karp, Shana Ashwood, and Annika Fasnacht.

We are grateful to the members of our families, Carmenza Gallo, Erika and Daniela Bailey, Jeff Honea, and Sandy and Katie Moore, who endured not only our lengthy preoccupation with this subject, but also the extensive travel required to carry out the fieldwork.

We are extremely indebted to the staffs of the programs that we studied. They patiently hosted our visits, answered our questions, gave us available data, and provided lists of employer participants. They also facilitated our student observations and shadowing. We would particularly like to thank Gina Lord, Virginia Detrick, Stu Weiss, Mark Tropia, Pat Leaveck, Irv Cumming, Larry Nelson, Harry Heinemann, Charlene O'Neill, Helen Niedermeier, Bonnie Silvers, Kristy Nguyen, Mary Jane Clancy, and Kathleen Foster. We also thank the many employers who responded to our surveys, and particularly the employers who allowed us into their workplaces to shadow the interns.

Finally, we owe our greatest debt to the students who allowed us to spend many hours observing them at and talking to them about their internships. The information that we collected from them has formed the foundation of this book. It is primarily through their cooperation that we have been able to make a contribution to the understanding of the educational value of work-based learning. So it is to them that we dedicate the book.

CHAPTER **1**

Work-Based Learning and Education Reform

During the 1990s, the United States economy enjoyed an unprecedented period of growth and low unemployment. Although the economy began to cool off at the turn of the century, even during the height of the boom, large sections of the nation's educational system remained in deep trouble. Increasingly, young people without some post-secondary education could not expect to earn enough money to support a family; yet large numbers of people still failed to finish high school, and another third who earned their high school degree did not acquire any additional education (U.S. Department of Education, 2000a). Moreover, many high school graduates did not have high school level skills—hundreds of thousands of students entering post-secondary schools had to take remedial instruction to prepare them for college-level work (U.S. Department of Education, 1999). Beyond these well-known problems, researchers found that most high school students were not engaged in their schooling and made an effort only so that they could get into college (Johnson, Farkas, & Bers, 1997). Learning was often far down their list of priorities. Yet almost all students who finish high school can gain access to some post-secondary institution. Therefore, many students do not see strong incentives for working hard in high school (Rosenbaum, 1997).

As these problems persisted throughout the 1990s, reformers increasingly called for higher expectations and more stringent standards for high school graduation and even promotion from grade to grade. High school students' participation in occupationally specific courses dropped 14 percent between 1982 and 1994 (U.S. Department of Education, 2000b). On

1

average, high school students earned 4.7 vocational credits in 1982; by 1994, that number had dropped to 4.0. At the same time, however, academic course-taking increased by 23 percent. In some states, examinations that had previously been taken only by the minority of students headed for four-year colleges were made the standard for high school graduation. Increasingly, the success of elementary and secondary education systems was judged on the basis of the performance of their students on tests of academic achievement and on traditional measures such as college-going rates.

The emphasis on high standards leaves open the question of what approach educators will use to achieve those standards. Perhaps the most common response has been to stress and often require all students to take the types of academic courses traditionally used to prepare students for college. Although these are effective for many students, they fail to engage and motivate others. Moreover, even students who successfully negotiate the academic curriculum are often coasting.

Over the last 15 years, some education reformers have argued that integrating experiences outside of the school with classroom learning is an effective approach to engaging students in their studies and helping to prepare them for education and work after high school (Hamilton, 1990; Jobs for the Future, 1994). Often these experiences involve work in private- and public-sector organizations. Reformers make a variety of claims about the educational benefits of this type of work-based learning, and in many cases these have struck a responsive chord.

> Dressed in a clean shirt and tie, a young man named José sat at a desk in the first-floor housekeeping office of a nondescript hotel near a busy airport. As a summer intern from a travel and tourism academy in a big city, his job this morning was to answer phone calls from guests and staff, figure out what needed to be done, and delegate the work to the appropriate person. Room attendants called to report that they had finished cleaning rooms, and he entered the information into a computer. Guests notifed him that they needed towels, or soap, or a repairman; he sent someone out. At 9:20, the phone rang and he answered: "Good morning, housekeeping, this is José." Hanging up, he wrote a note on a pad just as the housekeeping assistant manager, Ruth, walked in and told him that the rooms on the 14th floor were checked out. He told her that an attendant on that floor wanted her to call back. The phone rang again: "Good morning, housekeeping, this is José . . . okay." He informed Ruth that Room 929 wanted matches; she told him they don't stock matches, and called the bell captain to see if he had any. Another guest called to ask whether they had special equipment for the disabled. Ruth said yes and instructed him to get the room number; he did, and said, "Someone will be there shortly." The phone rang again, José answered, and informed the assistant manager that the guest who wanted matches was "getting a little hostile." José bummed some matches from a visitor, and Ruth sent a houseman up to the room to deliver them. . . .

As the morning wore on, José kept answering the phones, handling the room attendant reports, and updating the duty list.

This book explores the potential for using work-based learning as part of a broad education reform strategy. It is our contention that work-based learning, if it is done well, can play an important role in strengthening the educational preparation of many young people. Although students can learn job-specific skills in internships or apprenticeships, these types of experiences can have broader academic and developmental benefits as well. Thus work-based learning can be a productive part of a secondary school education designed explicitly to prepare students for college.

Most adults realize the importance of learning outside of school. Much of what makes them effective, they learned on the job or in the community. And during the last decade, many education reformers have argued that learning in the workplace should be a much more significant part of the country's basic education system. One of the major educational initiatives of the Clinton administration envisioned a system of internships or other types of work-based learning for a greater number of high school students. Yet despite enthusiasm for the notion of work-based learning, reformers have had difficulty convincing teachers and parents that acquiring experiences in the workplace is an optimal use of educational resources and of students' time. As reformers in the 1990s worked on increasing the number of internships, they often found that it was easier to find employers willing to take interns than to find interns willing to fill those slots (Hughes, 1998).

Ironically, during the 1990s work-based learning was seen as an integral part of a new and innovative educational strategy, even though internships and apprenticeships have been around for centuries. Moreover, at the same time that some educators and parents see work-based learning as a serious threat to good education, it is accepted as a fundamental aspect of graduate training. And post-graduate education in the U.S. is considered the best in the world. Professionals with no experience (i.e., who have had no work-based learning), regardless of the perceived quality of their education, are not considered skilled workers (Bailey & Merritt, 1997). Indeed, professional education is moving to incorporate more formal work-based learning and more authentic experience earlier in the period of training. Medical training programs are now getting their students into clinical settings earlier and even law schools are questioning the wisdom of the traditional training that gives students no concrete idea about what they will be doing as lawyers. In any case, law students have traditionally understood the importance of summer internships in which they could actually get some experience.

Despite this increased commitment to work-based learning for higher levels of education, work-based learning at the secondary school level has remained a marginal academic strategy. Even vocational education, a program that would seem to be most likely to involve work-based learning, is primarily classroom-based. To be sure, several hundred thousand students every year enroll in cooperative education programs in which they earn credit for work supervised by their schools, but these students are, for the most part, headed directly to work after high school. Thus cooperative education is often associated with traditional vocational instruction for the "non-college bound." Formal apprenticeships also enroll a few hundred thousand students a year and there is a general perception that apprenticeships, especially in construction, produce highly skilled and effective workers. But these apprentices are often in their mid-20s and many are high school graduates. For the most part, formal apprenticeships are not part of a secondary-level education.

One could argue that in cooperative education, apprenticeships, and professional training, work-based learning is, in effect, a transition strategy for young people who have already chosen their occupational direction. Once someone has chosen to be a doctor or a carpenter, then it makes sense that they should get experience in the actual activities of their chosen profession—that they should be inducted into the "community of practice" associated with that profession (to use a term that has become popular in current discussions of education and learning on the job). The underlying (and usually unarticulated) logic of the current structure of secondary school education is that during the period of study before the young person has chosen a career goal, or at least in the early stages of preparation, students are better served by concentrating primarily on learning academic skills using school-based pedagogy.

Increasingly in the United States, secondary schools must prepare all students to enter at least a two-year college. Young people with no more than a high school degree have very restricted occupational options. Therefore, high school is no longer a place to prepare directly for work. If work-based learning is considered primarily a strategy to prepare students for imminent work, then it would seem to have at most a marginal role in high school. To some extent, an analogous situation is taking place in community colleges in which increasingly programs are expected to at least hold open the door to transfer to a four-year school, even for students who enter the program explicitly aiming at a two-year terminal degree (Morest, forthcoming).

Thus the controversy arises, not so much over the wisdom of work-based learning in the abstract, but rather over when it should take place within the overall trajectory of a young person's education. Most educators agree that work-based learning can be useful as a last educational step before a young person starts work in a particular occupation. But as the

1990s progressed, work-based learning advocates increasingly argued that the approach was not only a means of transition to work once an occupational direction had been chosen, but rather a strategy for exploring career possibilities and gaining the underlying foundation of knowledge and skills needed by everyone to prepare for adulthood.

> Maureen, an intern from a rural New England high school, worked as an assistant to the music teacher in a nearby central school. One morning, Maureen consulted with Mr. P, a substitute teacher, on the agenda for the day in his 5th- and 7th-grade class. Mr. P told Maureen what activities the regular teacher had planned, and asked her some questions about the normal classroom practices. She answered him with confidence. The class got underway a bit late, and the kids were a little restless. Maureen went to the side of the room and flicked the lights several times, getting the kids' attention. After taking attendance, the teacher informed the class that they would be doing practice and assessment exercises that day. He looked at Maureen to see how they should keep track of the students, and she told him they could write the kids' names on the board. Mr. P and Maureen then grabbed a pile of assessment forms and handed them out to students. For the next 35 minutes, they worked individually with students, watching them play songs of their choice and evaluating them on hand position, notes, rhythm, and tempo. At one point, Maureen knelt to a student's level and asked if he wanted to play a duet; he didn't know what that meant, and she explained, then played a short song with him. The boy smiled broadly. Maureen walked over to a girl who seemed to be struggling a bit with the rhythm and tempo of the music. She meticulously went over the notes with her, demonstrating the beat by clapping and explaining the rhythm. When another pupil played a selection correctly, Maureen smiled and said, "You did very well! You learned a lot today."

This book is about work-based learning as a basic educational strategy, especially for secondary school students (and to some extent for those in community colleges). We have five broad goals.

The first is to clarify questions surrounding work-based learning and to encourage practitioners, policymakers, and researchers to identify their views and objectives. There has been some controversy about work-based learning, based on a lack of clarity about its purposes. For example, if work-based learning can improve academic skills, then which academic skills are involved? Can work-based learning replace academic classes? If so, how many and which ones? Or should work-based learning be primarily about career exploration, or about general youth development? Advocates have not been clear about exactly what they expect to achieve with work-based learning, exactly what it is *for*, thus leaving skeptics and others confused.

Second, we want to make the arguments much more systematic and concrete. When work-based learning advocates have identified objectives, they have generally been vague about why they believed that the strategy would achieve those objectives. For example, what type of program design might deliver academic skills as opposed to career exploration? What specific experiences can improve academic skills? Unless those mechanisms are specified, it will be difficult to understand whether work-based learning is effective and to figure out what characteristics lead to effectiveness.

Third, we want to begin to subject the various claims about the benefits of work-based learning to more systematic theoretical and empirical scrutiny. We do this both by reviewing the theoretical and conceptual discussions of the topic, and also by examining work-based learning programs themselves and the experiences of dozens of young people participating in these programs.

Fourth, the book strives to develop a better understanding of what we call work-related pedagogy. This effort will be built on our understanding of the mechanisms through which learning takes place both on the job and in the classroom. We will provide some guidelines that can help program operators find or design high-quality work-based learning experiences, and then enhance students' learning from those experiences back in school.

Fifth, we also want to focus attention on the cost side of work-based learning. One unique aspect of work-based learning is that it incorporates the workplace into the core educational system. Even if in principle this is a good idea, it requires the cooperation of the employers. We want to understand the extent to which difficulties with recruiting employers will stand in the way of a broad-based, work-based learning system.

What Is Work-Based Learning?

Learning takes place in every workplace, as one saw from the earlier vignettes. This learning can be narrow and employer-specific, or general and applicable to many situations. Our focus is on work-based learning as a specific educational strategy for high school students. The goal of this strategy is to enhance the traditional objectives of schooling—teaching academic skills, preparing students for citizenship and work, and helping them to develop into mature and responsible members of society. Work-based learning comes in many forms.

Full-scale apprenticeships are the most ambitious. Much of the thinking about youth apprenticeship in the U.S. is based on knowledge about the German system, in which two- to four-year apprenticeships start at about age 16, and combine work and classroom instruction that is closely coordinated with the activities on the job (Hamilton, 1989). The U.S. does have about half a million registered apprentices, and the system enjoys a positive reputation, but these are usually older students, often high school graduates. As a result, the system is not looked to as a component of secondary school education reform.

Internships are usually a much less ambitious and much less well-defined form of work-based learning. Typically, students spend from a few weeks to many months in a position that may be paid or unpaid. The learning intensity and the links to school curricula vary widely. In some cases, positions are chosen to match the in-school curriculum; in some cases, the links are made through a seminar in school in which students discuss their experiences on the job; and in other cases, there is very little connection between the internship and schooling. Cooperative education placements, which involve several hundred thousand high school students, are a form of internship. Traditionally these have been for students in vocational education programs designed to place them in employment immediately after high school. Co-op programs have been the foundation of many of the recent work-based learning initiatives, with program operators trying to broaden their educational objectives (Urquiola et al., 1997).

A variety of other forms of experienced-based learning are also common and indeed have been popular for many years. These include service-learning; volunteer work; 4-H and other agricultural-oriented programs, such as Future Farmers of America; and a variety of clubs and extracurricular activities such as Vocational Industrial Clubs of America. Although these programs have loyal and enthusiastic supporters, for the most part they have not been incorporated into the work-based, learning-oriented, education-reform initiatives of the last 15 years. One exception to this may be service-learning. Schools are increasingly promoting community service to students and linking it to classroom activities, in the belief that such experiences can improve student education and personal development (Eyler & Giles, 1999; Kleiner & Chapman, 2000).

> In the basement of a major urban hospital, the physical therapy clinic occupied a large, open room lined with parallel bars, wheelchairs, and faux staircases. One Wednesday morning, Rob, a student in a medical careers academy, got out the equipment that would be needed for several patients waiting near the door. A therapist, B, finished getting an elderly man started, then joined Rob in helping a female patient walk up and down the hall using a walker. After one pass she took a break, and Rob went over to the bulletin board to arrange name labels on a chart that tracked the appointments and arrivals of the patients. B and Rob went back to the woman patient, who complained that she needed oxygen; they hooked her up to a tank and walked her up and down the hall again. D, the PT manager, instructed a therapist on the care plan for each patient, and Rob helped him out. He walked behind a frail patient as T, another therapist, guided her through the parallel bars, ready to catch her if she should fall. D directed B and Rob to walk a particular patient 50 feet and then come

back; she explained that there were distance markers on the ceiling. An elderly woman also waiting in the exit line announced that she had to go to the bathroom; she repeated the statement, but no staff responded. Rob went over and said he was sorry that transport was slow in picking her up—but he did not take her, believing it was not his place. Later, he admitted feeling uncomfortable about the woman's situation and the staff's lack of response.

According to a 1992 national survey of public secondary schools, almost 20 percent of such schools sponsor at least one school-based enterprise, another form of work-based learning (Stern, 1992). In school-based enterprises, groups of students, under the supervision of a teacher or adult adviser, organize and staff businesses or services within the school itself. (See Stern et al., 1994, for a book-length discussion of SBEs.) They may run a school store, provide printing and duplicating services, or make and sell garments. One advantage of a school-based enterprise is that the activities are under the complete control of the school itself. At the same time, there may be only limited scope for these activities and schools are often reluctant to compete with local businesses. Virtual enterprises eliminate the problem of competition with real businesses. There are currently over 50 virtual enterprises in the New York City high schools that buy and sell virtual products from one other.

The least ambitious and the easiest to implement form of work-based learning involves student visits to workplaces, though this category of activity also varies in intensity. In individual job shadowing, students follow and observe workers over a period of hours or even days. At its best, this gives young people a chance to learn what is involved with a particular job and to talk to experienced workers. Important mentoring relationships can also develop out of job shadowing. Group tours of workplaces are the most easily arranged form of student visits, yet they can only give students a superficial understanding of the nature of the work and requirements for the jobs.

Finally, in addition to school-based enterprise, educators have used a variety of strategies to simulate some of the characteristics of the workplace. An emphasis on open-ended group projects is one of the most common. Such projects can simulate features of work such as working with others, taking responsibility, and developing approaches to solving problems when there is no "correct" answer and when there are a variety of alternative strategies.

Therefore, what is referred to as work-based learning by education reformers is, in fact, a continuum of activities that vary along several dimensions. One important dimension concerns the control that the school has over the experience. The school has most control over project-based learning or school-based enterprise whereas it has least control over paid internships. Another dimension, which is related to the extent of control, concerns the difficulty of setting up a work-related experience. It is easier to set up a group visit to a workplace than to organize a two-year sequenced apprenticeship. Other important dimensions are the extent to which the experience is actually involved with the employer's production process; the investment of time for the student; the potential conflict or connection with school-based studies; the intensity and nature of the learning that takes place in the experience; the nature of the relationships that the student forms with other adults at the worksite; and the extent to which the placement provides the student with a realistic experience of what she would encounter if she were employed in these positions. In many cases, these different dimensions conflict with each other. For example, programs over which the school has most control and that are easiest to set up are less likely to provide the most realistic experience. In some jobs a realistic experience may not provide much of an opportunity to learn or reinforce academic skills being taught in school. And a more intense work-based experience is likely to create a greater potential conflict with time spent in the classroom or on homework. Thus program designers need to have a clear idea of exactly what they are trying to achieve when they organize a work-based learning program.

Even though much of what we have to say in this book is relevant to many of the types of work-based learning, we focus primarily on paid or unpaid internships, including cooperative education placements, that last from a few weeks to several months. We do not focus on the more ambitious and longer-term apprenticeships, as these are so difficult to organize and present such a potential for conflict with school-based learning that they are not a realistic option for broad-based education reform in the United States (Bailey, 1993). Project-based learning is a central component of a constructivist educational strategy and there is extensive literature on this approach (Thomas, 2000). There is already a major study of school-based enterprise (Stern et al., 1994). Worksite visits and job shadowing may have important benefits, but they are also easier to carry out; therefore the costs and benefits do not have to be weighed as carefully. On the other hand, organizing high-quality internships does take staff time and resources and requires the development of extensive relationships with employers. And internships potentially take time away from classroom instruction and homework. Given these costs and conflicts, reformers need to develop a clearer sense of what they hope to and what they can achieve from internships and similar forms of work-based learning. This is the objective around which this book is organized.

Work-Based Learning and Teenage Employment

National data show that nearly two-thirds of high school seniors work for pay (U.S. Department of Education, 2000c). What if anything distinguishes such work from the internships that are the subject of this book and what can we learn from the experiences of those students about the potential costs and benefits of work-based learning?

There is abundant, somewhat conflicting literature on the benefits and costs of working while in high school (see Mortimer & Finch, 1986; Shoenhals, Tienda, & Schneider, 1998; Stasz & Brewer, 1998; Stone & Mortimer, 1998). Some researchers have found a negative relationship between the number of hours worked during the school year and both high school and post-secondary school attainment measures (Marsh, 1991). Unfortunately, this research is not able to fully sort out the direction of causality—for example, whether students with lower GPAs tend to work more hours or whether the work lowers the grades. The observed effects may be spurious because they do not take into account pre-existing differences between students who work and those who do not (Shoenhals et al., 1998). In any case, few internships require long hours during weeks when school is open. And working during the summer, when many schools schedule internships, is not associated with the same negative effects (Marsh, 1991).

One consensus of the research seems to be that the nature and characteristics of the jobs do have an influence. Part-time work can be a very formative experience as employment represents a new social role for an adolescent. Thus the influence of a particular job on a youth likely depends on whether the experience is a good or bad one (cf. Stern & Briggs, 1999). One study finds that "the quality of the work (i.e., its stressful or rewarding character) is a more important determinant of adolescent psychological functioning than either work status or its intensity" (Finch et al., 1991, p. 606). Mortimer and Yamoor (1987) point out that the opportunity for self-direction in a work setting can have positive consequences for a worker's self-concept and interest in work.

These results do suggest some clear implications for the design of internships. Moreover, there has been some research that compares the characteristics of internships and of regular jobs that students find without the supervision of the school. This research finds that the negative relationship between hours worked and grade point average is less strong for high school students in co-op placements than students in nonschool-supervised jobs (Stern et al., 1997).

In addition, surveys of 1998 seniors who were attending schools participating in school-to-work partnerships[1] found that the workplace opportunities offered through the schools had important advantages over

---

[1]These data are from the Mathematica Policy Research national study of the implementation of the School-to-Work Opportunities Act. See Chapter 3 for more details. See also Stern et al., 1990.

the workplace activities students reported finding on their own. School-developed positions tended to be in a wider range of industries, and tended to more closely match students' career goals. Students with school-arranged paid jobs were more likely than other students to spend at least half their time in training on the job. The former type of students were also more likely to report discussing possible careers with adults at their workplace, and were more likely to receive a performance evaluation from school or employer staff. Students who had obtained positions through school more often reported using academic or technical skills learned in school at the workplace, and were more likely to draw on their work experience in school assignments or discussions, thus experiencing more substantive connections between their studies and work experience.

Several researchers have observed that youth perceive school and the workplace as conflicting, not complementary, and argue that more efforts should be made to integrate the two (Marsh, 1991; Stern & Briggs, 1999). Stern and Briggs suggest a stronger connection between school and work so that the two might reinforce rather than undermine each other (p. 1).

Policy and Legislation for Work-Based Learning

Work-based learning has had a long but varied history in the development of education in the United States over the last century. In 1917 the Smith-Hughes Act was passed, formalizing federal support for vocational education. Many educators supported this legislation at the time, as it was seen as a means both of meeting employers' need for skilled factory labor and of keeping working-class and immigrant youth in school because they would see its usefulness in preparing for specific jobs. However, other educators, such as John Dewey, spoke out against it, arguing that it would create a tracking system that would isolate and stigmatize immigrant and lower-class youth (Lazerson & Grubb, 1974). Thus, Dewey and others opposed vocational education as it was developed following the Smith-Hughes Act, although much of what Dewey wrote can be interpreted as being favorable to work-based learning. Indeed, the association of work-based learning with popular images of vocational education has often been the source of confusion and controversy regarding the educational value of work-based learning.

Work-based learning, primarily in the form of cooperative education and apprenticeships, remained a vital, but marginal component of American education during the middle 50 years of the century. Throughout these decades, work-based learning, as it was practiced, continued to be seen as a capstone educational experience designed to help students make the transition from school into the occupations in which they intended to work as adults. By the last quarter of the century, educators began to set broader goals for work-based learning. The influential report of the Coleman commission (1974) blamed schooling, in isolating young people from adults and from productive work, for actually retarding youth's transition to adulthood. The report called for placing young people into work situations earlier, to bring about "social maturity." Thus Coleman saw work as a tool for social development. Presumably, work would provide a valuable educational experience, even if the work took place in an occupation not related to the eventual employment. In his influential 1990 book, *Apprenticeship for Adulthood*, Stephen Hamilton further developed the notion that work-based learning had broader social and psychological benefits.

The 1990 reauthorization of the Perkins Vocational and Applied Technology Education Act (VATEA) emphasized academic as well as vocational skills, thus breaking down the divide between the two, in mandating their integration in secondary schooling. Although the implementation of the Act occurred primarily in traditional vocational terms, much of the discussion that accompanied the Act emphasized the potential to use occupational education as a vehicle to teach academic skills. Secondary vocational educators began to emphasize that many of their students went on to college. Indeed, Tech Prep, an important component of the VATEA, called for explicit articulation between high school and post-secondary occupational programs. Thus vocational education was experiencing a transformation from an emphasis on education *for* occupations to education *through* occupations, to use Dewey's phrase. This change was signaled by the 1995 publication of a two-volume collection of essays edited by Norton Grubb titled *Education Through Occupations*. These essays were based on research done over the previous 10 years by the National Center for Research in Vocational Education (NCRVE), which was funded by the U.S. Department of Education. The notion that vocational education could serve broad academic and developmental ends had moved into mainstream educational discourse, even if it had not reached mainstream education practice.

Yet the 1990 reauthorization of the Perkins Act did not particularly emphasize work-based learning. Work-based learning was much more prominent in the 1994 School-to-Work Opportunities Act (STWOA). This legislation emphasized many of the themes of Perkins—integration of academic and vocational education and Tech Prep, for example. Although the Act was associated in the public's mind with vocational education, the authors clearly saw it as a broader educational strategy in which pedagogies traditionally associated with vocational education and occupational themes would be used for general educational goals. Work-based learning played a central role. For example, the legislation supported "a planned program of job training and work experiences" (U.S. 103d Congress, 1994, Section 103) that would be coordinated with career awareness activities and academics in the classroom. A stated purpose was "to encourage the development and implementation of programs that will *require* paid high-quality, work-based learning experiences" (U.S. 103d Congress, Section 3, emphasis added).

In its origins in the 1980s, many advocates of the school-to-work strategy saw educational approaches with a strong work-based learning component as particularly important for students not headed for college. School-to-work was designed to help the "non-college bound" get good jobs after high school or perhaps after a year or two of post-secondary school. But during the 1990s, this rationale shifted. School-to-work became a strategy appropriate for "all" students, as the Department of Education said, as it is good preparation for career *and* college. From this perspective, work-based learning is not seen as primarily a capstone educational experience to help students move from school to work, but rather it is a foundation experience also meant to prepare students for additional education.

What accounted for the growth of interest in work-based learning and its subsequent transformation to a comprehensive educational strategy with broad academic and even psychological and developmental goals? After all, work-based learning had existed for decades in secondary schools and was an accepted part of graduate training. Even the education-*through*-occupations notion had been articulated by Dewey as early as 1917. Moreover, influential education reforms advocated by *A Nation at Risk* (National Commission on Excellence in Education, 1983) emphasized an increase in traditional academic courses for high school students, which would seem to suggest a de-emphasis on work-based learning.

Three trends accounted for the growing emphasis on work-based learning during the late 1980s and early 1990s. Two involved developments in research on learning and pedagogy—the growing popularity of "constructivist" pedagogy, and developments in cognitive psychology that emphasized the effectiveness of "learning in context." The third trend concerned the apparent economic strength during the 1980s of Germany and Japan relative to the United States.

Advocates of constructivism are critical of a pedagogic approach that involves the straightforward presentation of material by a teacher or expert to the student. In a contructivist approach, as we will explain in detail in Chapter 2, students are expected to be guided by their teacher in such a way that they "construct" their own knowledge. This is closer to the type of learning characteristic of apprenticeships, as opposed to the classroom lecture, and this at least opened the door for a more favorable view of work-based learning. Nevertheless, most advocates of constructivism visualize it as taking place in schools and indeed are often suspicious of education that seems to cater too much to the needs of the workplace, which presumably work-based learning does. Thus school-to-work advocates, while making use of constructivist theories and research, have never formed a strong alliance with the reform networks based on constructivist notions.

In the 1980s and 1990s, cognitive psychologists argued that students learned most effectively if they were taught skills in the context in which they would use those skills. This research (which we also review more fully later) draws attention to the importance of context and social interaction in learning. Learning that does not occur in contexts of interaction and is not practiced in different domains turns out to be "brittle" or to not "transfer" very well from one context to the next (Anderson, Reder, & Simon, 1996; Brown, Kane, & Long, 1989; Lave, 1988). Work-based learning advocates generally invoke contextual learning as a justification for their approach; indeed the school-to-work legislation stated that "many learn better and retain more when the students learn in context, rather than in the abstract" (U.S. 103d Congress, Title VIII, Section 2).

Thus, theories about constructivism and contextual learning created an environment favorable to work-based learning. Relative international economic trends seemed to provide evidence that education systems that emphasized work-based learning and that had strong ties to employers and the workplace were more effective at least at preparing the workforce. The School-to-Work Opportunities Act in particular was motivated by anxiety over the economic position of the United States with respect to other industrialized countries—especially Japan and Germany, the two countries that seemed at the time to be challenging U.S. economic predominance. Although the Japanese and German education systems had significant differences, both placed a great deal more emphasis on learning on the job and on close relationships between employers and schools. The economic performance of these countries and the stronger performance of their students, especially on math and science tests, seemed to suggest that the U.S. might benefit educationally and economically by strengthening the connections between school and work and by making better use of the workplace in the education of young people (Commission on the Skills of the American Workforce, 1990; Dertouzos et al., 1989). Moreover, these countries seemed to do particularly well at preparing their middle-level workforce—those workers who had graduated from secondary school and perhaps had some post-secondary education but did not have bachelor's degrees. Given this history, it is not surprising that the influence of the German apprenticeship system is clearly evident in the STWOA.

But seen from the beginning of the twenty-first century, much has changed in the circumstances that led up to the initial passage of the STWOA. Clearly the economic motivations that pushed the initial interest in emulating the German system have died down. The performance of neither the German nor the Japanese economies created compelling arguments to emulate their education systems. Indeed, European educational systems that have traditionally relied heavily on work-based learning were at least slowly moving away from those strategies (Vickers, 1995).

Thus the growth of interest in work-based learning grew out of a particular conjunction of pedagogic and economic developments. But the situation changed. Clearly the economic context has moved against the advocates of work-based learning. The pedagogic arguments still seem relevant, although it is fair to say that their application to work-based learning has been somewhat superficial. Most reports or policy statements that call for work-based learning invoke these pedagogic strategies without a systematic analysis of how and under what circumstance they might apply.

Employer Participation in Work-Based Learning

Whatever the pedagogic benefit of work-based learning, it will not spread if employers are not willing to provide internships and other work placements. Germany, like other European countries where work-based learning is widespread, has a culture of employer participation in education and workforce development. Some analysts have been skeptical that employer participation would be adequate for a widespread system of internships in the United States (Bailey, 1995; Osterman, 1995; Stern, 1995). Indeed, earlier drafts of the 1994 School-to-Work Opportunities Act had a larger role for employers and these were scaled back partly due to skepticism about employer participation. Although programs often use the schools themselves as work placements, assigning students to jobs in administrative offices or to help out in classrooms, in-school placements do not provide a sufficient basis for a broad program. Eventually, many employers will have to be willing to work closely with educators and to provide places for young people to work and learn. Yet employers have rather weak incentives for participation.

The question of employer participation needs to be addressed for two important reasons. First, recruiting employers may take a great deal of effort and resources, so at some point the cost of those required resources may outweigh the benefits the program may bring to the students. That is, the teachers and staff who work with the employers and monitor workplaces might spend their time more productively in developing in-school activities. Second, the willingness of employers to participate will influence the quality of the work-based learning experiences. Assuming that the educationally optimal work-based learning experience does not occur naturally, then employers would be called on to change their behavior in order to ensure quality experiences. But if they only participate reluctantly, educators will not be in a position to ask that they make the effort to create higher-quality experiences.

Outline of the Book

This book proceeds through several sections in order to describe and analyze the current state of the art in work-based learning. Following this chapter's review of the history of work-based learning and its place in the policymaking around school reform, we use Chapter 2 to establish the theoretical and empirical basis for the rest of the book. In the first section of the chapter we describe the four claims made by advocates about the benefits of work-based learning: that it reinforces and improves academic learning by participants; that it enhances students' work-related skills and their understanding of careers; that it advances their social and emotional development toward effective adulthood; and that it engages them in new modes of thought seldom found in schools. We then lay out a brief description of the learning theory on which our test of those claims is based. This step is important to our argument about work-based learning: Whether or to what extent each claim is warranted must be decided upon based on observations of actual students in actual programs. Grounded in a combination of ideas from pragmatism, symbolic interactionism, constructivist psychology, activity theory, and the notion of situated cognition, this theory argues that if you want to claim that a person is learning certain kinds of knowledge and skill, you must be able to *see* that person engaging that form of knowledge in situated practices in some setting— whether in a workplace or a school classroom.

This theoretical foundation provides the rationale for our research methodology, which we describe in the final stage of Chapter 2. Using a form of ethnographic inquiry, we observed 25 students in their internship sites and schools, interviewed them and their work supervisors and instructors, and collected artifacts from those settings. This method goes well beyond the questionnaires and other measures used in many other studies.

Chapter 3 starts by defining the extent of work-based learning nationwide and examining the characteristics of student participants in the strategy. Some of the material in the chapter is based on general sources, but much of the information comes from student surveys conducted to assess progress in achieving the objectives of the School-to-Work Opportunities Act. Although work-based learning certainly predates the legislation, the Act was a well-financed, high-profile, national effort to promote work-based learning, so an analysis of the spread of the approach through the

Act can give a good indication of its potential. The central conclusion of the chapter is that the form of work-based learning that grew most in the years following the passage of the Act was short-term job shadowing rather than more intensive activities such as internships. In addition, based on students' own descriptions of the internships and jobs that they obtained through their schools, there appears to have been little improvement in the educational quality of these experiences over the life of the legislation. Thus, despite the emphasis the Act placed on intensive work-based learning activities, schools did not succeed in either expanding the range or enhancing the quality of these activities substantially.

In Chapter 4, we begin to address the causes of that limit by exploring the participation of employers in providing work-based learning. This chapter is based on fieldwork in 12 different programs that emphasize work-based learning, as well as a telephone survey of 334 employers providing internships to 5 of the 12 programs. We also surveyed 323 nonparticipating employers located in the same labor markets as the participating employers. Our central conclusion is that employer participation is not the primary factor thwarting the growth of work-based learning. First, we were surprised to find that in the cities that we surveyed, already about one-quarter of the employers had provided or were providing some type of internship. Moreover, program operators did not see employer recruitment as their most important problem. To be sure, much of the motivation on the part of the employers was philanthropic, and some of our results suggest that a significant expansion of the number of employer participants would probably require convincing employers that they have something to gain out of participation. Nevertheless, we conclude that expansion is still possible; operators have not yet run into onerous barriers caused by reluctance on the part of employers to provide slots. To be sure, some of the programs that we visited have since closed, but in none of those cases was the problem a lack of cooperating employers.

At this point, reluctance on the part of parents and teachers is apparently a much more serious problem. Many of them are simply not convinced that work-based learning has an educational value that justifies in particular the time that students need to devote to their work-experience placements. This resistance leads to our analysis in the second section of the book, in which we examine arguments for the educational benefits of work-based learning.

Each of the next four chapters, then, examines one of the major claims about the benefits of work-based learning. To tip our hand in evaluating these claims, we present these claims in order from the most pessimistic to the most optimistic. Chapter 5 looks at the evidence that might support the claim that academic learning is reinforced and extended through work experience. Although there are some positive instances of this happening, we find the claim generally weak, especially if one insists that "academic reinforcement" leads to higher scores on standardized tests. Chapter 6 then addresses the question of whether students acquire new skills and learn more about careers through work-based learning. Evidence here is rather more supportive, as one might imagine—although the extent and quality of the learning may not be as great as some maintain.

In Chapter 7, we explore the possibility that young people undergo social and psychological development when they take part in work-based learning programs. After reviewing some of the literature of the youth-development movement, we look for evidence that interns often have the kinds of experiences through which development can happen: taking responsibility; being treated like adults; interacting with others in meaningful and productive ways. As we will show, a good deal of such opportunity is available to students in work-based learning programs. Chapter 8 looks at the modes of thought that interns participate in—the ways they are expected to define and solve problems, the resources they draw on in collaboration with co-workers, and the general strategies of thinking that they come to use—and find that there are many senses in which their thought processes go beyond what happens in school. These experiences might not improve students' scores on standardized tests, but they do build thinking skills that could make young people more effective not only in the workplace but in more advanced forms of schooling. That is, if we redefine the academic impact of work-based learning away from tests and measures and toward higher-order forms of thinking and learning, the claim might be more tenable. We do not have good evidence on this effect of work-based learning, but our observations raise some tantalizing possibilities.

Next, we turn to the issue of pedagogy: how students' experiences of work are organized in such a way as to maximize their learning. Chapter 9 looks at the pedagogical processes in the workplace itself, creating a framework for educators who need to understand how interns come to participate in various kinds of knowledge-use. Frequently, we discovered, naturally occurring processes make it possible for students to learn a great deal without the intervention of the school. This chapter seeks to provide the conceptual tools for educators to recognize when that happens, and when it does not.

Finally, Chapter 10 explores some of the principles and strategies of effective pedagogy in the classroom. Once the students return to school, we ask, how can teachers and counselors make the most of those experiences? We identify some of the practices used by experiential educators, and ask whether these practices manage to engage students in the kinds of thinking—and learning—that the program designers promise. These two chapters should be of practical use to educators and employers who want to strengthen the educational value of work-based learning placements.

Chapter 11 summarizes some of our findings and reiterates the core conclusions we reached during the study. It highlights the principles by which we believe effective work-based learning programs must be run, and argues that these benefits can accrue to all students, not just the non-college bound—but including them as well. When it is done right, this pedagogy shows great promise for engaging students in meaningful learning, connecting them to their communities and their future careers, and building their senses of themselves as intelligent, responsible, and effective adults.

CHAPTER 2

The Questions and the Approach

Why should students and teachers bother with work-based learning? It is difficult to organize; it requires the collaboration of sometimes reluctant employers, who are not trained educators; and it potentially takes time that could be devoted to classroom studies or homework. Advocates have several answers to this question: through work-based learning, academic skills are reinforced; students learn what it means to work in particular occupations and what they need to do to prepare themselves for those occupations; young people learn both specific and general skills that they will need on the job; and youth mature and develop psychologically. We add an argument of our own: Work-based learning develops what we refer to as "new modes of thought" in students. We explore each of these claims in Chapters 3–8. In each chapter, our strategy is first to clearly identify the implicit and explicit features of the arguments in favor of work-based learning, and then to test the claim against the data from our firsthand observations and interviews with participants in some programs.

In this chapter, we introduce these arguments briefly, identifying their sources and implications. Then we explain the learning theory on which arguments for work-based learning are based. Much of the discussion among educators and policymakers of work-based learning makes casual reference to theories about contextualized learning or situated cognition without detailed and concrete analyses about how these theories might relate to the realities of programs. The fundamental reason for our making our theoretical perspective clear is this: Any argument in favor of or against a claim about learning (whether in the workplace, in the classroom, or in the laboratory) has to be justified in terms of a theory of what learning is and how it occurs.

Our view of learning theory points toward such a justification, not only as a conceptual argument in favor of work-based learning but as a rationale for the particular methods that we used to examine work-based learning empirically. At the end of this chapter we describe our data and sampling and we discuss the methodology we used in constructing the analysis. And in the following chapters we will use our conception of learning theory to analyze our own claims and those of advocates.

The Claims

What are the major claims made for work-based learning by its advocates? What is the logic and the rhetoric of experiential education? In this section we briefly review four broad arguments.

Academic Reinforcement

One core claim is that work-based learning has a role in strengthening high school students' academic skills and preparing them for college. Work-based education advocates increasingly suggest that work-based learning can have this effect. For example, this is the argument outlined by Bailey and Merritt (1997a) in *School-to-Work for the College Bound*. Of course, the influence of work-based learning on academic skills depends very much on what one means by "academic skills." This term is generally accepted to mean the mastery of the basic subjects taught in school. In practice, this translates into being able to perform well in school and particularly on tests or assessments. Increasingly, high school students, teachers, and administrators are concerned with performance on standardized tests. This is important both for admissions to post-secondary institutions and for public assessments of the performance of schools; in many states, schools are ranked publicly (in the newspapers) by the scores of their students on these tests.

From this point of view, the relevant question for our research is whether work-based learning can improve the in-school performance of students, particularly on standardized tests. Education reformers perhaps do not realize how significant a change this is in the justification for work-based learning. In the 1980s, reformers looked to work-based learning because they believed that schools were not doing a good job preparing young people for *work*. The question that reformers are asking now is whether the workplace can do a better job than the school in preparing students to perform in *school*.

Thus, the first claim for work-based learning that we address is that participating students will come out with stronger academic skills, such as reading and writing, and will ultimately do better on standardized tests.

Skills and Careers

Perhaps the least controversial argument in favor of work-based learning is that students acquire various practical skills and that they learn about industries and career options. At face value, this assertion seems obvious, almost intuitively defensible, because stories about interns are replete with images of their performing specialized and skilled activities: the apprentice cabinetmaker assembles a chest of drawers (Moore, 1986); the museum intern gradually becomes an accomplished tour guide (Moore, 1986). These performances clearly reflect a capacity to use situated knowledge to accomplish important organizational purposes.

One focal point of this argument relates to the 1991 report of the Secretary's Commission on Achieving Necessary Skills, *What Work Requires of Schools.* The SCANS panel identified a range of skills, both technical and social, that high school graduates ought to master. Work-based learning advocates maintain that there is both theoretical and empirical support for the belief that their program achieves these goals. Lauren Resnick's influential article entitled "Learning in School and Out" (1987) argued that thinking practices in school settings contrast sharply with those in the everyday world, including workplaces. If that is the case, say the supporters, actual work experience is theoretically likely to enhance those work-related skills more than classroom-based learning. Moreover, researchers from Hamilton (1990) to Stasz and Kaganoff (1997) point to clear evidence that students do develop skills through these experiences.

Another goal, which was articulated in the School-to-Work Opportunities Act, was "to expose students to a broad array of career opportunities" (U.S. 103d Congress, Title VII, Section 3). Advocates maintain that work-based learning is a strong way for students to explore different industries and careers, which would help them make sound vocational choices for their futures (Urquiola et al., 1997).

Youth Development

Another broad argument in favor of work-based learning holds that it promotes the psychological development and maturation of young people. The provision of opportunities to grow and learn through work-based learning assists young people in making the transition from youth to adulthood. And, if work-based learning accelerates the maturation process, one result may be that students will be motivated to take their studies more seriously.

The transition generally involves exploring and then taking on adult roles and, in the process, acquiring a sense of identity or self. The formation of the self is a lifetime process of constructing an identity through interaction with others in different social contexts, but adolescence is generally when the first coherent version of the self and a strong sense of self-ownership and self-dependence emerge (Erikson, 1968; Kegan, 1983; Schneider, 1994). In modern American society the transition to adulthood is protracted; it starts with puberty and for some youth is not resolved until the mid-20s or even early 30s, when the first good job is obtained.

Work-based learning, the argument goes, entails participation in the adult community, where youth can have supportive relationships with adults. Youth may also be treated as capable and responsible persons—that is, as adults. Having a role of some importance in the adult world may contribute to a more mature self-concept. Thus, the advocates maintain, work-based learning provides a rich ground for enhancing the personal development of young people.

New Modes of Thought

Finally, there is a category of claims only beginning to emerge in the work-based learning literature: that direct work experience gives students opportunities to use modes of thought that they do not typically encounter in school. Based on the recent literature on forms of cognitive activity (Bruner, 1996), this argument suggests that, at work, students have to do more than absorb information and repeat it in tests; they have to formulate problems, solve them using the environment in unpredictable and innovative ways, and share the thinking process with others in their community of practice. If this claim can be supported, it implies that students engage in thinking at work that is qualitatively different from that which they do at school. Moreover, since studies of the changing workplace maintain that these new forms of thought will be crucial to any future success (Commission on Skills in the American Workforce, 1990; Moore, 1994; Secretary's Commission on Achieving Necessary Skills, 1991), advocates believe that work-based learning programs will equip students more effectively for that new world of work.

The Learning Theory

If these are the claims made by advocates of work-based learning, and if we want to test those claims, we must first address this question: What do we mean by *learning*? What are the core features and conditions of that process? How does one go about it most effectively? In this section, we briefly review some of the central tenets of our approach to that question. This account will be sorely abbreviated, but its purpose is only to alert the reader to our theoretical and methodological premises. But first, a little history.

At least since the ancient Greeks, philosophers and psychologists have asked what role experience plays in learning. Some of them have tended either to deny or to ignore that role, focusing on mental processes divorced from actual experience. For example, in *The Republic* (1984), Plato regarded education as the process of bringing forth knowledge already in the learner, as a sort of recollection or reminiscence. His theory of forms argued that what is real is the ideal form of a concept—goodness, love—not a material or experiential manifestation of it; the latter as merely epiphenomenal. Similarly, Descartes, in asserting the classic mind-body duality, rejected sense experience as a basis of reliable knowledge. In *Discourse on Method* (1960), he argued that the only path to truth was reason.

Starting with Locke (1690) in the seventeenth century, some philosophers maintained that the human mind at birth is a blank slate, and that all ideas emerge from experience and the associations it produces. American behaviorists from the nineteenth century, such as Watson (1998) and Skinner (1965), built on this conception in their notion of learning as the changes in behavior resulting from stimulus-response arcs. That is, they regarded experience as determining human behavior: If a person responded to an external stimulus in some way, and the consequences of that response were aversive, the behavior would be less likely to occur again, and vice versa. Interestingly, this approach was not actually concerned with knowledge as an intrapsychic phenomenon, because its proponents argued that such processes are irrelevant to the scientific study of behavior. In this theory, which dominated American academic psychology for decades, the learner is seen as essentially passive, a blank slate on which external stimuli act. Skinner asserted in *Beyond Freedom and Dignity* (1972) that such notions as freedom and will are erroneous in their belief that the person chooses to behave in a certain way.

Another strand of theory (see, for example, Durkheim, 1915; Levy-Bruhl, 1910/1966; Parsons, 1954) sees knowledge as existing in a reasonably stable form in a reasonably stable society, a social order in equilibrium. Culture consists of various kinds of knowledge that are transmitted to and internalized by newcomers. This cultural transmission is crucial to maintaining social equilibrium because it ensures consensus among members. So learning is regarded essentially as socialization or acculturation, the induction of the neophyte into this body of culturally defined knowledge and the acquisition of functional forms of knowledge and cognitive skills by the learner. The process is essentially passive; appropriate social mechanisms and persons teach the learner socially appropriate knowledge. Teaching in school treats this knowledge and skill as decontextualized, as disembedded from the routine contexts of its use. The theory assumes *learning transfer*. If you learn something in one context, you can import it into another.

We find neither Plato's focus on the ideal form of a concept, nor Locke's opposite focus on the empirical, nor Parsons' functionalist view of the learning process very useful in analyzing work-based learning. Instead, we draw eclectically on several other traditions: pragmatism, constructivism, activity theory, and the concepts of situated cognition and situated learning. A few major thinkers stand at the foundation of this experiential theory. In the late nineteenth century, William James in *Talks to Teachers and Students about Psychology* (1983) articulated many principles consistent with this approach, although he was clearly not referring to experiential education as a practice: one learns best through one's own activity; sensory experience is basic to learning; effective learning is holistic, interdisciplinary, and specific; respect for individual differences is crucial.

Following James's lead, John Dewey, in such works as *Experience and Education* (1938), focused on experience as the key element in the educational process. He claimed that we should start with the experienced world as the object of education, not with some inaccessible, objective reality outside experience. He saw learning as the process of making determinate the indeterminate experience, and argued that the proper procedure for doing so was the scientific method: a sequence of perceiving a problem, articulating it, forming a hypothesis for solving the problem, testing the hypothesis, and experiencing the real consequences of our actions in the world. According to Dewey, education happens through direct contact with the world, through manipulating real things, through learning their social uses. This pragmatic philosophy clearly forms a solid theoretical argument for the potential benefits of work-based learning, where this direct experience is so obviously present.

Another foundation for our approach has been called *constructivism*: The notion that the learner, rather than simply receiving, storing, and retrieving knowledge provided by external sources, works on ideas and experiences and constructs knowledge (see, for example, Magoon, 1977). From Piaget (1967) to Bruner (1975), from Kohlberg (1981) to Belenky and colleagues (1997), thinkers in this tradition insist that the learner is an active participant in the learning process, not a passive vessel.

In a related line of inquiry, L. S. Vygotsky (1978), a psychologist of the 1930s, argued that thinking, learning, and development have to be understood as embedded in—not simply related to or affected by—sociohistorical activities and contexts. That is, a person's cognition not only is shaped by its social and historical context, but entails that context, using it as part of the process of thinking. This developmental approach makes two principal claims: that "higher mental processes in the individual have their origin in social processes," and that "mental processes can be understood only if we understand the tools and signs that mediate them" (Wertsch, 1985, pp. 14–15). The individual achieves the capacity to engage in more complex forms of cognition only by interacting with others in a meaningful social context. The social dimension of consciousness is prior to the individual dimension, and the individual dimension is derived from the social. Even more significant, this interaction is mediated by certain culturally provided tools, including symbol systems (e.g., language) and machines (e.g., computers), and these tools can be understood only as embedded in a social and historical context, as manifesting the accumulated and emergent knowledge of a social group. Vygotsky's work and that of his successors in *activity theory* (Luria, 1976; Wertsch, 1981) has recently been influential in many circles, and his conclusions seem to suggest the benefits of work-based learning—and to indicate the proper approach to the study of that practice.

After a long period during which these ideas had little impact on American psychology, when behaviorism and functionalism were ascendant, their influence began to grow in the 1970s. Toward the beginning of that decade, Michael Cole and his colleagues published *The Cultural Context of Learning and Thinking* (1971), arguing that Western psychometrics misrepresent the cognitive capacities of non-Western (especially nonschooled) people. This work spawned a number of studies in crosscultural psychology, all of which concluded that the basic forms of cognition vary across social and cultural contexts (Cole & Means, 1986). These ideas gained more and more followers over the next two decades, all committed to the premise that cognition must be understood as embedded in specific social and cultural situations.

One version of that argument was developed by Sylvia Scribner, one of Cole's colleagues, who studied what she called *working intelligence*, the capacity for thinking and problem-solving in such everyday situations as the workplace. Her pioneering study of dairy truck drivers identified some of the properties of everyday cognition—through experience, workers developed methods to carry out complex tasks (Scribner, 1986). In a similar vein, Robert J. Sternberg (1986) described the nature and scope of what he called *practical intelligence*. An anthology edited by Barbara Rogoff and Jean Lave, *Everyday Cognition* (1984), presented a number of studies of the process of thinking and learning in such situations as ski slopes and grocery stores.

Lave, who worked with Cole and Scribner in Africa in the 1970s, has emerged as a key figure in the construction of a dialectical conception of thinking and learning. In *Cognition in Practice* (1988), she articulated both a critique of functionalist theories and a new analysis of cognition. Drawing on studies of apprentice tailors in Liberia, grocery shoppers, and members of Weight Watchers, she showed how mathematical (and other) thinking is embedded in what she called *activity-in-setting*, the emergent relations between the thinking person, the activity in which that person is engaged, and the context in which that activity appears. This theory takes cognition out of the hermetically sealed cranium and places it squarely in the social world.

Later, John Seely Brown and his colleagues (1989) wrote an influential article that was among the first to use the term *situated cognition*. Critiquing conceptions of learning that "assume a separation between knowing and doing, that treat knowledge as an integral, self-sufficient substance, theoretically independent of the situations in which it is learned and used," they wrote:

> The activity in which knowledge is developed and deployed . . . is not separable from or ancillary to learning and cognition. Nor is it neutral. Rather, it is an integral part of what is learned. Situations might be said to co-produce knowledge through activity. Learning and cognition, it is now possible to argue, are fundamentally situated (Brown et al., 1989, p. 32).

Conceptual knowledge, by this theory, functions like a set of tools, the use of which is framed by the community that uses them. Etienne Wenger has recently elaborated this concept in *Communities of Practice* (1998).

Another step in this field was taken when Lave and Wenger collaborated in writing their book *Situated Learning* (1991). They wrote:

> Learning viewed as situated activity has as its central defining characteristic a process that we call *legitimate peripheral participation*. By this we mean to draw attention to the fact that learners inevitably participate in communities of practitioners and that the mastery of knowledge and skill requires newcomers to move toward full participation in the socio-cultural practices of a community (p. 29).

There are both more- and less-radical interpretations of that definition of learning. In his forward to *Situated Learning,* William Hanks took Lave and Wenger to be "locating learning squarely in the processes of coparticipation, *not in the heads of individuals*" (1991, emphasis added). A more moderate position (Salomon, 1993b) recognizes the partially social character of thinking and learning, but also acknowledges that individuals do think and learn intracranially as well. In either case, one can argue not only that learning happens within a situated activity, but that (in some respects, at least) it *is* that activity.

Another element of the theoretical background for a conception of work-based learning goes variously by the terms *socially shared cognition* (Resnick et al., 1991) and *distributed cognition* (Salomon, 1993a). With some minor variations, researchers in this school of thought maintain that a cognitive activity is not only situated, but shared; that is, the activity is carried out not by a single individual but by a complex system of persons, tools, and symbols. A classic analysis of this process is found in Edwin Hutchins's (1993) description of a team of naval personnel navigating a ship through a river. The cognitive tasks involved in this activity—fixing the ship's position, interpreting the nautical charts, setting the heading—

are distributed among six people and several tools that they use. It does not make sense to analyze the thinking done by any one member of this system, because it can be understood only in relation to (and as a part of) that done by other members. Certainly individuals think, but the nature and meaning of that thinking has to be interpreted in the context of the larger system of activity.

One other important strand of theory informs our conception of learning in the workplace: the notion of *organizational culture*. From more of an anthropological perspective than a psychological one, these theorists argue that social interaction in any given situation is held together by participants' shared understanding of purposes, activities, relations, and rules. Ward Goodenough (1957), a seminal writer in the field known as cognitive anthropology, defined culture as the knowledge one needs to participate competently in the roles and activities constituting a social system. This conception of culture suggests the intriguing position that it is the sharing and use of this sociocultural knowledge that, in fact, makes interaction— and learning—possible in specific situations. The extent to which participants in a given social encounter need to share the same knowledge may be less than some of these scholars thought (see, for example, Wallace, 1970); the underlying premise is that people in interaction share and use some basic knowledge or understanding about the event, about persons and their relations, about material objects and processes, and about the sequencing and constructing of activities. To some extent, these theorists claim that this knowledge is organized into "rules, maps and plans" (Spradley, 1972) that guide and inform participants' actions and interpretations.

More recently, some of these concepts have been applied to organizational culture: the beliefs, norms, and interpretive frameworks shared by members of a specific organization. Applebaum (1984), for example, proposed an extensive set of dimensions along which organizational cultures may be described and compared: the nature of social relations in the workplace, including interactions among peers, across genders, and between people at different points in the structure of authority; conceptions of time and space; patterns of authority and power; uses of language; rules concerning dress and demeanor; norms regarding work practices, and so forth. In the same vein, Martin (1992) listed the following elements of organizational culture: "dress norms, the stories people tell about what goes on, the organization's formal rules and procedures, its informal codes of behavior, rituals, tasks, pay systems, jargon, jokes understood only by insiders, and so on" (p. 3). Although there are disagreements about the nature and significance of organizational culture (see, for example, Hamada & Sibley, 1994), the concept affords us another productive tool in the analysis of work-based learning as it identifies some features of the *curriculum of experience*.

This notion of organizational learning certainly suggests that young people will need some experience within a given organization before they can become fully effective participants in that organization. This is an obvious role for work-based learning, however, our objective in this book is to explore the more general benefits of work-based learning, not just those that apply to a specific organization.

This brief review of some of the literature on thinking and learning has taken us from the pragmatism of James and Dewey through the developmental theories of Vygotsky to the activity theory of Luria, from the constructivism of Bruner through the notions of situated cognition and learning in Scribner, Lave and Wenger. Although these theorists disagree with each other in some major and minor ways, we draw on a syncretic version of their work both to support the fundamental practice of work-based learning and to justify our method of studying that practice.

Here, then, is our formulation of the most compelling points from these precursors to our approach. For the purposes of this inquiry, we use the term *learning* to refer to the process of the construction, reorganization, or transformation of knowledge and its use.[1] Each person can be said to use knowledge in the course of an activity. This claim, of course, requires a conception of knowledge as well. Knowledge may take a number of forms:

Facts are widely accepted statements about conditions, phenomena, or processes in the world. These include such statements as "the last Dutch governor of New York was Rip Van Dam" or "the law prohibits stores from refusing to accept returned goods unless they post a sign to the contrary."

Theories are sets of propositions meant to explain certain phenomena. Examples of theories include: "schoolchildren learn more when you have engaged their interest" or "graduated exercise speeds the recovery of stroke patients."

Procedural skills are the capacity to perform certain manual or conceptual operations, routines, or procedures. Interns that we observed, for example, learned to set up an equipment cart needed by anesthesiologists in operations and learned to calculate the reading level of a text.

Social skills are the understanding of and ability to participate appropriately and effectively in interpersonal relationships, dynamics, and poli-

---

[1] Although our focus in this book is on individual learning—how does a student benefit from work-based learning?—this concept of learning can be generalized to groups or communities of practice. Thus in the literature on learning, rather than referring to individuals, analysts discuss "activity systems." An activity system is one or more persons engaged in socially meaningful and purposive action mediated by various cultural tools. From this perspective, the activity system, which can be a person, an organized group of people, a community of practice, or even an institution, is what is engaged in learning.

tics. The interns whom we observed learned such lessons as "treat patients with care and respect" and "don't do more work than the other members of your project team."

Strategies are higher-level approaches to solving problems in the context of larger conceptions of purposes and conditions, or what Perkins (1993) calls the "executive functions." Thus an intern who was working as a tour guide learned to engage the classroom teacher as much as possible in the planning and execution of the tour. Another intern learned to divide the curriculum-development labor among the specialists, and coordinate their work (Moore, 1986).

Styles of inquiry, justification and explanation are patterns of approaches to asking and answering questions. Perkins (1993) refers to this form of knowledge-use as "higher-order thinking." For example, "doing cultural history" means interpreting the thoughts and feelings of people in the past. One intern we observed learned that the practices in physical therapy must be tested by means of the scientific method rather than by anecdote.

Worldviews or perspectives are general stances toward the world. These might include the notion that "history gives meaning to your life" or the view that one must "beat the competition."

Finally, *values* are shared claims about the relative goodness or badness of persons, phenomena, events, or relations. Interns we observed learned that "every patient is equal" or that "speed, efficiency, and accuracy are paramount."

This taxonomy, which represents what Simon et al. (1991) call *working knowledge*, is the static element of the analysis of knowledge and learning, the kind of *stuff* one knows at work. Its purpose is heuristic, simply to suggest one way of talking about what one means by knowledge. It also contains an intentional ambiguity in the term *capacity*. Some people think of knowledge as a possession, as something a person *has* (usually in mind). Others prefer to define it as an activity, as something one *does*; this stance often uses the term *knowing*. We straddle the fence on that debate. Knowledge can exist in the abstract and does not in some sense disappear between occasions of its use (see, for example, Pea, 1993; Perkins, 1993). But the most significant state of knowledge is its *use* in practice, its contribution to the way people make sense of and participate in activities.

Closing the circle now in this definition, we can see learning as the process of a person changing his or her use of knowledge. The change may mean the addition of some new facts: an intern working as a museum tour guide hears her supervisor mention that Rip Van Dam was the last Dutch governor of New York; interns learn about the causes of paralysis from a journal article that is posted on the bulletin board in the physical therapy unit; or a student gives the curriculum firm editors new information about consumer law. It may mean the reorganization of strategies: the tour guides agree to reverse the order of the film and the artifacts cart; an intern in a hospital begins to post a chart listing patients who have come and gone each day. It may even mean the transformation of fundamental perspectives and values in the community of practice: the editors at a curriculum development firm learn to be more competitive and businesslike in their work with clients.

Building on the earlier review of foundational theories, these images of learning assume that it is a constructive process embedded in situated activity, not a decontextualized phenomenon that only takes place inside the head. This conception of learning as situated, distributed, and activity-based gives us a picture of the phenomenon quite different from the disembodied view of the idealists and the Cartesians, the decontextualized view of the functionalists, and the deterministic view of the behaviorists. Instead, we see learning as the changing use of knowledge. The crucial issue for analyzing and evaluating the experiences of students in work-based learning programs, then, becomes the examination of the way they participate in these systems and settings in which knowledge is used, and of the way they encounter various kinds of knowledge as they take part in workplace activities. The issue is not what knowledge is generally in the environment, but what knowledge the students engage over time.

Even though almost none of the theorists talk explicitly about work-based learning (or even the broader category of experiential learning) as the focus of their arguments, the essential common point remains: Learning is a process that entails individuals' and groups' interacting with and through shared forms of knowledge in constructing certain shared activities. Learning is not, contrary to Plato, a matter of bringing out the knowledge already in the learner. Nor is it, contrary to Watson and Skinner, a matter of the individual being shaped by the consequences of behavior. Rather, the image of the learner as an agent, an actor, is key: The person does not simply undergo an experience, but participates in it, constructing its meaning as it evolves. She takes part in the activities of a community of practice, and in the process engages—not just absorbs, but works with—situated knowledge. She becomes an increasingly effective member of that community, contributing to the group's construction of meaning and accomplishment of practical goals. That process of making better (richer, more complex, more expert) sense of the community of practice is learning. The process is situated, active, bound up in relations with other people, and mediated by cultural tools and symbols.

This theory supports the practice of work-based learning in that it insists on the centrality of situated experience in learning. It argues that, if one is to learn about a concept, then one must experience that concept in practice. Even in a more traditionally academic vein, for example, it means that learning historical ideas requires engaging and working with those ideas in a meaningful context, not simply receiving them in a passive way. (This is the insight of the school-based constructivists: that students learn actively, not passively.) So to the extent that educators not only want students to learn work-related ideas and skills, but to learn how the ideas and skills are used, this theory tends to support the claim that work experience will engage students with that knowledge more effectively than will book-oriented, teacher-driven, abstract instruction.

But our learning theory does not necessarily support the practice of work-based learning. First, as Resnick (1987) argues, there are different forms of knowledge-use in school and out; and as a society we value the in-school forms as well as the out-of-school ones. If we want young people to learn to think like historians, they should become active participants in historical inquiry, which does not necessarily have to take place outside of school. Second, direct experience in the workplace may or may not, in fact, entail students' participation in the kinds of knowledge and skill claimed by advocates. In Dewey's (1938) sense, some firsthand experiences may indeed be miseducative, in that they thwart or discourage further learning by boring students, annoying them, or humiliating them (also see Behn et al., 1974, "School is Bad; Work is Worse"). Still, the theory generally gives basic support to the practice of work-based learning if we determine that we value the kinds of knowledge and skill encountered in work experience.

Moreover, this theory justifies our approach to studying work-based learning. The fundamental premise of our methodology is that supporting or rejecting any of the claims made earlier in this chapter demands that one be able to demonstrate that the putative learner has actually engaged the use of the sort of knowledge underlying the claim. It is not enough to show that the knowledge exists in the internship site: for instance, that a hospital uses a great deal of knowledge about biology and chemistry. Rather, one must document the subject's participation in an activity in which that knowledge is used. Some work-based learning advocates are rather too glib about asserting that interns learn from experience, that being in a knowledge-rich environment is inevitably educational (see Moore, 1999). If, on close inspection of actual experience, you cannot find a student engaging a certain kind of knowledge (if, for instance, she works in a hospital but never actually does anything that requires her to use biological knowledge), then our learning theory suggests that one should not claim that she is learning that knowledge. This position seems intuitively obvious when stated explicitly like this, but the fact is that many claims about work-based learning are made without the empirical justification required. In our study, we attempted to test empirically the leading claims of work-based learning advocates.

The Research Methods

Given the essential questions about how and what student-interns learn in the course of a work experience, and given our basic theory about what learning is and how it occurs, we determined that the most appropriate research method was a variant of ethnography, or participant-observation. That approach, borrowed from anthropology and some forms of qualitative sociology, follows through on the theoretical premise that if student-interns are learning, we should be able to *see* that learning in the contexts in which they work. We decided to observe and carefully document the activities in which some work-based learning students participated, and to discover the social relations and contexts within which those activities occurred.

In an intriguing sense, our methods of study were similar to the students' methods of participation: Both they and we had to understand new organizational cultures, new activities-in-setting, new social relations. We had to make sense of the contexts, and the factors shaping them: the formal organizational roles; the distribution of functions, responsibilities, and power; the implicit rules underlying participants' situated performances; the tone and character of their interactions. We had to track important activities in the workplaces, to see how members collaborated to accomplish their shared goals: leading a class on a tour of a history museum; treating a patient in a physical therapy clinic; monitoring the cleaning staff in a hotel. We had to document these experiences as they emerged, as the students' role relations and knowledge-use changed. These are the kinds of things we were looking at and for.

First we had to choose some examples of students in work-based learning placements. Members of the research team generated a sample of appropriate programs by soliciting recommendations from experts in the field; our primary criterion was that the programs included relatively intensive work-based learning, meaning the students spent a significant amount of paid or unpaid time in a workplace, not simply observing but taking part in work activities. The experiences had different names in different programs: internships, externships, apprenticeships. We eventually worked with 14 different programs in different parts of the country.

In the first phase of the study (described in Chapter 4), we investigated employer participation; conducting case studies of 12 programs, a telephone survey of employers participating in five of the programs, and a survey of a comparison group of nonparticipating employers in the same labor markets (see Bailey, Hughes, & Barr, 2000; Hughes, 1998).

Then, to explore work-based pedagogy and the potential benefits of work-based learning for the students, we looked more closely at the work-site activities in five of the programs in several different cities in the Northeast. In some cases, the workplace was chosen first, based on the willingness of the employer to host researchers. We then hoped that the student assigned to that workplace would agree to participate in the study. In only one case did that not happen. In other cases we used the opposite strategy, asking for student volunteers first and then hoping the employer would go along. In all, there were 25 separate focal students, placed in sites such as these: a major teaching hospital in a large city, where student-interns were in the operating room, the physical therapy clinic, and so on; a 5th-grade music class; the legal department of a major metropolitan transportation agency; the accounting division of a large advertising firm; the payroll department of a university; a small veterinary clinic in a rural area; and the operations office of a hotel.

Most of the students were in high school, and several were enrolled in a community college. We did conduct field visits to the schools or programs to interview faculty and staff. Some provided seminars back at school related to the work-based learning component, and some did not. We observed any classroom-based links to the work-based learning. In the case of one academy program that followed a set written curriculum for the school-based classes, we undertook a detailed study of all the coursework. For the other programs, we collected and studied a variety of syllabi and lesson plans.

Once the student-subjects were selected, we first interviewed each one at length about his or her background, family, school experiences, interests, plans, and expectations for their internships. Then we arranged to visit each student's placement site several times over the course of the internship. The visits generally lasted 3 to 5 hours, and took place at three points in the term: toward the beginning, middle, and end. We also interviewed the direct supervisors of the interns, getting information about the organization, its purposes for sponsoring interns, and the supervisors' strategies for working with the students. At the end of the internships we again interviewed the students, asking specific questions about what they believed they had learned.

During the worksite visits, the researcher observed the activities in the workplace, especially those involving the student-intern. Researchers took extensive field notes, using techniques suggested by Schatzman and Straus (1973): writing observational notes (ONs) describing events in as much grounded detail as possible; theoretical notes (TNs) offering first-cut interpretations of what was witnessed; and methodological notes (MNs) that were reminders to collect certain information or watch certain activities. (See the appendix, pp. 223–234, for excerpts from the research guide for the project.)

Table 2.1 Work-Based Learning Student Cases

Names*	School/Program	Internship
Shin-Kap	Community college co-op	Office of local orchestra
Carrie	Community college co-op	Office of local orchestra
Etienne	Community college co-op	Trade division of consulate
Irina	Community college co-op	Trade division of consulate
Carola	Community college co-op	Transportation-authority legal office
Carmen	Community college co-op	Ad-agency accounting office[†]
Ali	Community college co-op	Computer networking[†]
Abdul	Community college co-op	Computer networking[†]
Nell	HS health program	Radiology
Fiona	HS health program	OR/anesthesiology
Matthew	HS health program	Postsurgical unit
Rob	HS health program	Physical therapy gym
Renee	HS Economics & Finance academy	University accounts-payable office
Maria	HS E&F academy	Consulting firm general counsel office[†]
Alison	HS E&F academy	Bank's purchasing dept.[†]
Hiroshi	HS E&F academy	Investment bank's warehouse[†]
Catherine	HS E&F academy	Investment bank's mutual-funds dept.[†]
Fred	HS academic internship program	Animal hospital
Dan	HS academic internship program	Construction site
Adam	HS academic internship program	Independent filmmaking
Maureen	HS academic internship program	Central-school music class
Isabella	HS Travel & Tourism academy	Travel corp. office of corp. services[†]
Paul	HS T&T academy	Travel corp. hotel group[†]
José	HS T&T academy	Hotel housekeeping dept.[†]
Sinda	HS T&T academy	Travel-industry magazine[†]

*All names are pseudonyms.
[†]Indicates paid internship.

When the field notes were collected, the researchers read them carefully and tried to tease out the kinds of information discussed earlier: how participants in the worksites interacted to accomplish their shared goals; how they organized themselves into roles; how power and authority were used; and so on. They looked for the ways in which the interns became participants in the work-related and off-task activities in the site, and for the ways in which the interns used various kinds of situated knowledge in that work. Over time, we tracked the trajectory of subjects' learning, their participation in these various communities of practice; we saw them occupying different roles, enacting different social relations, performing new tasks using new kinds of knowledge.

In the remainder of the book, then, as we discuss the claims made by work-based learning advocates, we will place them in the context of the field observations and the interviews of these 25 students. We will describe the extent to which these claims are supported by what we saw happening, the extent to which students actually engaged the forms of knowledge represented by the claims. That is the strategy: to go back and forth between the hypothetical and claimed benefits of work-based learning, and our detailed study of some representative students in some intensive sites. The findings add a great deal of substance to the debates about the utility and efficacy of work-based learning.

CHAPTER 3

Student Participation in and Use of Work-Based Learning

JOSHUA HAIMSON AND JEANNE BELLOTTI

A central goal of work-based learning initiatives is to match students with work experiences that more closely correspond to their interests and offer more learning opportunities than the jobs they can obtain on their own. This, however, takes time and effort. To provide high-quality work-based activities, school staff must recruit employers, determine which positions are likely to be appropriate for individual students, and encourage students to take advantage of these learning opportunities. Even where school staff are interested in developing these activities, effective work-based learning programs must also elicit the active participation of students and employers. Students must be interested enough to take time away from their regular jobs or extracurricular and social activities. Similarly, employers must be willing to provide useful employment and learning opportunities for young people. The enthusiasm of each of these three groups—school staff, students, and employers—can have a positive feedback effect, heightening the receptivity of the other two. For example, eager students and school staff can encourage employers to expand their involvement.

To assess the feasibility of expanding or enhancing work-based learning activities in secondary school, we must first get some sense of the current and potential market for internships among both students and employers. To understand the market for internships, one needs to gauge both the scale of student and employer participation, as well as factors that appear to facilitate that participation. It is also helpful to examine the qualitative features of the work-based activities schools develop, how they differ from the jobs students find on their own, and the extent to which any advantages of schools' internships are likely to appeal to specific groups, including both students and school staff.

This chapter focuses on students' involvement in, and perceptions of, work-based activities. It also describes some of the qualitative advantages of the paid and unpaid internships students obtain through school relative to the positions they find on their own. The next chapter explores employer perspectives and motivations. Later chapters also discuss the important role of the school staff in developing and supporting work-based activities.

In this chapter, we first ask how many students participate in various types of work-based learning activities. We examine the extent of student participation in paid and unpaid internships and other school-sponsored work experiences (all these activities are referred to as internships); worksite observation activities (such as group worksite tours and job shadowing, where students follow and talk with employees at a workplace); and school-based enterprises. The principal focus of this book is on internships, however, it is important to set the analysis in context by examining both brief and more intensive work activities. To the extent that any of these activities already involve a substantial number of students, there is an even greater need to focus educators' attention on the role these experiences play (or could play) in students' lives.

We have some evidence as well of the extent of recent growth in participation in these work-based activities. We focus on growth during the years following the implementation of the School-to-Work Opportunities Act (STWOA), which was enacted in 1994. In particular, we examine differences in the high-school experiences of two cohorts: the classes of 1996 and 2000. This analysis can provide a sense of how federal, state, and local school-to-work initiatives—combined with other trends—affected student involvement in various types of workplace activities.

Second, we examine the extent to which specific subgroups of students differ in their rates of participation. Although the federal school-to-work initiative sought to involve all students in work-based activities, some groups of students were more likely than others to participate in specific activities. The findings from this analysis point to some factors that may impede or facilitate participation among certain groups and issues that schools should consider in promoting work-based activities.

Third, we identify some of the qualitative advantages of the paid and unpaid internships students obtain through school. We contrast the characteristics of such internships with those of students' regular jobs, thus providing a measure of the "value added" of internships, according to the perspectives of the students themselves. Since most students work at some point during high school, educators should consider this "value added" in gauging the benefits of work-based learning.

Fourth, we examine two ways in which students can use their high school work-based experiences after they graduate. We identify which work-based activities students say, in retrospect, were the most helpful in clarifying their career goals, comparing these ratings to students' assessments of career-focused, school-based activities. We also gauge how many high school graduates retain positions they obtained through school staff and how these positions differ from other jobs they find after high school. The chapter concludes with some suggestions about what educators and policymakers might do, both to expand the number of students involved in intensive forms of work-based learning, and to strengthen the educational value of those experiences.[1]

Most of the data and analysis in this chapter rely on student surveys conducted in eight states for the National Evaluation of School-to-Work Implementation. Surveys were administered to, and school transcripts were collected from, random samples of three cohorts of 12th graders drawn from the classes of 1996, 1998, and 2000.[2] In addition, follow-up surveys were conducted with the first two cohorts about 18 months after students left high school. The students participating in the survey are random samples of all students in these cohorts attending schools who were covered by the eight states' school-to-work initiatives.[3] Much of the analysis, and particularly the measures of growth in work-based activities, will

---

[1]It is worth noting that the next chapter follows the same outline but focuses on employers. That is, it first discusses measures of the extent of participation in internships, then identifies the characteristics of participants and explores their motivations, following with a discussion of internship quality (in that case, from data collected from employers), and ending with suggestions to facilitate strengthening and expanding employer participation.

[2]Mathematica Policy Research, Inc. (MPR) conducted this evaluation for the U.S. Department of Education. Additional information on these data sources, as well as additional substantive findings from the National Evaluation of School-to-Work Implementation, is contained in Hershey et al. (1997).

[3]All eight states—Florida, Kentucky, Maryland, Massachusetts, Michigan, Ohio, Oregon, and Wisconsin—received grants during the first and second years (1994 and 1995) of the national school-to-work initiative. The students were randomly sampled through a three-stage clustered design. First, the school-to-work local partnerships were randomly selected from the eight states, then high schools were randomly selected from these partnerships, and then, students were randomly selected from the schools' 12th-grade classes.

rely primarily on the surveys with the classes of 1996 and 2000. To help interpret some findings, the chapter also draws on site-visit discussions and other interviews with school and employer staff.[4]

Our counts of work-based activities are not confined to those sponsored by federally funded school-to-work initiatives but cover all work-based activities in these schools, including those developed by preexisting programs and concurrent initiatives. Many schools had preexisting work-based activities; students responding to the survey did not distinguish those activities from the ones developed by school-to-work programs. Moreover, concurrent educational initiatives other than those sponsored by STWOA—such as schools' service-learning programs—affected the schools' mix of work-based activities.

Scale and Growth of Work-Based Activities Between 1996 and 2000

Most students participate in some work-based learning activity during high school. The 12th-grade surveys conducted in the eight states asked students about their participation in three types of activities: worksite observation activities (job shadowing and group worksite tours), school-sponsored paid and unpaid internships, and school-based businesses. About four-fifths of the class of 2000 reported participating in at least one of these activities. However, some activities attracted more students than others.

Reflecting their broad appeal, worksite observation activities—specifically, job shadowing and worksite visits—have attracted the largest number of students and have been growing recently. Parents, students, and school staff often find these relatively brief activities attractive because they offer some exposure to careers without substantially interfering with students' other school or after-school activities. Among the class of 2000 in the eight survey states, about 43 percent reported participating in job shadowing and 62 percent in worksite tours at some point during high school. Moreover, job shadowing grew significantly during the late 1990s (see Figure 3.1).[5] The growth in job shadowing probably reflects the promotional efforts of such national organizations as Junior Achievement, The National Alliance for Youth, Monster.com, the U.S. Departments of

---

[4]As part of the school-to-work evaluation, the researchers conducted two rounds of site visits and one round of follow-up phone interviews to 31 local school-to-work initiatives in the eight states. The site visits were conducted between 1996 and 1998. The follow-up phone interviews were conducted in spring 2001.

[5]The fraction of students participating in work-site tours also appeared to grow, but this growth was not statistically significant (see Figure 3.1).

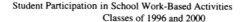

Student Participation in School Work-Based Activities
Classes of 1996 and 2000

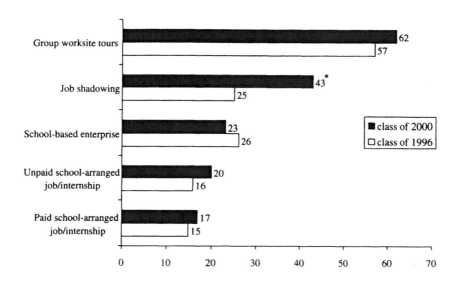

*Difference between class of 1996 and 2000 is statistically significant at the 1 percent level.

Source: Eight-state 12th-grade survey of classes of 1996 and 2000, Mathematica Policy Research, Inc.

Fig. 3.1

Labor and Education, and the National School-to-Work Office (while it was in operation).[6]

A smaller number of students participate in paid and unpaid internships, yet these more-intensive activities still manage to attract a substantial proportion of students. During their four years of high school, about 32 percent of the members of the class of 2000 obtained a paid or unpaid position that they found with help from school staff. Schools' paid and unpaid work-experience positions attracted roughly comparable fractions of students (20 percent and 17 percent, respectively). Most internship experiences are concentrated toward the end of high school, the period during which many students clarify their career goals and prepare to enter the

---

[6]These organizations developed National Job Shadowing Day beginning in 1998. In addition, "Take Our Daughters to Work Day," sponsored by the Ms. Foundation for Women, gained momentum around the same time.

workforce or higher education (Figure 3.2). These overall participation rates are more or less consistent with nationally representative data on the prevalence of internships among high school students.[7]

However, despite some encouragement provided by the school-to-work initiatives, student participation in intensive work-based activities did not grow substantially during the late 1990s. The proportion of students who reported obtaining a paid or unpaid internship grew only slightly between the class of 1996 and that of 2000, and these changes were not statistically significant (Figure 3.1). Nor was there any appreciable growth in the fraction of students participating in school-based enterprises.

There are several reasons why schools may have had difficulty expanding participation in extended internships. Site visits to school-to-work initiatives in the eight states indicated that some schools chose to replace preexisting co-op programs with new work-experience initiatives, resulting in little net growth in internship opportunities. Moreover, in most schools visited, the modest resources schools secured through their school-to-work grants were insufficient to develop a substantial number of new internships.

Some educators have also expressed concerns that work-based learning may impinge on the time students spend on their academic studies. Indeed, more than two out of five (42 percent) of the students who obtained a paid internship through school during the school year said they spent more than 20 hours per week at the employer's workplace (Figure 3.3). Moreover, 79 percent of these workplace experiences lasted more than 10 weeks. Although the positions students obtain through school involve about the same number of hours of work per week as the jobs students find on their own, the fact that many school-sponsored internships are time-consuming may still contribute to a perception that work-based learning can interfere with students' academic performance.

Even though the fraction of students with paid or unpaid internships did not appear to rise between the classes of 1996 and 2000, growing numbers of students reported having multiple unpaid internships. In particular, about 4 percent of the class of 2000 reported having an unpaid internship during more than one grade or summer, compared to only 1.8 percent of the class of 1996. Although internships continued to be concentrated toward the end of high school, a growing fraction of students also reported having some unpaid experience during 9th or 10th grades

---

[7]For example, using the 1997 National Longitudinal Survey of Youth, Rivera-Batiz (2000) found that about 15 percent of high school students in the 10th–12th grades had participated in an apprenticeship or internship, and more than 20 percent had participated in cooperative education (these two groups were not mutually exclusive).

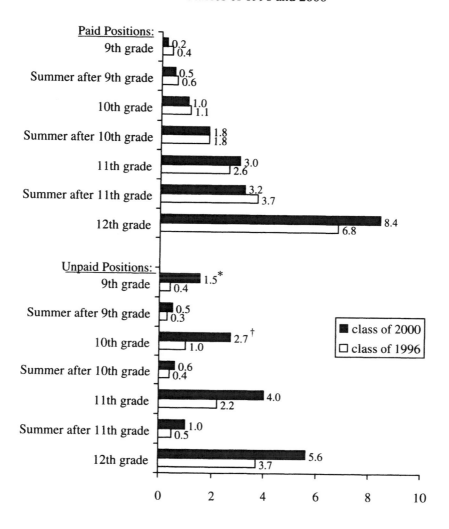

Timing of Students' Paid and Unpaid Work Experience
Positions Obtained Through School
Classes of 1996 and 2000

Paid Positions:

9th grade — 0.2 / 0.4
Summer after 9th grade — 0.5 / 0.6
10th grade — 1.0 / 1.1
Summer after 10th grade — 1.8 / 1.8
11th grade — 3.0 / 2.6
Summer after 11th grade — 3.2 / 3.7
12th grade — 8.4 / 6.8

Unpaid Positions:

9th grade — 1.5* / 0.4
Summer after 9th grade — 0.5 / 0.3
10th grade — 2.7† / 1.0
Summer after 10th grade — 0.6 / 0.4
11th grade — 4.0 / 2.2
Summer after 11th grade — 1.0 / 0.5
12th grade — 5.6 / 3.7

■ class of 2000
□ class of 1996

0   2   4   6   8   10

*Difference between class of 1996 and 2000 is statistically significant at the 5 percent level.

†Difference between class of 1996 and 2000 is statistically significant at the 1 percent level.

Source: Eight-state 12th-grade survey of classes of 1996 and 2000,
          Mathematica Policy Research, Inc.

Fig. 3.2

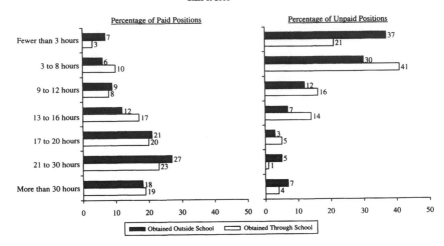

Distribution of Hours per Week in Work-Based Experiences
that Students Obtain During the School Year:
Class of 2000

Note: The distribution of hours per week for paid and unpaid positions obtained through school was not significantly different from that for positions obtained independently at the .05 level, two-tailed test.

Source: Eight-state 12th-grade survey of class of 2000, Mathematica Policy Research, Inc.

Fig. 3.3

(Figure 3.2). The expansion of unpaid internships during the early grades of high school may reflect efforts by state and federal agencies to promote service-learning activities—unpaid or volunteer activities designed to develop civic skills and complement some part of the school's curriculum.[8]

Mix of Students Participating in Work-Based Activities

Federal policies encourage schools to provide all students with comparable access to career-focused educational activities, including work-based activities. The federal Perkins legislation—the main funding source for vocational education—has several provisions relating to access, as did STWOA. Educators want to prevent any stereotypes from discouraging student participation in activities that may interest them. In addition, some work-based

---

[8]For example, during the past decade, the federal Learn and Serve program has expanded its efforts to promote community service among high school students. Maryland—one of the eight states covered by MPR's survey—now requires all students to perform some type of service learning during high school.

learning advocates believe that most students, regardless of their back-ground or post-secondary plans, can benefit from work-based activities.

There are four dimensions of access and diversity that are important to educators, each of which relates to different subgroups of students. First, during the past decade, some educators have sought to design or reconfigure work-based learning programs so that they attract not only those who plan to enter the labor market after graduation but also those who are college-bound. Second, federal vocational education policies encourage schools to find ways of overcoming any gender-based or race-based stereotypes that may impede some students' participation in particular career-focused activities. Third, although the most recent version of Perkins eliminated the set-aside grant funds to serve special populations—including students with disabilities—this legislation still requires states to serve these populations and report their success in doing so.[9] Fourth, STWOA sought to ensure that some work-based activities are available to students in both rural areas where low population densities make it harder to reach jobs and depressed urban communities where employment opportunities may be scarce.

Drawing upon the eight state surveys, we can examine the extent to which each of these subgroups participate in specific workplace activities. In particular, we examine whether rates of student participation vary substantially, based on students' (1) college plans; (2) race and ethnicity; (3) disability status; (4) gender; and (5) urbanicity. We examine these groups' participation in each of the three main types of activities: worksite observation activities, paid and unpaid school-arranged internships, and school-based businesses. Overall, the participation rates for all these subgroups were not substantially different from the average for all students (Table 3.1). These findings suggest that most schools have succeeded in engaging a fairly diverse mix of students in work-based learning activities. However, as discussed in the following, we do find some modest but notable differences in participation rates across these groups.

Students who do not plan to attend college appear to be somewhat more likely than their college-bound peers to obtain a paid position through school. Some well-established work-experience programs—including school co-op programs—have been designed primarily for students who do not plan to attend college. These programs often try to help students identify or prepare for a full-time job after graduation. The eight-state survey indicates that these programs continue to attract substantial

---

[9]The other special populations are economically disadvantaged students, foster children, female or male students preparing for nontraditional occupations, single parents, and displaced homemakers. Our survey did not contain sufficiently large samples of each of these groups to examine each of their participation rates.

Table 3.1 Participation in Work Activities by Student Subgroup

| | Paid Job/Internship Found Through School | | | Unpaid Job/Internship Found Through School | | | School-Based Enterprise | | | Job Shadow or Worksite Tours | | |
| | Class of | | | Class of | | | Class of | | | Class of | | |
	1996	2000	Change	1996	2000	Change	1996	2000	Change	1996	2000	Change
All students	15.0	16.9	1.9	16.3	20.2	3.9	25.5	22.7	-2.8	61.5	70.2	8.7
Plans to attend college after high school												
Have plans	14.0	14.6	0.6	17.0	21.8*	4.8	25.6	21.6	-4.0	59.5†	69.6	10.1
Have no plans	16.5	21.6	5.1	14.5	16.6	2.1	25.5	25.8	0.2	66.2	71.3	5.1
Completed college prep curriculum												
Completed	11.0†	12.6	1.6	18.4	20.6	2.2	24.5	20.8	-3.7	56.5†	66.5	10.0
Did not complete	17.0	22.1	5.1	15.9	20.3	4.4	28.1	24.7	-3.4	67.1	71.5	4.4
Race/ethnicity												
African-American	21.4*	23.3	1.9	18.7	21.0	2.3	30.2	22.7	-7.5	61.2	74.4	13.2
Hispanic	14.2	31.4	17.2	16.3	24.5	8.2	25.4	22.0	-3.3	55.8	72.1	16.3
White/other	13.7	14.0	0.3	15.9	19.3	3.4	24.9	22.8	-2.1	62.3	69.4	7.1
Gender												
Male	14.0	17.0	3.0	12.4†	15.3†	2.8	24.0	23.1	-0.9	61.3	67.5	6.2
Female	15.7	16.7	1.0	19.7	24.8	5.1	26.9	22.3	-4.7	61.7	72.8	11.1

Table 3.1 Participation in Work Activities by Student Subgroup *(Cont.)*

| | Paid Job/Internship Found Through School | | | Unpaid Job/Internship Found Through School | | | School-Based Enterprise | | | Job Shadow or Worksite Tours | | |
| | Class of | | | Class of | | | Class of | | | Class of | | |
	1996	2000	Change	1996	2000	Change	1996	2000	Change	1996	2000	Change
Disability												
Has disability	21.9[†]	9.3	−12.6*	20.3	17.3	−3.0	25.5	23.9	−1.5	60.5	70.0	6.5
Does not	14.0	17.3	3.3	15.8	20.1	4.	25.5	22.1	−3.5	61.6	69.8	8.2
Urbanicity												
Urban	19.5	26.6	7.1	17.5	21.9	4.4	24.4[†]	22.7[†]	−1.7	53.2[†]	67.9[†]	14.7
Suburban	13.2	12.9	−0.3	14.7	17.5	2.7	23.4	18.9	−4.5	62.1	65.2	3.1
Rural	12.2	11.9	−0.3	18.3	24.1	5.9	32.5	31.4	−1.1	72.5	85.4	13.0

*Differences among subgroups participation rates (or changes in participation rates) are statistically significant at the 5 percent level.
†Differences among subgroups participation rates (or changes in participation rates) are statistically significant at the 1 percent level.

Source: Eight-state 12th-grade survey of classes of 1996 and 2000, Mathematica Policy Research, Inc.

numbers of students who are not planning to attend college. About 22 percent of the seniors in the class of 2000 who had no concrete plans to attend college during the year after graduation reported obtaining a paid internship or job with help from school staff at some point during high school, compared to 15 percent of those who did have college plans. However, the difference between these two groups' rates of participation in paid internships is not statistically significant.

College-bound students, on the other hand, are more likely than other students to obtain unpaid internships. About 22 percent of the college-bound group participated in a school-sponsored unpaid internship or job, compared to only 17 percent of noncollege-bound students. This pattern may reflect differences in the family incomes of college-bound and noncollege-bound students. If they have higher family incomes, college-bound students may be able to forgo wages in exchange for an educational work experience with potential long-term payoffs. In addition, these students may be more motivated to seek volunteer experiences that can impress college admissions staff.

African-American and Hispanic students have somewhat higher rates of participation in paid internships than do white students, and this difference may be partly due to the racial gap in college enrollment rates. About 23 percent of African-American students and 31 percent of Hispanics had a paid position they found through school, compared with only 14 percent of their white peers. These racial differences appear to be due partly to the fact that a somewhat smaller percentage of African-American students had concrete plans to attend either a two- or four-year college than did white students. However, even among students planning to attend college, a larger fraction of African-Americans than whites were involved in paid internships.[10] African-American students also have lower overall employment rates than white students, which suggests that internship programs could be offering employment opportunities to some African-American students who might otherwise have difficulty finding after-school or summer jobs.[11]

---

[10]Indeed, even after controlling for school effects and a variety of background characteristics (including parents' education levels, welfare receipt, grades, and urbanicity), African-American students were more likely to obtain a position through school. (These statistical analyses did not control for family income or social networks.)

[11]The NLSY97 data reported by Rivera-Batiz (2000) also shows greater minority participation in school internships. Of all students in the sample who had at least been in 9th grade, 17 percent of the black, non-Hispanics; and 21 percent of the Hispanics; but only 14 percent of the white non-Hispanics had participated in an apprenticeship or internship. Twenty-five percent of the blacks and 21 percent of the whites and Hispanics had participated in a cooperative education program.

The involvement of students with disabilities in school-sponsored internship programs appears to have declined during the late 1990s. Within the class of 1996, the fraction of students with disabilities who had a paid internships was significantly higher than that of other students (Table 3.1). Between the class of 1996 and 2000, the rate of participation in paid internships among students with disabilities declined substantially, whereas it rose for other students.[12] Even though the 1998 version of the Perkins legislation eliminated set-asides for special populations, schools are still expected to make all vocational and co-op work-experience programs available and accessible to diverse students, including those with disabilities. However, it is possible that the elimination of the set-asides may have contributed to the apparent decline in these students' involvement in work-experience activities. Alternatively, or in addition, this trend could reflect schools' efforts to attract a broader range of students and to reduce any stigma associated with programs that had previously sought to involve many students with learning problems and other disabilities.

Female students responding to the survey were somewhat more likely than males to report participating in unpaid internships during high school. It is possible that these differences in male and female participation rates reflect (and perhaps even contribute to) the emerging gender gap in college enrollment. Consistent with the national trends, female respondents were more likely than males to develop plans for attending college and to enroll in college shortly after leaving high school. Unpaid internships generally attract students planning to attend college, in part because they sometimes can impress college admissions staff. The larger numbers of females involved in school's unpaid internships may also reflect the fact that many of these opportunities tend to be focused on education and health occupations, fields that have traditionally been dominated by young women. To attract more male students, schools might need to expand the range of unpaid internship opportunities available.

Rural students are most likely to engage in activities designed to overcome the transportation hurdles they often face. Even though rural students have employment rates comparable to those of other students, visits to rural schools suggest that the range of positions available is constrained by the limited range of industries in those areas and by students' difficulty reaching workplaces. School staff sometimes can transport groups of students to a wider variety of worksites. School-based enterprises also allow

---

[12]Although the rate of participation of disabled students within the class of 2000 appears to be appreciably smaller than that of other students, this is not significantly different. However, the participation-rate changes between the class of 1996 and class of 2000 are significantly different for disabled and other students.

students to develop work-related skills without having to travel to a work-site. Indeed, worksite tours and school-based enterprises have attracted larger percentages of students in rural communities than in suburban or urban areas.

Quality of Intensive Work-Based Activities

Schools have sought to create paid and unpaid workplace experiences that provide greater learning opportunities than are found in the jobs students obtain in other ways. Most students try to work at some point during high school and succeed in obtaining at least one paid job. Although students can learn something from nearly any work experience (if only about em-ployers' general expectations), many of the jobs students find on their own offer few structured learning opportunities, which bear little relationship to their career interests or school curriculum. Schools can try to help stu-dents identify positions that correspond more closely to their interests or that provide better learning opportunities.

The paid and unpaid internships that schools arrange appear to have several attractive qualitative features. Using the eight-state student survey, we contrasted the characteristics of the positions students obtained with help from school staff with those of the positions they found in other ways. The advantages of the internships are apparent based on simple cross-tab-ulations and chi-square tests for statistical significance (see Figures 3.4 and 3.5). Moreover, regression analysis suggests that these apparent advantages are not attributable to any observable differences in the types of students who tend to secure positions through school and those who find their own jobs or internships.[13] Based on the work experiences reported by students in the class of 2000, four advantages of the positions students obtain through school are evident.

---

[13]We estimated linear regression models in which the dependent variables were the qualitative features of students positions (e.g., whether or not they discussed careers with their employer) and the independent variables included a variable indicating whether or not the student found the position through school, as well as control vari-ables relating to the following student characteristics: gender, race and ethnicity, ur-banicity, 9th-grade GPA, disabilities, receipt of cash welfare, and parents' education. The estimates from these regressions indicate that the magnitude of the qualitative dif-ferences between the positions students obtain through school and those they find on their own remain approximately the same as those reported above (within about 1.5 percentage points) regardless of whether or not one controls for these student charac-teristics. The significance levels of these differences also remain unchanged. These re-gression adjustments, however, do not control for any unobserved differences between students who find jobs through school and on their own.

Industries in Which Students Have Paid Positions:
Class of 2000

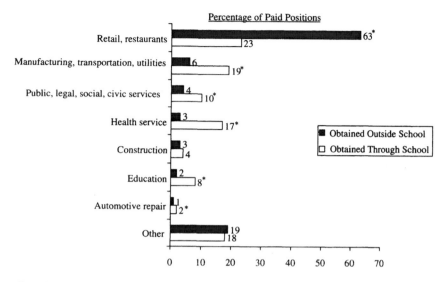

*The difference between positions obtained outside school and through
school is significant at the .01 level, two-tailed test.

Source: Eight-state 12th-grade survey of class of 2000, Mathematica Policy Research, Inc.

Fig. 3.4

First, schools develop positions in a wide range of industries, increasing
the chances that students can work in settings relevant to their career interests. The paid positions that schools develop are particularly diverse (Figure 3.4). These positions are less likely than jobs students find on their own
to be in the retail or restaurant sectors and are more likely to be in public,
legal, and social services; health services; and education (industries of interest to many students). Unpaid positions obtained through school are in
less-diverse settings; more than 40 percent are in schools (data not shown
in figure). However, in describing the occupation of volunteer jobs in
schools, students responding to the survey indicated that they were quite
varied and included tutoring students, completing administrative tasks,
and helping to manage sports teams or events.

An analysis of students' career goals suggests that they are more likely to
correspond to the positions students find through school than to the regular jobs they find on their own. For students reporting a clear career goal
focused on a particular industry, the 12th-grade survey of the class of 1996

Learning Opportunities in Workplace Experiences:
Class of 2000

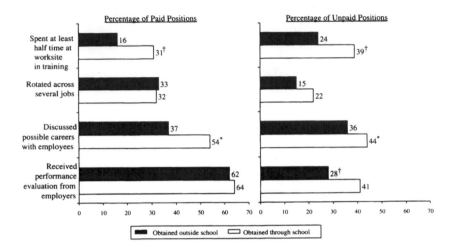

*The difference between the positions obtained outside school and through school is significant at the .05 level, two-tailed test.
†The difference between the positions obtained outside school and through school is significant at the .01 level, two-tailed test.

Source: Eight-state 12th-grade survey of class of 2000, Mathematica Policy Research, Inc.

Fig. 3.5

provided a rough measure of the match between the industry of the students' most recent position and their career goal at the time of the survey.[14] Although only about 23 percent of the positions students obtained through school matched their current goals, this was considerably better than the 4 percent match rate for students who found their own jobs. Match rates were the highest for those obtaining unpaid positions through school (38 percent).[15]

---

[14]This analysis could be conducted only for the 44 percent of students who identified clear career goals in an industry that could readily be matched with their jobs. Vague career goals (such as "business") and goals that did not focus on a specific industry (such as "computers") could not be matched. It is also important to recognize that students' career goals at the time of the interview may have differed from their goals at the time they started working in the position.

[15]Some of these apparent matches may have been less than ideal. For example, although many of the students interested in careers in education obtained unpaid positions in schools, these positions often did not involve any teaching or tutoring.

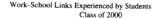

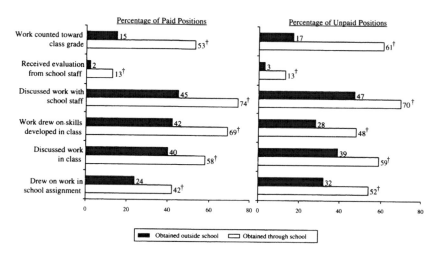

Work-School Links Experienced by Students
Class of 2000

*The difference between the positions obtained outside school and through school is significant at the .05 level, two-tailed test.
†The difference between the positions obtained outside school and through school is significant at the .01 level, two-tailed test.

Source: Eight-state 12th-grade survey of class of 2000, Mathematica Policy Research, Inc.

Fig. 3.6

Second, students with school-arranged internships often receive training or discuss career options with employer staff. Students' opportunities to perform challenging tasks in a workplace depends in part on how much training they receive. Students were asked to estimate the fraction of the time at their workplaces they spent "doing regular work" and the fraction they spent "being trained or practicing skills." In paid jobs, they were more likely to spend at least half their time in training if they had found their job through school (Figure 3.5). They also were more likely to have chances at the worksite to discuss career options with adults. About 54 percent of students who had secured paid positions through school reported discussing possible careers with adults at their workplaces, compared with 37 percent of those who had found their positions independently.

Third, school internships offer feedback on students' worksite performance. Students in unpaid positions arranged through school were more likely than those finding their own positions to receive performance evaluations from employer staff (Figure 3.5). As one might expect, students obtaining both paid and unpaid school-arranged positions were also more likely to discuss their work experiences with school staff and to have their worksite performance count toward a grade at school (Figure 3.6).

Finally, students who had obtained positions through school often make some substantive connection between their studies and work experience (Figure 3.6). For example, compared with those who found their own position, students in school-arranged internships more often reported that workplace tasks made use of academic or technical skills they had learned in school. They also were more likely to draw on their work experiences while completing school assignments or participating in class discussions. Although most of the assignments that drew on students' work experiences were made in vocational classes, a substantial minority of students reported receiving these assignments in their English, math, or science class. However, visits to high schools suggest that links with the academic curriculum are somewhat thin. For example, teachers sometimes ask students to write short essays or presentations about their work experiences without necessarily linking these assignments to any other parts of the curriculum. Although this may enhance communication skills and give students an opportunity to reflect on career goals, it may not substantially develop students' analytic skills.

The differences in the quality of positions that students find through school and on their own cannot be explained by the duration of these experiences, but longer internships do appear to offer more learning opportunities. Among students who obtained a paid internship through school, those who worked more than 12 hours per week were more likely than those working fewer hours to be evaluated by their employers, discuss their work experience during class, and have work linked to school through grades.[16] Among those with unpaid positions, students working 3 or more hours per week were more likely to receive performance evaluations from their employers, discuss careers with their employers, receive training at least half the time, use what they learned on the job in vocational or academic classes (specifically, mathematics or English), and have their job linked to a class assignment and grade.[17]

In developing and scheduling internships, school staff need to balance the objective of providing sufficient time for workplace learning with the interest in ensuring adequate time remains for their academic studies. The trade-off is less difficult in the case of unpaid internships, which usually are short and whose quality may be enhanced by modest increases in the

---

[16]These findings are based on an analysis of the surveys of the class of 1998.

[17]Visits to schools and students' workplaces suggest that this pattern reflects the constraints and priorities of school and employer staff: in developing workplace activities that involve a larger time commitment from students, school and employer staff are more likely to design activities that offer students some chances to develop skills, discuss career options with employer staff, and secure feedback on their performance.

number of hours students plan to spend at a worksite (to at least 3 or more hours per week). The trade-offs are somewhat more complex in the case of paid internships. The survey data suggest that students spending at least 12 hours per week at a worksite have higher-quality experiences than those spending less time. However, regression analysis also suggests that working longer hours (specifically, 20 hours or more) in paid positions is associated with slightly lower grades, after controlling for students' prior academic performance and background characteristics.[18] Even if this association is spurious, these findings and similar ones from other studies can lead educators to question the value of intensive internships. Internship programs might try to develop more internships of intermediate duration with enough time for some workplace learning without appreciably interfering with students' other learning activities.

Although the positions students find through school appear to have several attractive qualitative features, these features did not become more pronounced or change substantially during the late 1990s, despite some efforts to enhance internship programs (Figure 3.7). Site visits to schools participating in the eight states' school-to-work initiatives identified many efforts to strengthen traditional work experience programs or to create new programs. However, schools typically secured only modest federal or state funds for these efforts. Moreover, high-quality internships often were costly for employers to develop and maintain.

The only significant change was some growth in the extent to which students discussed their paid internships with school staff (Figure 3.7). Whether as a result of improvements in traditional programs or the introduction of new programs, it appears that school staff may be more closely monitoring or supporting students' internship experiences. However,

---

[18]The cumulative grade point average of students who worked more than 20 hours per week at their most recent job or internship was 0.08 points lower (on a 4.0 scale) than those who did not work at all. This negative association exists regardless of whether students obtained their position independently or through school staff. By contrast, students working fewer than 20 hours per week appear to receive grades similar to those who did not work during high school. These results are based on regression analyses that control for students' 9th-grade GPA and background characteristics, including race, gender, parents' education level, urbanicity, welfare receipt, and disability status. Other studies on this issue have similar findings—namely, that only the most time-consuming jobs appear to interfere with students' academic achievement (National Academy of Sciences, 1998). The students who choose to work long hours may already be less engaged in their studies for reasons that are not directly related to their jobs. Moreover, regardless of whether these associations reflect the negative effects of time-consuming jobs, they may be contributing to teachers' perceptions that working long hours can be detrimental to students' academic success.

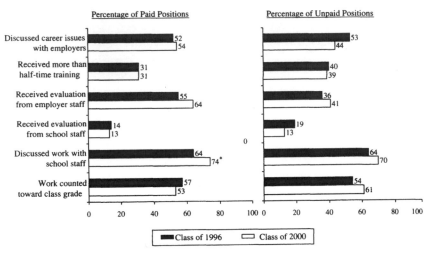

Selected Quality Indicators in Positions Obtained Through School
Changes from 1996 to 2000

Percentage of Paid Positions   Percentage of Unpaid Positions

*The difference between the class of 1996 and class of 2000 is significant at the .05 level, two-tailed test.

Source: Eight-state 12th-grade survey of classes of 1996 and 2000, Mathematica Policy Research, Inc.

Fig. 3.7

since there appear to be few other qualitative changes in students' paid positions, it is uncertain whether these more frequent discussions with school staff have affected students' internship experiences.

Ways in Which Students Use High School Work-Based Activities After Graduation

There are many ways in which work-based activities potentially provide lasting benefits to students. These activities may help students clarify goals, get a sense of employers' expectations, develop useful skills, or secure a job after they leave high school. Even though the survey data do not allow one to estimate the impacts of work-based activities on students' outcomes, we can make use of the follow-up surveys conducted 18 months after students left high school to get a sense of some of the potential benefits of these activities. First, the survey data allow us to gauge the extent to which graduates perceive that specific high school work-based activities were helpful in clarifying their career goals. Second, we can determine how many students obtained a school-arranged job or internship that led to a job after they graduated. Third, we assess how the quality of the post-secondary jobs students obtain through high school staff positions differs from the jobs students found in other ways.

After students graduate, they may have useful insights into the value of various high school activities in clarifying their goals. These insights take into account changes in their goals and what they have learned about careers since leaving high school. The class of 1996 and 1998 follow-up surveys asked students whether they recalled participating in various career-focused activities during high school. Students who said they had participated in a particular activity were asked how helpful it was in "figuring out what you want to do or don't want to do in a career." These data should be interpreted with caution because some students may not know whether they would have chosen the same career goal had they not participated in a particular activity.[19]

Overall, participating students indicated that job shadowing and extended workplace activities were among the most helpful high school activities for purposes of clarifying their career goals (Figure 3.8). The highest ratings were assigned to job shadowing, followed by paid school-arranged jobs and internships. Many students also rated as very helpful certain types of career-focused classes—such as academic classes designed for students with specific interests and vocational classes. However, relatively few students viewed school-based career development activities—such as career exploration classes—as particularly helpful. In addition, group worksite tours and school-based businesses were viewed as less helpful.

Based on these survey findings, students appear to value those workplace activities that tend to provide some one-on-one contact with employer staff. It is noteworthy that students viewed job shadowing as considerably more helpful than group worksite tours, even though both are fairly brief activities with similar goals—exposing students to some of the jobs adults perform. Job shadowing usually differs from worksite tours, however, in that students are more likely to have some choice about the employee they shadow and have more opportunities to speak with that person individually. In addition, both internships and job-shadowing experiences may engage students more fully, since they often require a student to help plan the activity and report on the experience after it has been completed. These findings suggest that students may need individualized workplace experiences, as well as some opportunity for reflection about

---

[19]Furthermore, students were only asked how these activities helped them to develop career goals. Clearly some of these activities may have been useful in other ways including in developing students' skills or other competencies. Nonetheless, most students may have a sense of how various experiences were useful in formulating goals.

Perceived Value of High School Career-Focused Activities
in Clarifying Career Goals
Class of 1998

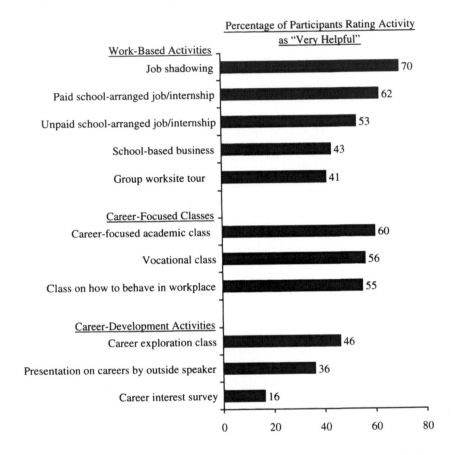

Source: Eight-state follow-up survey of class of 1998, Mathematica Policy Research, Inc.

Fig. 3.8

their experiences in order to develop an understanding of the jobs available in an industry and to clarify their goals.

Students also can derive some lasting benefits from school-arranged jobs and internships when they lead to paid positions after graduation. Only a fairly small proportion—4.6 percent—of the high school graduates from the classes of 1996 and 1998 in the eight states found their first job after high school with help from school staff. Another 2.8 percent of students found positions through a post-secondary program. The most common method of finding their first jobs after high school were referrals from family or friends, using classified ads, or contacting employers directly. An even smaller proportion of students—3.2 percent—worked in school-arranged internships during high school that led to a full-time position.[20]

While noncollege-bound youth are sometimes targeted by high schools' job-placement programs, these students were not significantly more likely than other students to find their first jobs with the help of school staff. Only about 5 percent of those not currently in a two- or four-year college at the time of the survey had found their first job with the help of high school staff. In fact, the fraction of students who obtain jobs through high school staff does not vary considerably based on most student background variables—such as race, gender, and urbanicity. Even among vocational concentrators—who tend to have higher rates of participation in co-op work experience programs—only about 6 percent reported that they found their first job through school.

Although relatively few students obtain paid positions after high school with help from either high school or post-secondary school staff, these positions have some attractive features. Comparisons of the jobs high school graduates obtained through school staff with the positions they find in other ways suggest that the former often have three distinct advantages.[21] First, the jobs high school graduates find through school tend to provide more intensive training (Table 3.2). According to respondents of the follow-up survey, nearly 70 percent of these jobs offer some training, compared to only 62 percent of the positions they found in other ways. Second, about 43 percent of jobs found through high school staff and 49 percent of positions they found through post-secondary staff corresponded to students' career goals, compared to only 23 percent of jobs found in other ways. Third, jobs found through school are somewhat more likely to offer to pay for employees' educational tuition. However, the average pay and most other fringe benefits are about the same for jobs students find through school and other jobs. The apparent advantages of the positions students found through high school staff persist even after controlling for

---

[20]Overall, about 27 percent of students in the classes of 1996 and 1998 had some school-arranged paid or unpaid internship during high school. This implies that about 12 percent (3.2/27) of those with at least one school-arranged position during high school ultimately obtained or retained a job after high school with the same employer.
[21]The first two of these qualitative advantages are similar to those associated with the school-arranged jobs and internships that students have during high school, as discussed above.

Table 3.2 Characteristics of First Post-Secondary Jobs: Differences Between Positions Found Through School and Other Positions

Job Characteristics	First Job Found Through High School	First Job Found Through Post-Secondary School	First Job Found Through Other Means
Percentage of jobs that:			
provide at least some training	70.3	70.0	61.5*
correspond to career goals	43.1	48.5	23.3*
help pay tuition	20.7	14.3	10.2*
Average hourly wage	$7.40	$7.43	$7.33

*The differences among jobs found through high school, post-secondary school, and other means are statistically significant at the 1 percent level.

Source: Eight-state follow-up survey of classes of 1996 and 1998, Mathematica Policy Research, Inc.

the characteristics of students, suggesting that schools actually enhance the quality of the positions students find.[22]

The higher quality of the jobs students find through high school suggests that other students might benefit from this type of assistance. Since nearly all students seek some type of job after leaving high school, and since many students work near their former high school, schools might consider widening the employment opportunities available to students. However, given the small number of graduates who currently find jobs through high school, it is difficult to know what additional resources would be required to substantially expand schools' internships and job-placement assistance, or whether schools could feasibly identify opportunities for a much larger group.

Conclusions

Although brief worksite activities attract the largest number of students, a substantial proportion obtain a paid or unpaid internship through school

---

[22]The results of logistic regression models indicate that these advantages persist even after controlling for differences in the observable characteristics of students who find jobs through school and those who find jobs in other ways. In particular, these models controlled for students' race, parents' education, gender, whether or not a student was a vocational concentrator in high school, and students' cumulative high-school GPAs. The regression adjustment does not allow us to control for any factors, such as motivation, that we do not observe.

at some point during their four years of high school. One important implication flows from this observation: a large amount of student and staff time is currently being devoted to internship programs. This substantial commitment of resources suggests that educators can benefit from a clear understanding of the potential costs and benefits of work-based learning for particular groups of students, which is one of the objectives of this book.

Internships appear to play a somewhat different role in the lives of college-bound students than they do in those planning to enter the labor market after graduating from high school. Specifically, college-bound students are most likely to accept unpaid internships, whereas other students appear to be more interested in paid work-based learning positions. In matching students to particular internships, school staff should be sensitive both to students' post-secondary plans and to their stated reasons for participating in internship programs. College-bound students may be less interested in earning wages or finding a position that leads to a full-time job after high school; instead, they may seek opportunities to define a career goal that can inform their selection of a college major or at least provide a focus for the essay they must submit on their college application. At the same time, school staff responsible for placing students in internships must refrain from imposing their own stereotypes on students based simply on their grades or apparent readiness for college; instead, staff should work with individual students to determine what they might want (and be able) to get out of their internship experiences.

Our data provide cautiously optimistic conclusions about the quality of the internships high schools develop for students. For the most part, these internships are not in the retail sector that traditionally employs teenagers. Also, a majority of internships are linked to school in a variety of ways. Most interns discussed their work in class or with school staff and used skills developed in class on the job. In general, the internships students find through school appear to offer more learning opportunities than do the positions they find on their own.

However, to the extent that we can judge from a four-year period, the schools covered by the eight states' school-to-work initiatives did not expand or substantially enhance student internships. Participation in paid and unpaid internships did not change appreciably between the class of 1996 and that of 2000. We found only slim evidence of improvement in the quality of paid internships. Instead, interest in involving a large, diverse group of students in work-based activities appears to have led schools to expand brief worksite observation activities that can easily be developed and that require a relatively small commitment of time from students.

The focus on briefer workplace activities may be disappointing to those who advocate substantial growth in more extended internships, yet it has two potential benefits. First, as noted, many high school graduates report that their job-shadowing experiences were very helpful in clarifying their career goals. Although these activities are not designed to provide opportunities to apply or develop skills, their role in clarifying students' goals is potentially quite useful. Second, if the enhanced interest in job-shadowing initiatives is sustained, these efforts have the potential to strengthen schools' internship programs. Specifically, students who have visited one or more worksites may be able to make a more informed choice of an internship and get more out of their workplace experiences. To realize this objective, however, school staff will need to consciously help students obtain job-shadowing opportunities in settings similar to those offering internships and to encourage students to reflect upon their job-shadowing experiences.

It remains uncertain the extent to which resources will be available in the future for enhancing and expanding internship programs. Given the lack of growth in internships during a period when many policymakers supported this objective, it seems unlikely that internship programs will expand in the near future as states increasingly focus on school accountability and ways of increasing students' academic achievements and test scores. Our analysis and fieldwork suggest that the concern that work-based activities might sometimes interfere with students' studies is an important constraint on the development of these activities. More generally, expansion of work-based activities is unlikely to occur unless school officials and parents perceive these activities as providing attractive learning opportunities. Schools could respond to these concerns in at least four ways.

First, to enhance work-based learning activities and to make them more attractive to educators and parents, schools could forge stronger connections between students' workplace experiences and the school curriculum. Although many students report some connection between their internships and assignments at school, case-study evidence suggests that these connections are not always particularly deep. Because few employers are willing and able to substantially reconfigure students' work activities to reinforce the school curriculum, school staff and students must be creative in finding ways to make use of workplace experiences. It is a challenge to make meaningful connections between the academic curriculum and work-based activities, and can require a substantial commitment from teachers and students, and sometimes from employers. Chapter 10 addresses this issue in depth and gives ways for school staff to enhance the learning from workplace experiences.

Second, to win support from school staff, it may be wise to limit the duration of paid, work-based activities and to schedule them so as not to conflict with students' regular classes. Some teachers might endorse paid work-based learning activities if they are sure that these activities are substitutes for regular after-school jobs that provide fewer learning opportunities. Even if these activities have this advantage, however, work-based learning advocates are likely to have difficulty securing broad support among educators unless internships are scheduled at times that do not interfere with students' classes, with only a moderate amount of time at the workplace. But since very brief internships tend to provide more limited learning opportunities, school staff could try to develop more internships of intermediate duration.

Finally, advocates may need to cultivate greater public appreciation for the types of competencies and knowledge that work-based activities are best suited to develop. Work-based activities occasionally can reinforce academic competencies, but this may never be their most important asset. Even when internships are connected to the school curriculum, they may not provide many opportunities to practice or reinforce academic skills. However, carefully designed internships do often provide opportunities to perform challenging tasks, receive feedback from employer and school staff, and learn about the world of work. These kinds of experiences have the potential to cultivate students' ability to define and solve problems, work productively with others, and develop a sense of self-confidence and direction. Whether or not these developmental benefits lead to higher levels of academic achievement, they can contribute to students' success in the labor market and in life. Much of the rest of this book provides evidence of the potential value of work-based learning in cultivating a diverse array of student competencies. By developing internships that realize this potential and documenting these contributions, supporters of work-based learning can demonstrate its value in expanding students' career options.

This chapter has been funded at least in part with Federal funds from the U.S. Department of Education under contract EA95010001. The content of the chapter does not necessarily reflect the views or policies of the U.S. Department of Education.

CHAPTER 4

Employer Involvement in Work-Based Learning

If work-based learning is to be effective, it requires the active participation of employers. During the 1990s, the most ambitious advocates hoped that many of the country's workplaces would play a central role in the education of a significant number of young people (Hamilton, 1990; Lerman & Pouncy, 1990). But employers are not in business to educate adolescents. Indeed, during the discussions and debates of the last 15 years about education reform, many observers have questioned the quality of training that American employers provide for their own employees (Commission on the Skills of the American Workforce, 1990; Dertouzos, Lester & Solow, 1989). These observations led many analysts to be skeptical about whether enough employers could be recruited to provide work-based learning opportunities for a substantial number of students (see, e.g., the articles published in Bailey, 1995). Thus, Osterman (1995) wrote that "the prospects for widespread employer participation seem bleak" (p. 79). Klein (1995) evaluated the economic incentives for employer participation, and wrote that further market-based encouragement would be needed.

The results of early research on this question were inconclusive. Mathematica Policy Research's study of the demonstration sites that were a model for the School-to-Work legislation found that the implementation of youth apprenticeship programs posed "a substantial burden on employers," and raised doubts about the potential for widespread employer participation (Hershey & Silverberg, 1993, p.9). Others were also pessimistic about employer recruitment (Office of Technology Assessment, 1995; Stern, 1995). Yet a study of 10 programs around the country from 1991 to

1994 (the National Youth Apprenticeship Initiative) found that although most of the programs began with a focus in one industry, almost all increased the number of participating industries and occupational areas over time (Kopp, Kazis, & Churchill, 1995). Another study of cooperative education sites found that "employer recruitment was not a significant problem and that there were generally enough employer slots for the referral of eligible students" (Lynn & Wills, 1994, p.23). Other researchers held positive views on the likelihood of widespread employer involvement (Kazis & Goldberger, 1995; Zemsky, 1994).

Employer recruitment is not simply a numerical problem. Even if an adequate number of work-based learning slots could be found, the educational value of an internship will depend on what the intern does on the job. Chapter 2 emphasized that it is not enough for students to simply be present in exciting, learning-intensive workplaces; they must be engaged in appropriate activities. One of the presumed benefits of internships is contact between adults and youth. But coexistence in the same workplace does not guarantee that students will begin to be incorporated into a community of practice where they can learn and grow. Reluctant employers who give in to the pleas of school counselors are not likely to devote the effort and staff time that could turn a boring job into a productive learning experience.

This chapter investigates employer participation in work-based learning. After explaining our methods and the data on which we base the analysis, we present evidence on the percentage of employers who were already providing internship slots at the time of our data collection. Are internships provided by a tiny minority of employers or is there a substantial foundation of participation on which to build? Policies to expand or improve internships must take account of the motivations of employers and the barriers that stand in the way of expanding the number of employer participants. We address these topics along with a discussion of whether employer recruitment is a significant barrier to program expansion. Then, as Haimson and Bellotti did in Chapter 3, we turn to measures of internship quality, this time based on information reported by employers. We are interested in measuring the absolute level of quality in internships, but we would also like to know what may lead to higher-quality internships. Finally, we present some recommendations for expanding and strengthening the participation of employers.

Methods and Data

We use both qualitative and quantitative data for this chapter. The qualitative data come from case studies of 12 programs in nine sites, located in both urban and rural areas. We collected the quantitative data in 1996 from a survey of employers participating in 5 of the 12 programs and from a survey of a comparison group of nonparticipating employers in those same five labor markets.

Students in all 12 of these programs participated in internships or apprenticeships. As explained in the preceding chapter, many school-to-work initiatives offer students one-day job-shadowing opportunities or short-term mentors from the business community; although these activities are certainly valuable, programs in which students spend regular and significant amounts of time at workplaces require the most commitment from employers. The 12 programs selected, which include some new as well as older, more established programs, are described in Table 4.1. In the fall of 1995 and the winter and spring of 1996, we conducted one and, in some cases, two site visits to each of the programs.

At each research site, we toured the programs and schools and interviewed students, teachers, counselors, principals, and intermediaries who helped broker the participation of employers. We observed classes, particularly any that purported to link the work-based learning component with the classroom curriculum. We also visited worksites and interviewed employers, including the human resources staff who coordinated the student interns, as well as the individuals who supervised and mentored the students. We asked whether the school-to-work programs were developed with employer initiative or input, how the sites recruited and worked with employers, and what methods program personnel were using to continue to recruit employers. One of our goals was to find out if there was attrition among participating employers in the already-established programs, and if so, why. We asked employers about their motivations for involvement, and what factors would encourage or discourage their continued participation.

From May to August 1996, we surveyed the employers involved in 5 of the 12 programs.[1] The five, each of which had more than 40 employer participants, are included in Table 4.1. These were: the urban alternative school; the urban community college cooperative education program; the county-wide Education for Employment system; the urban school district school-to-careers program; and the district-wide youth apprenticeship program. At the same time, we surveyed a matching sample of nonparticipating employers in those same labor markets, which we created from a Dun and Bradstreet database of all known firms by geographic region.

The questionnaire, which had an average response time of about 30 minutes, was in two sections. For participating employers, the first section asked for information about the firm's participation in the program, and was answered by the person supervising the interns or coordinating the firm's participation. In the nonparticipant version, the first section asked

---

[1]For a detailed description of the sample, data collection procedures, and survey instrument, see Bailey, Hughes, and Barr, 2000.

Table 4.1 Characteristics of Research Sites at the Time of Data Collection

	Urban Community College	Urban Alternative School	County-wide Education for Employment System	Manufacturing Technologies Partnership, Careers in Health, Financial Learning Academy	Urban School District School-to-Careers Program
Program started	1971	1972	1986; employer-initiated	MTP in 1991; Careers in Health 1980; FLA 1995 (also employer-initated)	In 1990 received foundation funds to extend academies concept; began in 1992
Program structure	Two-year program, approx. 2000 students complete two internships; attempt to match placements with students' majors	950 students in 10th–12th grades; academic and elective credits given for work experiences; students spend little time in the classroom	2300 students in 8th–12th grades; different varieties of work-based learning offered in the 11th and 12th grades; 24 career areas; half-day programs	MTP 89 students CIH 250 students FLAG 24 students MTP two-year program CIH one or two years FLA two years All are half-day programs	1000 students participating; curriculum starts in 9th grade but work-based learning only in 11th and 12th; "theme" areas are manufacturing, business, health, hospitality and tourism, printing, and transportation; these located in different schools

Table 4.1 Characteristics of Research Sites at the Time of Data Collection (*Cont.*)

	Urban Community College	Urban Alternative School	County-wide Education for Employment System	Manufacturing Technologies Partnership, Careers in Health, Financial Learning Academy	Urban School District School-to-Careers Program
Worksite structure	Some positions paid, some unpaid; students work for 13-week periods, part-time or full-time	Unpaid positions last for 8-week cycles; full-time or part-time; by graduation kids have had 8–12 work experiences	Varies by career area; ex: health students work 3–4 hours, 2–3 days a week in 12th grade; unpaid	MTP paid work 2 hours every day; CIH same schedule, unpaid; FLA at worksites 3 hrs., 3 days per week, work when projects available	Juniors work 1–2 days per week; seniors can work more; internships substitute for class time and are paid
Employer characteristics	Over 300 employers of all types	352 employers of all types	117 employers of all types	MTP: GM and 12 others; CIH: 3 hospitals, 1 HMO; FLA: 2 banks, 1 CPA firm	179 employers of all types in the "theme" areas

Table 4.1 Research Sites *(Cont.)*

	Medical Careers Program, Graphic Communication Program	High School of Economics & Finance	District-wide Youth Apprenticeship Program	Rural Vo-Tech Center Manufacturing Technologies Program
Program started	Medical Careers Program developed in 1993; graphics/printing program began in 1995 and is no longer operating	1993	1994; initiated by area superintendents and business leaders; is no longer operating	1994; started with business input; program no longer operating
Program structure	Full-day senior-year health-occupations program; 40 students maximum; students alternate between 10 weeks at school and 10 weeks at the hospital; printing program had same structure but only enrolled 7 students	Magnet high school; "theme" is business and finance; 3 internships required; 450 students in '95–'96	85 students; 2-year, full-day program; students alternate 1-week classes at magnet schools and 1-week full-time work; newly developed applied curriculum	9 students graduated 1996; 1-year half-day manufacturing technologies program; mornings either in applied classes or at worksite; afternoons at regular high schools

Table 4.1 Research Sites *(Cont.)*

	Medical Careers Program, Graphic Communication Program	High School of Economics & Finance	District-wide Youth Apprenticeship Program	Rural Vo-Tech Center Manufacturing Technologies Program
Worksite structure	Unpaid; students work about 3 hours per day during the two 10-week periods at the hospital; have classroom at hospital	2 unpaid and 1 paid internships; work done on Wed. afternoons or after-school hours; some connecting activities and theme curriculum	Students paid at prevailing wage rates; work full-time every other week during school year for up to 2 years with the same employer	Unpaid internships; first semester students rotate around firm, second semester stay in one area; work 2 hours per day, 2–3 days per week
Employer characteristics	General hospital; printing program was industry-initiated and supported by the local chapter of the Printing Industry of America; many employers interested	All types of employers: nonprofits, for-profits, city agencies, etc.; at least 40 employers	All types of employers; 44 at the time of our visit; Business-Education Partnership already existed; much use of employer organizations	4 firms in manufacturing; all firms on board since the beginning

about concerns the firms might have about participating in a school-to-work program. The second section (for both samples) asked for general characteristics of the company—such as employee demographics and turnover, and human resources policies—and was answered by a human resources manager.

Out of 548 participating employers and 900 nonparticipating employers, we gathered 334 complete responses from participating employers and 323 from nonparticipants, resulting in response rates of 61 percent and 35.9 percent, respectively.

The Scale of Employer Participation

Many firms in the United States have been providing internships, apprenticeships, and other forms of work-based learning for many years. For example, there are several hundred thousand students in cooperative education programs. It is important to know how many employers are now participating in some form of internship program. Our survey of nonparticipants does provide information that would allow us to make an estimate of the participation rate in the cities that we surveyed. Before interviewing respondents, we asked a screening question: if they were providing or had provided internships. Of the total of 468 establishments that responded to the screening question, 113 (24.1 percent) had provided internships. Table 4.2 displays the participation rates by firm size category. Clearly the largest firms are much more likely to provide internships. Over 40 percent of the larger establishments (50 or more employees) in the labor markets covered in the survey provided internships, but even the smallest group of establishments (0 to 10 employees) had a participation rate of one in seven.

Data collected in 1997 and 1998 by the Census Bureau from a national survey of employers are consistent with our findings. In 1997, 39 percent of private, for-profit business establishments with more than 20 employees

Table 4.2 Employer Participation Rates*

Size Category	Percentage of Firms in Size Category That Have Interns
0–9	16.6
10–49	25.9
50+	41.7

*Calculation is based on percentage of nonparticipants answering yes to screening question, and is reweighted to correct for industry oversampling.

were participating in some form of work-based learning[2] (Capelli, Shapiro, & Shumanis, 1998). Twenty percent were participating specifically in internships (Capelli, Shapiro & Shumanis, 1998). Probably encouraged by the growing number of states receiving funding from the School-to-Work Opportunities Act, between 1997 and 1998 there was growth in the proportion of employers participating in their local school-to-work partnerships and in employer involvement in work-based learning activities (Shapiro, 1999). It is likely that the strong economy at the time also created an environment conducive to the growth of employer partnerships, but the support of large, influential firms such as Citigroup and Charles Schwab, and employer organizations such as the Committee on Economic Development, probably also contributed to the expansion.

Thus, our conclusions about the extent of participation of employers are consistent with the conclusions from the preceding chapter on participation of students. In both cases, skeptics argued that a variety of problems would prevent the spread of work-based learning among students and employers. But simple counts of participants have shown that work-based learning was already a widespread phenomenon among both groups even before the enactment of the School-to-Work Opportunities Act. And in the case of employer involvement specifically, participation spread in the 1990s.

Why Do Firms Participate?

Any policy to expand or to improve the participation of employers in work-based learning must be based on a firm understanding of why firms would be willing to provide internships. The possible reasons can be roughly divided into philanthropic and self-interested motivations. Self-interest can, in turn, be divided into what we refer to as individual and collective self-interest (Bailey, 1995).[3]

Philanthropic motives: Many employers feel a commitment to their communities and look for opportunities to make some contribution to the general well-being of their towns and neighborhoods. Some employers try to do this through helping to strengthen the local education systems. This often involves donation of equipment; participation in "adopt-a-school"

---

[2]The types of work-based learning specified in the survey were internship, cooperative education, job shadowing, mentoring, registered apprenticeship, and youth apprenticeship.

[3]Theoretical reasons for employer participation are also discussed in Corson & Silverberg (1994), Hershey & Silverberg (1993), Klein (1995), Osterman (1995), and Urquiola et al. (1997).

programs; offering sites for field trips; explaining occupations and industries to young people; and individual mentoring or tutoring. But many employers have also agreed to help out by providing internships.

Individual self-interest: There are also many reasons why businesses might have an individual self-interest in providing internships. They may believe that their participation will generate goodwill, which could bring them both political and economic benefits. (This incentive to participate may be difficult to distinguish from the philanthropic one.) Or, interns might be seen as low-cost labor (especially if they are not paid). Some employers could consider internships to be a good way to get to know and train young people who might be enticed to stay on as part of the firm's permanent workforce. Working with schools to provide internships might be seen as a way to strengthen relationships with local schools, both to obtain advantageous access to the best graduates and to influence schools so that they will turn out more qualified graduates. Those who have studied school-to-work programs suggest that participating employers may reap unanticipated benefits to existing workers who supervise and mentor young people. These could include improved management skills, more enjoyment of their jobs, and greater attention to their own skill development (Kazis & Goldberger, 1995; Olson, 1997).

Collective interests: One of the most common arguments for improving education in the United States is that firms lack an adequately skilled labor force. Thus, some employers may be convinced that an education system with a strong work-based learning component will be in their collective interest if it generally improves the quality of the labor market from which they draw their employees, even if it does not provide an immediate bottom-line benefit. The problem with this argument is that the actions of one employer will not be significant enough to influence the overall labor market (unless the employer's firm is very large relative to the local labor market) and if enough employers do participate, then the general pool of recruits will improve even if some individual employers provide no internships. Because of this "free-rider" problem, the articulation of collective interests usually requires the participation of a strong intermediary organization, such as a union or employer group, which can encourage broad participation in recognition of the broad benefits.

Previous research concludes that the recruitment of entry-level workers and philanthropic (community-service) goals are the most important motivations for participation (Lynn & Wills, 1994; OTA, 1995; Pauly, Kopp, & Haimson, 1995). Another objective is to gain access to low-cost, short-term employees. Thus, although both self-interest and philanthropy are important, self-interested motivations have been found to slightly outweigh community service.

Whatever the initial reasons for participation, Zemsky (1994) reported that participating employers found the internships to be beneficial to themselves, as well as to the students (they believed). Kazis and Goldberger (1995) concluded, on the basis of fieldwork at school-to-work programs, that "once employers get involved in working closely with schools and young people, they tend to become more rather than less committed to intensive efforts" (p. 188). A 1997 national sample of employers found that firms that had close relationships with schools on a variety of measures tended to have lower turnover rates, although the researchers who reported these results cannot say for sure whether the close relationship *caused* the lower turnover (Shapiro & Iannozzi, 1998). Still, the researchers contend there are "real and substantial benefits" to individual employers who participate in school activities (Shapiro & Jannozzi, 1998, p. 158).

One project used case studies of six firms providing internships to try to measure the actual financial costs and benefits of providing internships (Bassi & Ludwig, 2000). The benefits included the value of student labor, reduced training and recruitment costs, higher productivity of students hired as regular employees compared with other entry-level employees, improved community relations, improved productivity and morale of employees, and increased diversity in the workplace. The costs included expenses for the development and administration of the programs, the time that supervisors and mentors worked with the students, intern salaries, and miscellaneous costs such as tools. Many of the benefits were difficult to quantify; however, the study found clear net benefits from participation for three of the six firms. The other firms were found to have net costs in the short-term, yet the authors suggest these might be outweighed by hard-to-measure long-term gains. One of the six companies had discontinued its program because of high costs and company personnel policies that restricted the eventual hiring of student apprentices—thus preventing the firm from benefiting from reduced training and recruitment costs in the long term.

What do our data, both from the fieldwork and the employer survey, tell us about the motivations of employers? As Table 4.3 shows, the majority of participants chose philanthropic reasons for participating whereas over three-fourths of the nonparticipants looked to internships for self-interest reasons. These comparisons should be made with caution since the answers for participants were based on experience whereas those for nonparticipants were hypothetical.

The Philanthropic Motivation

More than half of the participating employers who responded to our survey claimed some philanthropic reason for participating. One-fourth cited

Table 4.3 Most Important Motivation for Participation: Participants Versus Nonparticipants

Most Important Motivation to Participate Is/Would Be	Participants		Nonparticipants	
Local labor shortage	3.0%		4.3%	
Opportunity to test potential employees	5.8%		15.9%	
Part-time/short term hiring	10.3%		24.1%	
Improving public ed. system	33.1%		9.1%	
Encouragement from industry gps.	0.6%		1.4%	
Reducing benefits expenses	2.7%		1.9%	
Contributing to community	25.8%		11.9%	
Access to prescreened applicants	3.7%		5.1%	
Increased training is necessary	4.6%		5.0%	
Access to pool of qualified workers	10.3%		21.3%	

N = 329 for participants, 295 for nonparticipants. Standard errors of estimates are under 1.3%.

Primary Motivation Would Be Helping Community or Educational System				
Private, for-profit sites	47.7%	(3.8%)	17.7%	(2.5%)
Private, not-for-profit sites	76.8%	(4.3%)	32.3%	(6.8%)
Government sites	64.2%	(6.7%)	81.4%	(13.0%)

*Standard errors in parentheses.

an interest in contributing to the community as their primary motivation, and one-third said that their most important reason was to improve the public education system. Employers also cited the philanthropic motivation in face-to-face interviews. Nevertheless, in these interviews, employers rarely put this forth as the sole or most important incentive for their involvement. Many program coordinators, however, said that philanthropic arguments were important in convincing employers to participate. One school-to-careers coordinator from Philadelphia said that a selling point is to tell an employer: "Here are children from your own community that you can actually directly help." She stated that employers like to work with a particular school in their own community. Another internship coordinator said that she has certain employers to whom she can send the most troubled students; she knows that those employers will continue in the program however little they receive from their participation. The impression of teachers at the urban magnet school is that employers become involved because "they feel sorry for inner-city public school kids."

Yet coordinators from other programs stated that, although participating employers often cite philanthropic reasons for their involvement, the program operators do not usually emphasize altruism when making their pitches to employers. Some of those whose job it is to recruit employers told us that urging employers to "give back to the community" can backfire if the implication is that employers do not give to their communities already.

The Individual Benefits Appeal

A substantial minority—about one-third—of the employers who responded to our survey identified self-interested reasons as their motivations for participating. In our field visits, employers and program coordinators most frequently cited three broad reasons why internship programs might be in the direct interest of employers. These reasons included positive public relations, meeting firm labor needs, and improving the morale and engagement of incumbent employees.

Public relations: We were told by the staff of the urban School-to-Careers program that the city's hospitals use their participation in the program for public relations purposes. A bandwagon effect has even been created among the city's different hospitals. Thus, initial employer involvement can help program personnel succeed with further recruitment: the program is given legitimacy in the eyes of other employers, and nonparticipants may feel compelled to become involved so they do not look bad in comparison with participants.

Labor needs: Because student interns are either free or are paid on average a low hourly wage and given no benefits, some employers use school-to-work programs as temporary agencies; the costs of supervising students evidently do not outweigh the benefits of the students' labor. Ten percent of our survey respondents said that they participated so that they could hire part-time or short-term workers. Another 10 percent said that the program gives them access to a pool of qualified workers.[4]

The Financial Learning Academy program is an example of firms benefiting from flexible labor. The creation of the program was spurred by a local bank's concern about the area's labor pool, yet the program was structured so that the participating firms could use the students in the program as temporary help. When a firm has a project or task that a student

---

[4]In a survey of employers participating in work-based learning programs that was carried out by the Office of Technology Assessment, nearly two-thirds of employers cited recruitment goals as the most important reason for their participation (Office of Technology Assessment, 1995).

can assist with, the firm contacts a program staff member, who matches a student to the project. Students leave their worksite classrooms for these "earning projects" which can last from one day to several weeks, and at the time of our research, students were paid about minimum wage for this work. One such student helped a bank put into place a new computer-software system, but other "earning projects" are more mundane, such as microfilming and shredding. Firms participating in this program are clearly gaining low-cost, productive labor.

An employer who takes interns from the urban magnet school was clear about the firm's use of the students as "extra help," and said they probably could not take interns if they had to pay them. When we asked a focus group of students from this school why they thought employers become involved with them, the students said almost simultaneously: "Free labor!" The student responses were not all negative, but one student in particular had the impression from her internship that employers take interns not to give them a learning experience but simply to do their most tedious work.

Employers also use school-to-work programs to recruit permanent, full-time employees. A railway maintenance yard for an urban public transportation system is successfully using the city's school-to-career system to recruit apprentices; at this worksite, student interns follow a demanding curriculum created by the yard's assistant director especially for the program, and are paid $9.60 an hour (at the time of our research). The director of the now-defunct Youth Apprenticeship program pitched the benefits of trained labor and the problem of local skills shortages to potential participants. The Manufacturing Technologies Partnership (MTP) with General Motors had its origins in that company's need for skilled trades apprentices. Through this manufacturing school-to-work program, in partnership with the area education officials and the union, GM could rely on a steady stream of young recruits who came prepared for the apprenticeship examination. At the time of our research, three General Motors plants were taking over 30 students in the area, and the program had been replicated in other parts of the state. An additional 20 non-GM employers also took student interns because, according to the program director, "Skilled labor is impossible to find in this county."

Boosting the morale and enthusiasm of regular employees: Some employers say that having to teach their job to an interested young person renews employees' pride in their work. For example, the director of community relations at an urban hospital said that the hospital personnel working with the students received gratification from having young people look up to them. Thus, our findings agree with those of Kazis and Goldberger (1995), who state that "employers report . . . that having young people in their workplaces motivates existing employees . . . and improves the quality of supervision and coaching, for the adult workforce as well as for the young people" (pp. 188–189).[5]

The Collective Appeal

Possible responses to the survey questions about employers' motivations included items representing collective reasons; these were: "encouragement from industry groups or other employers" and "increased training is necessary for your industry to remain competitive." Table 4.3 (p. 78) shows that neither participants nor nonparticipants tended to choose either of these as their most important reason for participating (or, in the case of nonparticipants, for considering participation).

Another type of collective motivation that we found in the fieldwork is the goal of marketing an industry as a whole to young people. The owner of an electrical wiring company who participated in the youth apprenticeship program characterized his participation as a "selling job." He pointed out that the work done by his employees is perceived as dirty and nonglamorous, thus he appreciated having the opportunity to teach a wide audience, educators as well as students, about the more modern and technical aspects of his industry. In a different case, employers in the printing industry helped create the Graphic Communications program in an attempt to do a "selling job" of their industry to young people; the industry was suffering because of the difficulty of recruiting new talent.

An additional collective motivation found in our site visits was the goal of developing the labor force of the area as a whole. At one particular site, employers participating in the successful half-day medical occupations program hoped that the program would induce locally trained youth to remain in the area. Those involved in the financial program in the same town also spoke of their desire to upgrade the skills of the local labor force, which could ultimately benefit all the local employers.

Characteristics of Participating Employers

We can gain additional insights into the motivations of employers by comparing the characteristics of participating and nonparticipating employers. We have already seen that large firms are much more likely than small firms to provide internship slots, although a substantial number of smaller firms do participate. It is likely that program operators looking for placements go to the large firms first, since such firms are more likely to be able

---

[5]Also see Klein, 1995.

to provide multiple placements. Large firms are also more likely to have specialized community relations departments and human resources staff who can oversee an internship program. In addition, being more visible, large firms might have more incentive to engage in public service activities.

Another significant distinguishing factor appears to be the type of work organization in a firm. Compared to the nonparticipants we surveyed, participating employers provide more training for their employees in general, and tend to have more progressive human resource practices, such as job rotation, self-managed teams, quality circles, Total Quality Management, and profit-sharing. One interpretation is that internships are an integral part of a broad human resources strategy, suggesting that as (or if) firms move toward more progressive strategies, employer recruitment will be easier.

A striking finding from the surveys is that less than 50 percent of the participants are for-profit, whereas 90 percent of the nonparticipants are for-profit. It is clear that appeals to "help out" the community or local school system might be more effective with the not-for-profit and public sectors than such appeals would be with profit-making firms. Moreover, not-for-profits are often short of cash, and interns might be attractive as cheap labor. Cash constraints may simply make it impossible to hire additional employees, so such organizations may be faced with the choice of taking an unpaid intern or doing without anyone. Indeed, unpaid interns are much overrepresented among the not-for-profit participants.[6]

The survey also asked employers what would motivate them *not* to participate, or in the case of nonparticipants, why they did not participate (see Table 4.4). Participants were much more concerned than nonparticipants about students' lack of basic skills (nearly 27 percent of participants listed this as their biggest concern) and their unreliability or immaturity. Possibly reflecting dissatisfaction with the interns, an in-depth study of one of our survey sites, an urban community college, found a high attrition rate for employer participants. Indeed, half of the employers who participated in that program between 1984 and 1995 participated for only one internship cycle (Wieler & Bailey, 1997). Finally, as in previous studies, the present one finds that both participating and nonparticipating employers are much more concerned about the indirect costs of training students than

---

[6]We also conducted a multivariate analysis of the determinants of participation. In that analysis we controlled for the establishment size, the types of training programs and human resources programs, and for the sector (private, public, or nonprofit). According to that analysis, the most important determinants of participation were employment size and the types of human resources practices. Establishments in the public sector were more likely than private, for-profit firms to participate and that difference was statistically significant. The difference between for-profit and nonprofit firms was not statistically significant (Bailey, Hughes & Barr, 2000).

Table 4.4 Factors That Discourage Participation: Participants Versus Nonparticipants

Most Important Motivation Not to Participate Is/Would Be	Participants	Nonparticipants
Employee resistance	1.4%	5.1%
Lost productivity for trainers	15.4%	23.2%
Students might leave after training	4.8%	15.0%
Opposition from unions	3.4%	1.7%
Uncertain economic climate	3.9%	4.1%
Students lack basic skills	26.9%	9.0%
OSHA/ child labor-law violations	9.6%	10.1%
Students not always available	9.6%	10.2%
Students are unreliable or immature	22.1%	15.8%
Student wages are too costly	1.4%	4.4%
Problems working with schools	1.4%	1.4%

N = 208 for participants, 279 for nonparticipants. Standard errors of estimates are under 1.9%.

they are about the direct costs of paying students (though only about half of internships are paid).

Summary

What can we conclude from these data about the motivations and concerns of employers? Clearly, employers can have a mix of motivations. In all of the cases from the fieldwork, even the most philanthropically motivated employers also hoped to benefit individually through their participation. For example, the success of the alternative high school internship program rests on a key trade-off: in exchange for their willingness to help at-risk youth, employers get free labor. Yet, as a program staff member put it, the employers must have a great deal of altruism because otherwise "they wouldn't be doing it with all the problems the kids have." The employers are also proud to have helped young people turn their lives around.

It is hard to argue from the survey data that most firms are participating out of a conviction that it will advance their business in a direct way. There is some evidence in our study that philanthropic motivations could support a reasonably large school-to-work program; the alternative high school places hundreds of students each year and has been doing so for over 15 years. On the other hand, our survey shows that public-sector and not-for-profit organizations have been the mainstay of the participant pool. To further penetrate the for-profit world more successfully, program operators will have to convince employers that participation will be in their firms' interests.

Is Program Size Constrained by Employer Participation?

What are the overall implications of the mix of incentives and motivations associated with employer participation in work-based learning? Are program operators turning away students because they cannot find internships for them? To answer this question, we draw on information collected from our 12 case-study sites.[7]

The 12 programs fell into one of three categories. The first group was characterized by a scarcity of students. Programs in the second group had more trouble finding employers. And those in the third group were able to find adequate numbers of employers and students given the program target sizes.

Three of the 12 programs—the Medical Careers and Graphic Communications at one site, and the rural Manufacturing Technologies Program—had more difficulty recruiting students than employers. In fact, the latter two ceased to operate because of a lack of student enrollment. All three programs were developed with employer partners, but in the latter two cases, employer interest and participation was insufficient for program success. The Medical Careers program, although a stellar initiative, continued to have difficulty attracting enough students to fill available slots.

Once there was steady student demand, five of the programs—the High School of Economics and Finance, the district-wide Youth Apprenticeship Program, the urban district-wide School-to-Careers program, the Manufacturing Technologies Partnership, and the Financial Learning Academy—experienced difficulty securing large numbers of employers to provide work-based learning placements. At the time of our fieldwork, these were all relatively new programs, so staff were still working to build a larger base of participating employers. Some applicants were being turned away or had to wait for a placement. Nonetheless, as indicated by the student interest, these programs had achieved wide acceptance in their respective communities, and they were successfully placing many students in work-based learning positions.

Four of the programs—the urban community college, the urban alternative school, the county-wide Education for Employment system, and Careers in Health—had steady student demand and either high employer recruitment or retention. The longevity and relatively large size of these four programs demonstrates that, over time, programs can gain a reputation for benefiting both students and employers, and can become successful at recruiting both.

---

[7]See Hughes (1998) for more on the case-study research.

Thus, for 7 of the 12 programs we studied, employer recruitment was not an insurmountable barrier. And four of the five programs in the middle category continued to work to expand their base of employer participants (the apprenticeship program closed, but not because of employer- or student-recruitment difficulties). In addition, employers were involved in the initiation and development phases of all but two of the programs. The fact that the main problem of some programs was that they lacked students, rather than employers, is significant, as it calls into question the assumption that employer participation is the principal challenge to creating a school-to-work system.

The Quality of Work-Based Learning

In our survey of participating firms, we collected data on three measures of the quality of work-based learning: the type of occupation interns were placed in; the presence or absence of particular program characteristics; and the amount of internship time spent learning. Chapters 5–8 will examine the quality of internships in much more detail, based on our extensive observations of the activities of interns. But the survey measures do offer some sense of the potential learning opportunities represented by internships in the particular firm.

Type of Occupation

An important finding is that the internships were not concentrated in retail, the traditional youth-employing sector. The majority were in the service sector, in a diverse group of occupations that includes health, education, and business services. Nearly half of the internships were in administrative support positions—entry-level jobs in office and business employment. Interns were also overrepresented in technical occupations whereas relatively few were in machine operative positions and other areas of youth concentration. The overrepresentation in technical jobs is encouraging since employers often have difficulty filling these positions; this is further evidence that some employers may be using school-to-work internships to strengthen their pool of available labor.

Program Characteristics

The survey asked about the program components (or practices) that are often considered part of the school-to-work model. We believe the presence of these components indicates a better planned and implemented work-based learning initiative. The model has ten components (see Table 4.5).

Table 4.5 Common Components of School-to-Work Programs

Component	Percent of Firms Practicing
1. A written agreement between school and student	65.5%
2. A customized training plan designed specifically for each student	47.3%
3. Student learning at the worksite is documented and assessed	90.0%
4. A workplace mentor or supervisor who counsels students and teaches job-related skills	95.5%
5. Rotation of students among several jobs	61.5%
6. Training for mentors or supervisors	33.4%
7. Company provides classrooms at the worksite	20.2%
8. Company serves on the advisory board of the program	14.9%
9. Employer advises schools on content of curriculum	36.8%
10. Company staff teaches or makes presentations to students at the school	24.7%

Standard errors of estimates are less than 1.5%.

About 70 percent of the firms responded that their participation included between three and six of these practices. On average, the firms had four practices. The large majority of firms provided a mentor and claimed to document and assess student learning on the job. Internships in a large majority of the firms also involved a written agreement between the student and the school, and the rotation of students among several positions. In contrast, far fewer employers engaged in active participation with the schools—about one-third advised schools on the curricula; only one-fourth had staff make presentations at the school; and one-fifth provided classrooms at the site.

Findings from our fieldwork demonstrate that figures like these can present a misleading picture, however. When we asked students about their "mentors," we found that in many cases these individuals simply kept track of the students' hours. In several cases, the intern rarely saw his or her mentor at all; the term "mentor," then, was a misnomer. Also, even though the vast majority of firms responding to our survey replied that student work was documented and assessed, we found in our fieldwork that this often consisted of a superficial checkoff sheet completed by the student's supervisor.

Internship Duration and Learning Time

The amount of time it takes an intern to learn the assigned job is a measure of the amount of learning represented by the placement. A job that can be learned in a day has less educational value than one that takes a month to learn. Since internships take time away from other educational experiences, such as homework or extracurricular activities, as much time as possible during the internship should be spent learning.

We asked participating employers who responded to our survey how many weeks their internships lasted, how many hours per week the interns generally worked, and how many eight-hour days it took the student to learn his or her job or duties. We found that, on average, the internships lasted almost 23 weeks and it took 14 days to learn the jobs, so the interns were spending only about 14 percent of their time on the job learning. When we compared paid internships to unpaid ones, we found that paid placements had a higher mean percentage of time learning, and a higher program intensity score, an index measuring the number of program components (from Table 4.5). These quality measures were also higher for those firms who intended to hire their interns. The government sites had the highest program intensity, but the internship jobs in the private for-profit sector scored highest on the learning-time variable.

Regression analyses suggest that public and nonprofit organizations and those that expected to hire their interns as permanent employees tended to provide higher-quality internships (see Table 4.6). However, the not-for-profits had internships with the shortest learning times. It may be that nonprofits in particular try to provide beneficial learning experiences and therefore tend to follow program guidelines by introducing the types of practices measured by the intensity variable. Yet the nature of the jobs that they have available may not allow them to give interns positions that have an inherently high learning content. The regression analyses indicate that firms that paid their interns scored higher in terms of internships' learning times, yet the relationship between quality and whether the internship was paid was not strong. Significantly, the size of the organization was not related to any of the measures of work-based quality.

We also asked our survey respondents what level of education a regular (nonstudent) employee, in the same position as the intern, would have. Internships at sites where a college-educated worker would otherwise perform the work scored lower on our quality measures than at sites where a worker with a high school or two-year college education would otherwise do the work. This suggests that internships are best at sites where students are not too far behind other workers, rather than sites where the skill differentials are so great that students do separate work entirely. Not seeing

Table 4.6 Regression of Program Quality Measures on Firm Characteristics

	Program Intensity	Learning Time	% of Time Learning
	(Ordered Probit Regression)	(OLS Regression)	(OLS Regression)
Logarithm of establishment employment size	0.13	0.48	0.00
	(0.83)	(0.60)	(0.10)
Firms that hire	0.35††	3.29	0.04
	(2.65)	(1.19)	(1.54)
Firms that pay	−0.09	7.15*	−0.00
	(0.51)	(1.82)	(0.10)
Not-for-profit sector	0.29*	−7.77††	−0.05†
	(1.90)	(−2.41)	(1.77)
Government sector	0.64††	−2.80	−0.01
	(3.28)	(−0.70)	(0.37)
No. observations	274	261	229
Ln likelihood	−526.33		
Model chi²/ Model F-statistic	34.11(0.00)	4.95 (0.00)	2.03 (0.04)
Pseudo R²/ Adjusted R²	0.03	0.12	0.04

*T-statistics in parentheses.
†Significant at the 10% level.
††Significant at the 1% level.

the interns as potentially productive workers in their assigned tasks, the employers may pay less attention to them. The jobs that could otherwise be filled with workers without a high school degree also tend to score lower on the quality measures. These are probably typical teenage jobs that offer few opportunities to learn. Thus, this analysis suggests that internships are most productive when they involve jobs in which the interns could realistically be expected to be productive, but that still demand skills and abilities that the interns do not already have.

We mentioned earlier that firms that provided more training for their workers and that had more progressive human resources practices ("high-performance workplaces") were more likely to provide work-based learning. The data indicate that firms that engaged in these practices also provided higher-quality internships (on all of our measures except the ratio of learning time to program duration).

Discussion and Conclusions

Employer recruitment is not an insurmountable problem. A large number of employers are already willing to take on interns and many of the programs we studied had recruited and retained an adequate number of employers, and, in some cases, had been able to sustain a high number of participants for many years. These programs succeeded because of the staffs' understanding of local economic conditions and their skill at adjusting their strategies accordingly when those conditions changed, as well as their ability to form relationships with area employers. These educators wisely gauged the amount and depth of involvement they could expect from employers and the type and level of returns the employers required in order to continue their participation. If programs are to succeed and endure, the retention of employers is crucial, because recruiting new partners is difficult and time-consuming. Two of our long-running programs had different strategies with regard to retention: the urban alternative school retains employers through personal relationships and support while the community college keeps employers participating by not asking much of them.

The good news is that, for the most part, the internship placements in the programs we studied were not in the traditional youth-employing sectors and occupations. Furthermore, employer participation in the programs seemed to be associated with a cluster of progressive human resources practices. Not only were firms that used these practices more likely to participate, they were also more likely to provide higher-quality internships. This suggests that employer recruitment would become easier if these practices spread, even if participation is not necessarily in the direct short-term interest of the employers. Employer motivations for participation were rarely pure but were mixed and could change over time, and there appeared to be trade-offs between employer participation, student demand, and program quality. Thus, employer participation cannot be studied separately from other program features and concerns.

However, it is likely that the employer partners initially recruited were those whose participation was won most easily. Our survey results indicate that the chief motivation for many participating employers is philanthropic. Although altruistic motivations have clearly carried these programs a long way, further recruitment is liable to be more difficult—especially considering the extent of the resources spent to achieve the current level of employer involvement. Alternatively, in cases where the school-to-work movement has become better understood and more well known, it has probably been easier for program staff to find employer partners. Nonetheless, if work-based learning is to grow, more and stronger attempts must be made at marketing. The nonparticipating employers who responded to our survey indicated that they would need more bottom-line-oriented arguments to convince them to become involved.

After this analysis of employer participation, we are still left with the conclusion that the most important barrier to the growth of work-based learning is related to the extent to which parents, students, and teachers are convinced that internships have educational value. Indeed, preoccupation with employer participation can lead to neglect of other constituencies whose support is needed. In our field visits, school counselors were repeatedly blamed for either not presenting school-to-work programs as an option or for advising students not to enroll in them. Some teachers still believe that students are missing the "real work" of the classroom when they leave the school to go to a workplace. Thus, programs can fail when not enough of an effort is made to win these constituencies' acceptance. Indeed, the lack of student and parent demand may be a larger problem for work-based learning programs than the recruiting and retaining of a significant number of employers.

We are convinced that if there were a widespread conviction in our communities that work-based learning had significant educational value for a large number of students, then employer cooperation would be forthcoming. As a result, we will devote the rest of this book to examining the educational value of work-based learning and developing suggestions about how it could be strengthened.

CHAPTER 5

Work-Based Learning
and Academic Skills

This chapter addresses the claim that work-based experience will improve students' academic performance. The Office of Technology Assessment (OTA), in a congressionally mandated study of the School-to-Work Opportunities Act, suggested that one of the rationales for the act was as follows: "Academic work and occupational preparation in schools are to be upgraded and the two are to be integrated so that students can see how academics will be applicable in their work lives. Work-based learning experiences are to extend the academic and occupational instruction of schools. . . ." (OTA, 1995, p. 3). Yet interestingly, the legislation did not explicitly make the academic reinforcement claim. The act was more vague, stating that "students in the United States can achieve high academic and occupational standards, and many learn better and retain more when the students learn in context, rather than in the abstract" (U.S. 103d Congress, 1994, Section 2). The legislation went on to say that work-based learning, combined with school-based learning, "can be very effective in engaging student interest, enhancing skill acquisition . . . ," and the list continues. Yet academic skills were not specifically named (Section 3).

It is likely that the academic reinforcement claim came about as a response to opposition toward the spread of school-to-work programs. Originally, these programs were targeted toward the "forgotten half"—the middle half of high school students who exhibit no serious problems but are likely not headed for college (or at least four-year colleges) (Bailey & Merritt, 1997a). As the school-to-work strategy came to be seen by some as having broader potential—and when the legislation referred specifically to "all students"—opponents began to argue that work-based learning activities undermine academic learning. Opponents associated the initiative with vocational education, with the resulting view that education reform with a strong work-based learning component was "a threat to the college-prep curriculum" (Urquiola et al., 1997, p. 99; see also Vo, 1997). In the 1990s, higher academic standards and new academic tests were being implemented at the same time that school-to-work programs had been proliferating. Asserting that work-based learning contributes to, rather than takes away from, academic achievement was an apt rejoinder to critics. So the academic reinforcement claim spread.

Among work-based learning practitioners, the relationship between classroom learning and workplace learning tends to be generally assumed. That is, internship coordinators and cooperative education directors often use rhetoric that suggests that students can apply academic knowledge in workplace activities, and that learning in the workplace somehow reinforces school-based knowledge. As an example, the School District of Philadelphia (1998) distributed a handout to workplace mentors stating that: "within the context of the work site, students gain insight into how specific career-related jobs operate, which skills are most essential, and *how what is learned in school integrates with the real world*" (italics added). Since that claim seems to underlie much of the pedagogical practice and social policy in the field, it is important to subject it to more rigorous scrutiny.

The following section tests the common propositions about academic reinforcement. We first review some existing literature, including studies of how working affects youths' academic performance, and studies of the academic achievement of students in programs that include work-based learning. We then draw on empirical data from our research. The five work-based learning programs reported on here were chosen based on program staff's assertions that academics were a high priority in the programs, and that academics were integrated with the work experiences. Thus we believed these programs showed promise for academic reinforcement. In addition, we draw on the work of Stasz and her associates (Stasz & Brewer, 1998; Stasz & Kaganoff, 1997), and the earlier work of Moore (1981a; 1981b; 1986), all of whom also observed student-interns. This body of data provides a great deal of detailed description of what actually happens when students engage in work-based educational programs.

The Reinforcement Claim

James Herndon's story in *How to Survive in Your Native Land* (1971), about his student who could keep score flawlessly in the bowling league but who flunked every math test (even when Herndon gave him bowling-score math problems), demonstrates the serious disjuncture between classroom operations and real-world operations. The extensive literature by researchers like Scribner (1986) and Sternberg (1986) on the concept of practical intelligence, as well as the studies of real-world math by Lave (1988) and others, suggest that people rarely perform the kinds of cognitive operations outside of classrooms that they perform inside them. Cole, Hood, and McDermott's (1978) influential critique of experimental cognitive psychology argues that people don't think the same way in real-world situations as they do in laboratories. This is one of the core insights of the field of situated cognition: Cognitive activity varies across social contexts.

It may be at least intuitively obvious to say that people in workplaces *do* read, write, and compute. But it is also fair to ask whether the way they do those things corresponds broadly to what they do in classrooms. The situated and distributed cognition theorists suggest that it does not. There are some fundamental differences, they argue, between computation, writing, problem-solving, and memory in the classroom and in the workplace. Resnick's (1987) oft-cited article "Learning In School and Out" argues that there are broad differences between school learning and other learning: individual cognition in school versus shared cognition outside; pure mentation in school versus tool manipulation outside; symbol manipulation in school versus contextualized reasoning outside; and generalized learning in school versus situation-specific competencies outside school. Her point is that schooling is not organized so as to transmit the skills and abilities required for performance outside of school, and increasingly it is even failing at imparting academic competencies; she says "Modifying schooling to better enable it to promote skills for learning outside school may simultaneously renew its academic value" (p. 18). Resnick's contentions have been used in support of work-based learning programs; however, she does not directly advocate work-based learning but rather a transformation of the classroom "to redirect the focus of schooling to encompass more of the features of successful out-of-school functioning" (p. 19).

Thus there is now a body of research that demonstrates not the connection between, but the separation between classroom knowledge and that outside the classroom. Berryman and Bailey (1992) point out that "research, spanning decades, shows that individuals do not predictably transfer knowledge. . . . They do not predictably transfer school knowledge to everyday practice. They do not predictably transfer sound everyday practice to school endeavors, even when the former seems clearly relevant to the latter" (p. 46). Raizen (1989) also reviewed the literature and came to the conclusion that "research has documented the fact that people learn differently on the job and through experience than they do in formal school settings and, just as important, that they use what they know differently" (p. 23).

If school and work are so different, and individuals do not easily transfer knowledge gained from one to the other, it follows that in order to be fully prepared, young people should have both. It does not directly ensue that learning out of school will improve learning in school. Yet the reinforcement thesis makes three kinds of implicit assumptions about how academic knowledge and workplace experience may connect. First, school-based knowledge may be applied in work settings, and thus reinforced. The student may, for instance, use reading skills learned in school to comprehend instruction manuals, or she may apply arithmetic skills to accounting tasks. This process, we infer, yields a form of practice that solidifies school knowledge. In the terms of Bloom's (1956) well-known taxonomy, reinforcement may thus be achieved through work activities calling for knowledge and application.

Second, school-based knowledge might be explored and tested: The learner can think through the meaning, validity, and utility of school-derived knowledge in a practical setting. This process goes beyond mere application to enlarge the student's understanding and cognitive skills by requiring additional forms of thinking, such as comprehension, analysis, synthesis, and evaluation. The claim is that doing something in the work world with school-derived knowledge makes the student grasp the knowledge in more elaborate, profound ways. Here is where the notion of situated learning applies to work-based learning: If, as Brown and his colleagues (1989) argue, people learn more effectively when they use knowledge in a meaningful social context, then surely an actual workplace is one such environment.

For example, a student in an accounting office who has learned in class a particular technique for double-entry bookkeeping may have to determine whether the school version works successfully in solving situation-specific problems. She may have to consider several elements of the process (analysis) and assess them in relation to such workplace criteria as time demands and customer needs to make that decision (evaluation). Finally, she may need to draw on both classroom-based methods and local practices to construct a strategy tailored to the specific requirements of her work (synthesis).

Third, work-based learning may have motivational effects. During an internship, a student may recognize that academic knowledge actually has meaning in the world, thus providing an incentive to study. Students may also learn the schooling requirements for different careers; that is, if one wants to become a doctor, one had better start hitting the science and math books. In an evaluation of a group of travel and tourism academies, 69 percent of the seniors said that the summer internship "motivated me to continue my education" (Academy for Educational Development, 1995). In addition, for students who are not successful at the traditional in-school curriculum and as a result lack confidence about their abilities, capably completing an internship may encourage them academically. Bailey and Merritt (1997a) quote the director of a career academy as saying, "Many of my students come to me at-risk and leave college-bound," and point out that "this type of change in goals and aspirations of the student is the most obvious case in which school-to-work promotes academic learning. . . ." (p. 22).

Defining Academic Knowledge and Skills

To judge the reinforcement claim, one must first address a definitional question: what one means by academic knowledge and skills. Stasz and Brewer's (1998a) paper on academic skills at work points out the debatable nature of the term "academic skill." Academic skills have commonly been viewed as "measurable properties of individuals," referring to academic achievement tests, although the situative perspective has argued that knowledge and skills cannot be understood outside of the context in which they're applied (Stasz & Brewer, 1998a, pp. 7–8). Others refer to reading and math skills as "basic skills" that "must be learned as a foundation for all other learning" (Raizen, 1989, p. 19).

Thus it is appropriate for researchers to ask: What do work-based learning proponents mean when they refer to academic skills? What kinds of academic knowledge do students acquire in the classroom that might then be (or not be) reinforced in the workplace? How would we know these academic forms of knowledge if we saw them in the work world?

Work-based learning proponents seem to take a fairly straightforward, unproblematic perspective on that question: Students learn to add, subtract, divide, and multiply; they learn to read with comprehension and write grammatically; they learn to solve certain kinds of problems (e.g., algebra equations, chemistry formulas) and to recall certain kinds of information (e.g., names of authors, dates of events). That is, they learn to use the skills of computation, expression, memory, and problem-solving called for by school-based tests. It would be reasonable, then, to ask whether those same classroom skills are demanded by the work-based tasks that student-interns undertake.

The reinforcement argument also seems to imply that student-interns can apply higher-level theory and analytic skills. A student in an urban community center, for instance, might have occasion to connect his observations of poverty in the neighborhood with academic ideas about social class and economic development. A student in a medical lab might use school-derived concepts about anatomy and physiology in the course of an experiment. An accounting student might execute certain bookkeeping functions by means of classroom-learned procedures.

Once we establish the terms of our examination, we need to pursue the more empirical question of whether students actually have occasion to apply school-based knowledge, however defined, in a clear-cut, systematic, and explicit way. Do they, in fact, get the right kind of and enough practice in the use of such knowledge? Further, do they ever explore the school knowledge in a process that leads them explicitly to think through its implications or its adequacy? Are they held accountable for the competent display of this knowledge? If and to the extent that these processes occur, we might reasonably claim that workplace experience reinforces school-based learning—deepens it, strengthens it, enlarges it.

The results of one study imply that it might be difficult to link academic skills used at work with academics taught in the classroom. Stasz and Brewer (1998a) analyzed technical jobs (that required at least a high school diploma but less than a bachelor's degree) at four different firms to determine which academic skills were evident in the jobs and whether they were central to the work or only used occasionally. The researchers also tried to obtain a sense of the relationship of academic knowledge and skill to work practice in general. These researchers found that academic skills, particularly math and science, were essential to these jobs, but the skills varied according to the job, the community of practice, and the work setting. The level of academic skill used also varied. Most significant was that the academic skills were in a sense "hidden" in the work activity, as "the language that workers use to discuss academic skill does not necessarily correspond with the topics of subject areas defined in the school curricula" (p. 93). The authors conclude that because mathematics and science knowledge vary with work context, academics on the job have a "situated nature" (p. 94).

Finally, there is a curriculum design issue embedded in the reinforcement claim. Even when the knowledge connections between classroom and workplace are clear, as they may sometimes be, the organization of that information in the students' experience might or might not be educationally effective. The basic premise of the school curriculum, rooted in works by Ralph Tyler (1949), Jerome Bruner (1966; 1977) and others, is that exposure to the knowledge of a discipline must be structured in such a way as to build a student's understanding incrementally from the simple and foundational through the complex and advanced. We start teaching chemistry with fundamental information about elements, for instance, and then move on to more difficult ideas resting on that foundation. That sort of incremental exposure to disciplined knowledge does not often appear in naturally occurring work situations, even in research laboratories.

Rather, workers are assumed to have that foundational knowledge, and to perform their tasks by drawing on it. The sequence in which workers need certain kinds of knowledge stems from the production process in the workplace, and does not typically coincide with the sequence in which they originally learned it in school.

Of course, there are modern educators, often descended from Dewey, who believe that the first step in acquiring complex academic knowledge (biology, for instance, or even history) should be *doing* the discipline rather than *studying* it; one should be introduced to biology by participating in what biologists do, rather than by first building a tool kit of fundamental concepts and theories. That approach has great strengths—and may constitute a strong argument for work-based learning—but it raises the pedagogical question of whether it suffices for the purposes of education. In looking at the relationship between school-based and work-based learning, we need to ask not only about the *content* of the learning but about the *structure* of the student's engagement with it. A student working in a highly sophisticated environment—say, as an assistant in a medical research laboratory (Stasz & Kaganoff, 1997)—may or may not participate in the full range of knowledge-use that her biology teacher desires.

Existing Data

There is some existing literature that is germane to this topic. In this section we first briefly look at studies of the effects of part-time work on students' academic performance. Part-time jobs that students find themselves are not entirely comparable to school-organized, work-based learning placements, and indeed the national evaluation of school-to-work implementation finds that students rate school placements higher in learning opportunities than the jobs they find on their own (Hershey et al., 1999). Still, this area of research may be instructive. We then thoroughly review the new and growing body of literature that addresses the academic achievement of students in work-based learning programs.

Academic Achievement and Working While in School

National data show that the majority of American high school students work (National Center for Education Statistics, 1998), and so for some time, researchers have been interested in the effects of after-school jobs on schoolwork. The rather large body of research on this topic is somewhat conflicting in its findings, leading to neither a blanket endorsement nor a condemnation of school-aged youth working for pay. We will here touch on only some of the studies.

Some are concerned that working for pay while in school diminishes academic performance. Greenberger and Steinberg (1986) contend that work affects student outcomes negatively. Mortimer and Finch (1986), in an analysis of a longitudinal sample of young males, found that those who did not work at all during high school had higher grade point averages (GPAs) in their senior year, and higher educational and occupational aspirations. The authors did not find a strong process of selection that might have accounted for these results.

Another study found a negative association between academic achievement and hours spent in part-time work. Stasz and Brewer (1998a) analyzed longitudinal data on youth from two national databases, looking at the relationships between working while in school, academic outcomes, and participation in extracurricular activities. The common paths they found were the following: students tended to have either high academic achievement and high participation in extracurricular activities, or low academic achievement and a great deal of part-time work experience (no causality can be inferred).

However, Stern and Briggs (2001) posit in their review of many studies that the relationship between hours of work and performance in school tends to have an inverted-U pattern, meaning that students who work moderate hours perform at a higher level in high school than students who work more or not at all. Mortimer and Johnson (1997), who also reviewed the literature on adolescence and work, concluded that, under certain conditions, working can have positive effects on academic attainment. Working part-time or less does not appear to have deleterious effects on GPA, and in some cases seems to affect GPA positively. Schoenhals, Tienda, and Schneider (1998) analyzed longitudinal data, controlling for background characteristics that differed between students who did, and did not, work, and found no negative effects of employment on grades. Nor did youth employment lower the amount of time students spent reading or on homework.

Thus there is as yet no simple or conclusive answer to the question of whether working while in high school has positive or negative consequences for students' academic achievement. As Schoenhals, Tienda, and Schneider (1998) note, there is "an astonishing lack of consensus" (p.724), which is partly due to methodological disputes.

Participation in School-to-Work Programs and Academic Outcomes
Rigorous research on the academic achievement of students in programs that include work-based learning is scarce and thus far the results are mixed. Some studies find no effect, or negative effects. For example,

Hamilton and Hamilton (1997), in their study of 100 students participating in the Cornell Youth Apprenticeship Demonstration Project, found that the youths did gain job-related skills and knowledge, but there were no effects on their academic achievement. The authors conclude that improved academic achievement will have to be a central goal of such programs before effects will be seen. Similarly, Stasz and Brewer (1998) found from a survey of students in two different work-based learning programs that even though the students rated their work-based learning experiences positively, they primarily learned work-readiness-related attitudes and behaviors, and they perceived links between the internships and the classroom to be weak.

The 1996 High Schools That Work Assessment found that those students who were earning credit for part-time jobs connected with school had lower achievement in reading, mathematics, and science than students with part-time jobs that were not related to a school program (Bottoms and Presson, n.d.). (When dividing the sample by sex, however, the differences hold only for males.) The authors explain these results by noting that students whose jobs were connected with school worked longer hours than the other working students. Fewer of the former type of students took mathematics and science courses during their senior year, as they were instead enrolled in unchallenging vocational courses. It appears that for some students, school-related employment is substituting for higher-level courses, with the result of lower academic achievement.

Other research has yielded more positive findings. A comparison of students enrolled in the Flint, Michigan, Manufacturing Technology Partnership (MTP) program with a group of similar students not enrolled in the program found that the MTP students had higher grade point averages and higher average class ranks, as well as fewer absences (Hollenbeck, 1996). In addition, for the first cohort of students, participation in the program did not diminish the number of math or science courses taken. However, students in the second cohort of the program did take more vocational education courses, rather than math and science courses, relative to the comparison group students. Another study focused on a sample of black students from four Philadelphia high schools (Linnehan, 1998). This study found that participation in work-based learning for more than half the academic year had positive effects on the students' GPAs, compared with students who participated for a shorter period of time or students who were eligible for work placements but did not end up participating.

A study based on observations of student interns from three different programs found significant learning opportunities at the worksites (Stasz & Kaganoff, 1997). In a transportation academy, school learning appeared to enhance work, and in both a medical program and a school-based enterprise, work appeared to enhance school learning. A more in-depth study of the transportation program compared student outcomes with the outcomes of students from magnet schools and from the general school population. This study found that, for grade point average, credits earned, on-time credit acquisition, and attendance, transportation academy students performed better than students in the general population, and comparably to magnet school students who are screened before being admitted (Hanser & Stasz, 1999). However, this study did not entirely account for selection effects. In addition, although internships are a part of the transportation academy program, it is unclear if all the students included in the study had participated in work-based learning. In fact, since half the sample consisted of students from grades 9 and 10, it is likely that at least that half had not yet had work placements. Thus one cannot necessarily attribute any positive academic outcomes to the work-based learning portion of the program.

This is a problem common to other studies of student outcomes. The 1995–96 evaluation of 42 California Partnership Academies enrolling over 5000 students found that over students' four-year tenure in the academies, students improved their attendance and grade point averages (Foothill Associates, 1997). Yet again, even though internships are one element of the academy program, it is unclear whether all students participate in work-based learning. The report states that some academies have a community-service component whereas others offer internships, some of which are paid. And, the researchers found that the largest gain in performance occurred early in the four-year program, between the 9th and 10th grades. Again, it is likely that these students had not yet engaged in work-based learning. Thus even though student outcomes are positive, they can most likely be attributed to components of the academy program other than work-based learning. Another study compared career academy students with students in the general, academic, and vocational tracks at public schools in the same district, and found that the career academies enrolled more at-risk students than the other tracks, yet the students were as likely to attend college as students in the academic track (Maxwell and Rubin, 1997). In this instance it is impossible to determine whether that outcome is related to work-based learning; the report does not specify how many of the students studied participated in it.

The interim evaluation report of the New York State school-to-work system states that "students who actively participated in STW programs and activities demonstrated better academic performance than comparable students with little or no STW exposure" (Westchester Institute for Human Services Research, 1997, p. 33). These findings come from an analysis of transcripts and surveys of randomly selected high school seniors from seven school-to-work partnerships in the state. However, the report also notes that less than 15 percent of high school seniors have participated in structured work-based learning experiences, and "work-based learning generally does not involve a school-based component that extends or complements the knowledge and information gained at the worksite" (p. 27). Once again, we cannot use these findings as evidence that work-based learning improves academic performance.

The research in this area has mixed results so far. It seems that participation in a work-based learning program can improve academic achievement, but in some cases the positive effects are not clearly attributable to the work-based learning component itself. Stasz and Kaganoff (1997) raise the possibility that any positive outcomes of programs may be due to their characteristically small size and personal focus. We might expect results to be better for programs that make concerted efforts to integrate work-based learning with academics; yet a lack of information makes it impossible to compare the programs on that basis. Thus the evidence is as yet inconclusive. In the next section, we turn to our own and others' qualitative data on students' work-based learning experiences.

Testing the Claim

To test the claim that work-based learning can have positive effects on academic learning, we contend that one must be able to see its origins in the details of students' workplace experiences, in the texture of their participation in specific situated activities. This requirement escapes the danger of the facile assumptions about the relationship between academic learning and work experience captured in statements like these: "She worked in a hospital, so she must have applied her knowledge from biology class," or "He had to compose business letters, so his writing skills must have improved." These claims may or may not be true—it depends on the particulars of the students' experience. Thus to substantiate the claim, we would need to find several things in the data on students' experiences:

- Student-interns using forms of knowledge—content (facts, theories); skills (reading, writing, quantitative reasoning); and higher-order thinking (problem-solving, hypothesis-testing, analysis of cause-effect relations, etc.)—that are substantively analogous to the forms of knowledge acquired and used in school.
- Interns engaging these forms of knowledge often enough to strengthen them by means of practice.

- Interns having opportunities to explore, elaborate, and test these forms of knowledge in the context of situated activities where they can recognize the meaning and utility of school knowledge and its connection to situated knowledge-use.
- The engagement of the student-interns with this knowledge organized in such a way that they encounter a substantial range of the knowledge used in school, rather than just fragments of it.

This is not to argue that work-based learning needs to mirror or duplicate the school-based learning, but only that, if the academic reinforcement thesis is to be confirmed, students should be found actively engaging the school-like knowledge in the course of participating in work activity. Otherwise, the claim will be seen as merely rhetorical.

We analyzed data from our observations and interviews with 25 student-interns, to look for evidence of engagement in school-like knowledge at students' internships. We looked for students' engagement in content knowledge, as well as students' use of reading, writing, math, and science skills. We also looked for examples of work-based learning positively affecting motivation toward schoolwork. The following gives examples from our fieldwork, as well as examples, as appropriate, from the work of Moore (1981a; 1981b; 1986), and Stasz and her associates (Stasz & Brewer, 1998; Stasz & Kaganoff, 1997).

Content-Knowledge

We first look at the data on content knowledge, asking whether interns engage facts and theories that they might first encounter in school. Among other things, students in high schools acquire (take in, store, and retrieve) certain kinds of information and ideas: that the Erie Canal was opened in 1825; that economic struggles between the industrializing North and the agricultural South were among the causes of the Civil War; that falling objects accelerate at 14 feet per second per second. One empirical question for proponents of work-based learning, then, is whether students encounter this kind of knowledge in their internships. Sometimes, according to our studies, they do:

> A student working at a local history museum, as part of her training as a tour guide for elementary-school classes, learned the names of colonial governors and mayors; the dates of key events in English settlement; the dominant forms of transportation in the early nineteenth century; and so on (Moore, 1986).

> An intern working as a nurse's assistant in a hospital had a conversation with a physician in which he heard facts about the liver and its disorders. (case viiic)

> An intern working for a travel-industry magazine learned about the different countries featured in different issues of the magazine. (case xvii)

More often, though, it is difficult to locate content-knowledge in the workplace that corresponds in any clear way with the content-knowledge encountered in the classroom. What the tour guide may remember a year after the internship is not the name of the last Dutch governor of New York so much as how to deliver a lecture and how to manage the behavior of a group of 3rd graders. Matthew, the hospital aide, got only a single, fragmentary lesson on the liver, but he did learn how to make beds with people in them, how to demonstrate care and sensitivity in interactions with sick people, and when to ask questions. What Sinda, the young woman at the travel magazine, will remember most is that, when the magazine featured a map of Africa and spelled Zimbabwe wrong, the company reprinted the issue with the corrected spelling; "You can't mess up," she said in amazement, understanding that errors in the real world have consequences. These are not items of knowledge that would typically appear in a course syllabus or lesson plan.

Skill-Oriented Knowledge-Use: Reading, Writing, Math, and Science

What about more skill-oriented knowledge-use? One might expect to find that form of school-related learning more easily in the workplace. Again, however, our data tend to contradict that expectation. In our fieldwork, we did not often find students performing school-like tasks, or even tasks that implicitly drew on knowledge obviously derived from school. Even *reading* was not a significant part of their experience. To be sure, some (not all) did occasionally read at work: instruction manuals, organizational brochures and reports, and so on. Our best guess is that the grade level of those reading materials rarely exceeded 8th or 9th grade. Their reading was highly episodic, not sustained. Its function was usually to provide specific information that the student needed to perform a work task, or perhaps to construct a bit of background knowledge (about the overall structure of the organization, for instance). Understanding these materials was not difficult; they were fairly straightforward, declarative, informational. Interns did not need to interpret or analyze long texts. Moreover, we rarely saw students being held accountable for things they had read; rather, they were held accountable for performing the tasks for which they were doing background reading. Thus, in terms of reading skills, one could conclude that work-based experience did not provide much in the way of reinforcement: There was not much practice and virtually no testing.

One student in particular, Nell, was asked if her reading disability had caused any problems in her internship. She asserted that the lack of reading at her work placement was a positive thing:

> . . . there really isn't any reading. They just show you hands-on what to do. Which I like anyway. I learn best that way . . . (case viiia)

In a rare case, Maureen, who was interning as a teacher's aide, was given reading assignments by her supervisor, a music teacher:

> I do a lot of reading for him and the way I show him my knowledge is the way I am able to apply that knowledge in the class. Like I'm able to teach a certain way, and he can say, "Oh, isn't that a Kane and Kane way? You got that part, didn't you? Oh, isn't that Howard Gardner?" (case xiiidt2:8)

Through college-level outside reading, this student was exposed to different learning theories, which she could then apply to her work as a teacher's aide. This is an admirable instance of a student's connecting academic theory and real-world application, but it was unclear whether this knowledge was connected back to her in-school classes. The school programs did sometimes inject work-related reading into the students' assignments. For instance, a young man working at a veterinary hospital said students in his English class:

> could choose books to read and study according to their interest and/or internship. Fred picked *All Creatures Great and Small*, about a veterinarian. He said this book was more on the social aspect of being a vet, as opposed to the technical aspect. He found this interesting because he said he needs to work on the social aspect a bit. Occasionally he is annoyed by clients who complain about having to pay vet bills. . . . He thinks he should be more understanding of these clients. He tried to tie this book into some of his journal entries. This worked out okay, as opposed to previous books they were assigned to read. (observation xiiia2)

But the fact remains that in our observations of student-interns, we rarely saw them doing sustained, complex reading. Even the school-generated reading assignments were only tangential to the work itself.

Moore's research on the School for External Learning (SEL) and Stasz and her colleagues' work in Los Angeles included sites where interns did do substantial reading: the history museum in the SEL case, for example, or the medical research lab in Stasz's. To prepare for giving tours related to state history, the SEL student not only watched a veteran guide lead elementary-school classes around the galleries, but she spent a good deal of time in the Education Department library reading appropriate sources on such topics as colonial government and transportation (Moore, 1986). Similarly, the Los Angeles students in the medical careers program, who functioned as lab assistants, were sometimes assigned to go to the hospital library to find research articles related to current work; moreover, their supervisor occasionally gave them background reading on the fundamental science involved in the experiments (Stasz & Kaganoff, 1997). In both instances, the reading was substantial, challenging, and clearly related to work tasks. But these examples were in the distinct minority—most student-interns did not do much work-related reading.

Nor did most students that we or other researchers observed do much *writing* as they took part in work activities. Some positive examples show up in Moore's (1981b) SEL data: a reporter for a community newspaper; a legislative assistant for a city council member; even a cabinetmaker's apprentice who was required by the master to write commentaries on historical styles of furniture. In the fieldwork for our project, we did observe an intern in the legal department of a municipal agency being asked to digest the transcripts from cases, and producing memos for the attorneys. A student working with an independent filmmaker wrote his own short script. And the student working for the travel magazine did write an article for the magazine. But these students were in the minority: Few of the subjects in any of the studies did any sustained, significant writing.

Similarly, only a few of the students we observed engaged in substantial *mathematical* work, especially anything requiring complex operations and problem-solving. The young man working with the independent filmmaker had to create a budget for his film, and the young man working on the construction site said that he could see how geometry was used in carpentry. One student, Hiroshi, worked in the materials warehouse of an investment bank and used math in an inventory project:

> With a serious look on his face, he concentrated on counting numbers on a total report that consisted of product requests, and product transfer sheets. The number tally included: description, number of case quantity, quantity per case, number of cartons, and total quantity. In the beginning, he mentally figured the calculations. Later, he turned and got the calculator from a coworker's desk for more complex calculations. He turned to the coworker and asked her for some Post-its; he put one on each pile of papers and wrote P, C, or Q on it; and then proceeded to count through all the reports. Someone came in and asked him "Are all these reports from today?" and he said that most of them were. (fieldnotes, xi3, p. 3)

Another intern, Catherine, worked in an investment bank's mutual-funds department and performed significant computations for a task called "paying the brokers out." She described it as follows:

> But what happened was, usually what happens is that the fund itself will send us a report that kind of lists all the trades for the month and the bottom line would be that okay, that the following brokers made this much money in terms of commission on these trades that they've done over the month. And they would just give us the figures and they would send us a check for that amount so that we could go back to our branches and give the money to the brokers. Now, this month, I guess it was June, something happened. The report was not done. We didn't have a report from the fund. So we had to go back to our records, do all the math. They have like a system for it. . . . I was working with that for a while. I was just printing statements out. I had my pile, I would go back. I would find the average of things. I would add this, multiply by that. There's a lot of steps involved. It's not just like one thing. Everything needs to

be averaged out over the month. And yes, there was the math part, the printing out part, the writing it out part, separating it by fund, separating by branches, separating by the individuals, all that good stuff. (transcript xiit2, p.15)

The best example is a community college student, Carmen, who worked as an assistant accountant in an advertising firm:

> The work performed by [this] office appears to be basic procedural accounting. The work consists of four main accounting functions: management of cash flow and reconciliation of bank accounts, paying vendor contracts and expenses, reimbursing [company] staff for travel and business expenses, and payroll. . . . On the day [the researcher] visited, Carmen was engaged in a cash-flow management task . . . [which] basically involved identifying which checks in a stack already printed for mailing should be withheld to adjust the amount of funds remaining in the firm's four bank accounts at the end of the month. . . . She added the withheld checks up to get a total and then went . . . to enter the data into a Lotus spreadsheet used for monitoring cash flow. (observation iva1)

Carmen's work came as close to application of school-based knowledge as anything we saw: She used bookkeeping techniques learned in class to handle the accounts. And she adapted those methods to her specific setting—that is, she tested her school learning, went beyond it to make it useful in her work. For instance, she had to check expense vouchers for "reasonableness," which required that she develop a sense of what kinds of expenses were appropriate by the company's standards; this chore took her beyond classroom techniques for tracking expenses. In that sense, her work experience may have reinforced her school learning. But her duties stayed on a fairly rudimentary level, not getting into more advanced accounting practices.

None of the other interns whom we observed got real practice or testing experience in mathematics—and thus, by our reckoning, little reinforcement of school-based math knowledge. They did not even seem to engage in the kinds of everyday math that Lave (1988) describes among grocery shoppers or Scribner (1986) among dairy workers.

Some of the students in Stasz's study worked extensively with numbers. One medical lab intern tracked the statistical results of an experiment on rats' muscular reflexes; a computer program actually performed the necessary calculations, but the student-intern did have to understand what the study was about and how the results fit into that enterprise. In a school-based enterprise where students produced and marketed salad dressings, participants had to manage the books: keep track of expenses, sales revenues, profits, and so on (Stasz & Kaganoff, 1997). Certainly those tasks had characteristics akin to school math, and therefore represented a form of academic reinforcement—although many of the students in the program were probably not taking accounting or business math, but were presumably learning these practices *in situ* rather than reinforcing classroom-derived knowledge.

Again, we have some evidence that the degree to which school-based knowledge appears in work settings varies a great deal from situation to situation. If the data from these studies are at all representative of high school students' work-based learning experiences, one could conclude that interns rarely have occasion to practice or explore mathematics skills in the workplace. It might be, of course, that even a small amount of exposure to mathlike problems in the nonclassroom world motivates students to work harder at math in school. We simply have no data to confirm that hunch. In any case, with a few notable exceptions, the observations do not yield much to support the idea that work-based learning can help students strengthen their quantitative reasoning.

A careful reading of the descriptions of internships suggests that the reinforcement of *science* concepts and theories does occasionally happen, but more often is very difficult to find. Three of the students in the high school health program did come across school-based science knowledge in their hospital internships. Fiona is one example:

> One example I can think offhand is when I went to CAT lab, and I saw angioplasty being performed. And . . . when I went back into high school, we were studying the cardiovascular system and she talked about angioplasty. . . . So I thought that was a good connection because when we were learning about it, if I just heard about it then or read about it in a book, I probably wouldn't have remembered it or understand it. But because I actually went to the CAT lab, actually saw it and they had the nurse sitting there and we were looking at the screen and watching it, and like I was standing there saying yeah, I see blockage here and stuff like that . . . (transcript viiibt1, p. 29)

Fiona, while not able to do much hands-on work at the hospital, was assigned her own patient case studies, where she read patient charts, analyzed them, and then wrote up their cases, combining reading, comprehension, science, and writing knowledge and skills.

Fred, the veterinary assistant, observed operations and acquired some detailed knowledge of animal anatomy and physiology in the process. For instance, during the amputation of a cat's tail,

> . . . [the doctor and another technician] placed the cat on the newly clean operating table and stuck a tube down its mouth. Then they discussed how much of its tail to shave, began shaving, and vacuumed up the hair. Then they began "expressing" the bladder, which Fred explained to [the researcher]. . . . While the doctor and technician were performing these tasks, Fred remained at the sink just on the other side of the operating room, but he could see into the room perfectly. . . . He told me in a matter-of-fact way what was going on at each moment . . . Fred asked the doctor if the purpose of a cat's tail is to help

> the cat balance. The technician replied that probably balance is one purpose, but cats seem to do fine without them. Fred continued with his running commentary, saying, "She's sterilizing the area" as the technician rubbed some liquid all over the cat's tail and behind. The tech corrected him, saying the area would be "aseptic," not "sterile." Fred didn't mind the correction ... Fred asked, "How much of the tail is actually bone?" The doctor replied, "It's bone all the way down." (observation xiiia1)

At moments like this, the student was introduced (sometimes by observing the natural process of the work, sometimes by taking the initiative to ask questions, sometimes by playing a peripheral role in the activity) to interesting information that might also have been encountered in school. Theoretically, experiences such as these could help a student comprehend and retain classroom knowledge, and Fred saw a connection between his internship and the AP biology course he was taking, saying that in class they were learning the "underlying science" of some of the work that is done at the animal hospital. But Fred was doing poorly in the class, and he had trouble being very specific in explaining how his work in the veterinary hospital gave him an opportunity to apply and explore the knowledge he was acquiring in biology class. Since most of his work through the final observation involved fairly menial tasks—filing, cleaning up the operating area, and so forth—it is not clear that he experienced these school-to-work connections on more than a rhetorical level. Thus, even in some cases where the reinforcement effect could be argued, data supporting it are tenuous.

Matthew, from the high school health program, emphasized the differences, rather than the similarities, between his science education at school and that at the hospital:

> Oh, on my rotation I'm learning more about what would be done to fix a problem. While in the classroom I'm learning more about the parts of the body. Like learning about the heart. Like, specific things, like how it works. Where, like, if I were in cardiology or something, I would be learning about how they would fix it. Just more of the problems that go wrong. (transcript viiict2, p. 36)

Logically, one would need to know how something works before one can fix a problem, but this student saw these two fields of knowledge as separate, rather than connected.

The medical careers academy in Los Angeles gave students regular and systematic exposure to sophisticated scientific information and procedures; indeed, the level of science encountered by these students exceeded what they found in their high school classes. Stasz and Kaganoff (1997) point out that the teaching hospital where the interns worked had educational practices deeply embedded in its culture; that function stands at the core of the institution's mission. They also note, however, that staff were accustomed to teaching medical students, not high school students, and that they occasionally had difficulty accommodating the latter's learning needs. The students may or may not have been prepared for this level of science.

Motivation

A recent survey of over 1000 American teenagers was entitled *Getting By: What American Teenagers Really Think About Their Schools* (Johnson, Farkas, & Bers, 1997). The title reflects the study's findings: Most students say they could do better in school if they tried, but they have minimal interest in academic subjects. Majorities of student respondents said that the best thing about school is that they get to be with their friends, and they do not think they will need to know in the real world the things their school is teaching. Yet, a majority of student respondents to the survey also said that doing a job internship for school credit would result in them learning "a lot more." Unfortunately, the survey question did not specify what area this learning might be in. Still, it is a rather enthusiastic response from an otherwise disengaged population.

The motivation claim of the academic reinforcement argument for work-based learning is the notion that, by encountering school-related knowledge in the meaningful contexts of work activity, students will develop a stronger incentive to study hard in school. Fred's earlier claim about seeing the "underlying science" from his AP biology class in his work at the animal hospital represents a class of possibilities. The problem is that we simply have too little data to test this proposition; in a qualitative study it is too difficult to trace the impact of specific experiences on attitudes about another enterprise. Fred barely passed his AP biology class, but one could argue that the internship helped him to pass and that he might have failed otherwise or that, without the motivational effect of the internship, he would never have been so enthusiastic about a subject in which he did not do well.

A few students did claim that they were doing better in school because, through their internship, they had become more interested in a particular topic or field. Nell, with the reading disability, said that, although the program was harder and she was assigned more homework than the previous school year, her grades had improved. This was because she "cared more" because there was "more stuff that interested me" (transcript viiiat2, p. 35). Matthew said he had "straightened out" "because now I know what I want to do and I know what I have to do to get there. And I like this program and it actually makes a lot of learning fun" (transcript viiict1, p. 9). He agreed that the program was hard, but being interested in the topic made it easier. A student from the high school economics and finance program said, too, that "When I'm interested I study harder" (xit1, p. 8).

Thus, we do find some evidence for the motivation claim. Students may find certain occupations attractive (vet, CPA, surgeon), and may therefore be impelled to pursue certain kinds of study to attain those career positions. Students in "theme" programs may also find that classes using health or banking careers as a context are certainly more "fun" than classes in which the subject matter is entirely abstract. These effects are worthwhile, but it is not the same thing as discovering direct relations between specific academic knowledge and particular work practices. And sometimes the experience of work in the real world has a different kind of motivational effect: two other students, Renee and Maria, had such tedious internships that they became highly motivated to attend college directly from high school, rather than delaying post-secondary enrollment or combining it with work.

Summary

In Table 5.1, we summarize the results of the analysis of our cases, noting for each student whether the three claims for academic reinforcement (school-based knowledge is applied; school-based knowledge is explored and tested; and motivation toward school is positively affected) were met. For nine of the students (over one-third of our sample), over the course of multiple visits to the internship sites, and before-and-after in-depth interviews with the students, we found no evidence for any of the claims. For 16 students, we found evidence for one or two of the claims. Thus we have some instances of academic knowledge being reinforced through practical experience, but the evidence is far from overwhelming. As for the motivation effect, we found evidence in only seven of our cases. However, we must note that the community college students in general were already highly motivated and thus not affected by the experience in that way (with one exception).

Almost half (12 out of 25) of the students experienced instances of the simple application of school-based knowledge at work. The medical-site internships offered through the health programs were particularly promising in this regard; they did tend to involve scientific facts and knowledge. Regarding the testing and exploration of school-based knowledge, we found evidence for this in only three of the internships. These cases are instructive, as in each instance the internship matched the student's major field of study or was paired with an independent study course. These cases could be viewed almost as training in the students' chosen occupational fields, in which the work-based learning corresponded closely to, and built upon, academic and theoretical knowledge.

Yet what was more often the case was that the interns' tasks were productive for the work of the office or site, such as in the case of Alison, who created a spreadsheet listing vendor information for the corporate strategic-sourcing department of a bank, or José, who inspected hotel rooms for maintenance needs. Two of our community college interns, Ali and Abdul, had useful, challenging internships in a highly technical field (in which they hoped to gain permanent employment). These are certainly jobs that require cognitive ability, but one could not characterize them as having academic content or requiring academic skills. In the transportation program Stasz and Kaganoff (1997) studied, students reported that nearly 90 percent of their duties were either "general clerical/office work" or "computers/data entry." Except for the students who were taking courses in clerical skills and data entry in school, the academic reinforcement functions were minimal. Thus in general the work of the internships was functional to the organization, as would be expected, but hardly academic.

Moreover, the curriculum structure problem needs careful examination. In most cases, students' exposure to situated knowledge could be characterized as episodic, as driven by the contingencies of the work process rather than by a rational conception of the sequence of learning. When Fred, the Vermont veterinary assistant, went beyond the relatively menial work of cleaning up after surgeries and maintaining the office files, when he encountered knowledge-use of a more scientific nature, the specific content was determined by the particular patients that were brought into the clinic. There were a lot of neutering operations, for instance, so he had a number of opportunities to observe and ask questions about reproductive organs; in these instances he participated in practice and engaged in exploration. The tail amputation was rather unusual, a single exposure to that aspect of anatomy, which meant he was able to explore a bit—though it was not clear that he understood the broader context of the information.

As we indicated earlier, this sort of episodic exposure to complex knowledge at work could be the basis for more extensive and systematic investigations. That is the strategy that Dewey (1938) advocated. But, contrary to the assertions of those who translate his message as simply "learning by doing," Dewey, in fact, insisted on the carefully designed intervention of the educator to exploit and extend the learning potential in natural experience. He did not believe that such experience was educationally sufficient in its own right. This is a pedagogical issue.

Table 5.1 Work-Based Learning Student Cases: Academic Reinforcement Findings

	School/Program	Internship	School-Based Knowledge Applied at Work	School-Based Knowledge Explored and Tested	Motivation Effect from Work-Based Learning
Shin-Kap	Community college co-op	Office of local orchestra	No	No	No
Carrie	Community college co-op	Office of local orchestra	No	No	No
Etienne	Community college co-op	Trade division of consulate	No	No	No
Irina	Community college co-op	Trade division of consulate	No	No	No
Carola	Community college co-op	Transportation-authority legal office	Reading, text analysis	Yes—paralegal studies	No
Carmen	Community college co-op	Ad-agency accounting office*	Math	Yes—accounting coursework	No
Ali	Community college co-op	Computer networking*	No	No	Yes
Abdul	Community college co-op	Computer networking*	No	No	No
Nell	HS health program	Radiology	No	No	Yes
Fiona	HS health program	OR/anesthesiology	Science, reading	No	No
Matthew	HS health program	Post-surgical unit	Science	No	Yes
Rob	HS health program	Physical therapy gym	Science	No	Yes
Renee	HS E&F academy	University accounts-payable office	No	No	Yes
Maria	HS E&F academy	Consulting firm general counsel office*	No	No	Yes
Alison	HS E&F academy	Bank's purchasing dept.*	No	No	No
Hiroshi	HS E&F academy	Investment bank's warehouse*	Math	No	Yes

Catherine	HS E&F academy	Investment bank's mutual-funds dept.*	Math, accounting	No	No
Fred	HS academic internship program	Animal hospital	Science	No	No
Dan	HS academic internship program	Construction site	Possibly math	No	No
Adam	HS academic internship program	Independent filmmaking	Reading, writing, math	No	No
Maureen	HS academic internship program	Central school music class	Reading	Yes—theories of teaching	No
Isabella	HS T&T academy	Travel corp. office of corp. services*	No	No	No
Paul	HS T&T academy	Travel corp. hotel group*	No	No	No
José	HS T&T academy	Hotel housekeeping dept.*	No	No	No
Sinda	HS T&T academy	Travel industry magazine*	Geography, writing	No	No

*Indicates paid internship.

Alternative Possibilities

In the internships we studied, we did not find students frequently learning academic concepts or applying academic skills. One could argue that none of the programs we studied had a purposive design to that end. Should, and could, educators and employers structure internships to try to bring about the academic reinforcement effect?

Stasz and Kaganoff (1997) conclude that, although the connections between school and work were weak in the programs they studied, the students learned many valuable lessons and developed many skills. They question whether the lack of connection to specific academic classes made the work experiences less valuable, and say that making these explicit connections may not necessarily be a desirable goal. In particular, worksite supervisors and mentors do not tend to act as teachers toward students, and it would be difficult to design internships to follow or connect with a specific classroom-based curriculum.

More often what programs attempt is to connect workplace experiences to classroom subject matter through an occupational theme. Medical careers programs assign students to job rotations in hospitals or other health-care sites, and courses are taken in relevant science and health subjects. In economics and finance programs, students take accounting and business courses, and efforts are made to acquire internship slots in banks and other finance-related companies. In the travel and tourism program we studied, students have a special geography class, a travel and tourism class, and an English class that uses literature and assignments with a travel theme. During the summer between their junior and senior years, students are placed in internships in hotels, the regional airport, and various travel companies. A thorough analysis of the curricula for all of the courses for this academy found that there were few structured activities or assignments that made use of students' individual internships. Students did write short essays about their internships and their supervisors' work histories at the end of the summer, but once back in the classroom in the fall, the internship experiences were not integrated into the coursework. Thus the theme of travel and tourism encompassed the curricula and internships, but the two were not brought together in more specific ways.[1]

---

[1] And indeed, an earlier evaluation report on the Academy of Travel and Tourism recommended that "more attention be given to infusing academic instruction into the internship experience" (Academy for Educational Development, 1995). The report also stated that more care needed to be taken to ensure quality internship placements, and internship supervisors should receive a formal orientation and structured support.

One program, selected for our study because it was called an "Academic Internship Program," found it difficult to cluster the diverse group of students in the program—diverse both academically and with regard to the occupational fields of their internships—in an academic course. The teacher tried to create a curriculum that would integrate the students' interests in different occupational fields with English, using general work-related readings and journal-writing assignments. The students complained that the curriculum was too similar to that of their internship seminar (which involved many types of internship-reflection exercises), and the teachers agreed. As a result, the English class dissolved into individual study projects, in which the students read books related to their specific occupational field, created bibliographies of relevant works, and so on. In the end they wrote lengthy papers and presented them to panels of employers, parents, and school staff. Thus these students did complete academic assignments related to their chosen general occupational area.

There are ways to use and apply knowledge gained in the workplace to academic subject-matter. Rather than students using academic skills in a work context, which we found occurring infrequently, activities engaged in at the workplace can be used to bring about a better understanding of knowledge or concepts being taught in the classroom. The idea is that a student interning at a hospital who is able to observe surgeries would then understand human anatomy (at school, in biology class) more deeply and would better retain the knowledge. The student's authentic experience with biology would reinforce the classroom lesson in the subject. There is no assumption that school-based knowledge is being used by the student at the internship.

This more promising way to reinforce academics through work-based learning was found in one program. Rather than assuming that academic learning will be possible at the workplace, real-world situations and examples are imported into the classroom. In this particular program, a medical careers initiative, the teachers created assignments that called upon students to use their hospital internship experiences to illustrate and better understand academic concepts. For example, in their medical-related economics class, students were asked to use examples from their internships to illustrate the concepts "division of labor" and "productivity." The assignment read:

> Using your experiences working in a large hospital setting, discuss in what ways a hospital demonstrates specialization and division of labor to increase productivity. Then discuss ways that the hospital increases its investment in capital and in human capital to increase productivity. Provide some examples from your knowledge of the hospital. Finally, discuss ways that specialization and/or division of labor may not always prove effective for increasing productivity. Specific examples are required.

Students were instructed that they could discuss the questions with others, but they were to write their own answer in 300–400 words. This is one small example of a strategy that teachers could take to try to bring about academic reinforcement.

Conclusion

We have shown that academic reinforcement does happen in internships. The school-work connection does happen in some situations, sometimes as a natural consequence of the work itself and sometimes as an intentional pedagogical intervention; the latter circumstance is probably the more likely one. However, our examples suggest that many internships do not provide any academic reinforcement and for those that do, the reinforcement is episodic and not sustained. Unless an internship is explicitly designed to teach a broad range of material (such as the rotations of a medical internship), the work experience can be expected to reinforce only a small percentage of any high school curriculum. Fred's internship at the animal hospital, under the best of circumstances, would not do much to prepare Fred for most sections of the AP Biology exam. Work-based learning proponents who stand primarily on the academic reinforcement claim as a way to convince skeptics of the program's value are standing on thin ice.

We argue that there are other, nonacademic but equally important forms of learning that can come from work experience and that these forms give us good grounds for supporting work-based learning—*when it is done well*. That last phrase is crucial. Our experience with work-based learning teaches us that one cannot easily generalize about its impact. Poor placements can lead to dismal, miseducative experiences, but quality work-based learning can provide benefits above and beyond what students get even in excellent classrooms. We turn to these issues in the following chapters.

CHAPTER 6

Learning Skills and Careers
Through Work-Based Learning

A central argument in favor of work-based learning is that students acquire various practical skills and that they learn about industries and careers. At face value, this assertion seems obvious and intuitively defensible. The stories about interns are replete with images of their performing specialized and skilled activities: the apprentice cabinetmaker assembles a chest of drawers; the veterinary clinic aide tests a canine fecal sample; the accounting intern calculates cash-flow totals for her firm. These performances clearly reflect a capacity to use skills and knowledge to accomplish important organizational purposes. It also seems plausible that by working alongside skilled workers and professionals, the interns will learn about what it means to have a career in those fields—as a cabinetmaker, a veterinarian, or an accountant.

Like the claim for academic reinforcement, this one becomes more complex as one pushes on the concepts and the data. Analysts are engaged in important debates concerning the appropriate definitions of skill and expertise. They raise questions about what skills are, where they are located, the extent to which they are context-specific or transferable, and how they are developed. Placed in the tradition of learning theory outlined earlier, these issues resist easy resolution.

From our point of view, the concept of skill is important because the value of work-based learning relative to classroom learning hinges on what skills are and how they are learned most effectively. How much does a young person learn about being an accountant from listening to a lecture on career day by the accountant parent of a classmate? High school teachers can instruct students how to write a business letter or how to make a presentation, but how useful is that instruction once the young person is in an authentic work setting? If skills can be learned in classrooms, and then transferred to other contexts like workplaces, then perhaps work-based learning programs are unnecessary and too costly in time, money, and lost opportunities in school; if, on the other hand, students can learn these skills better in authentic workplaces, then the programs may be justified.

This chapter examines the claims about students' practical skills and learning about careers. After reviewing some of the literature on skills and expertise, we report on our field data to demonstrate the positive—yet sometimes not overwhelmingly so—evidence. Then we look at the research and theory on career learning, and similarly search for indications of whether our student-subjects displayed gains in that area. Consistent with our basic approach to learning theory, we look for indications that students in work placements encounter, engage, and use the kinds of knowledge related to the claims about skills and careers.

Conceptions of Skill and Expertise

Much of the literature on work-based learning takes a straightforward, commonsensical stance on skills and their acquisition. Skills are seen as discrete capacities, acquired and possessed by individuals, enabling them to perform various manual, intellectual, or social tasks. Some of these skills are highly site-specific: using a particular technique or tool to accomplish a particular operation in a single environment. Fiona, a high school intern in a big-city hospital, set up a very specialized anesthesiology machine for operating-room procedures; the techniques she used were not likely to be useful even in other contexts in the hospital, much less in another institution. To what extent, therefore, is this "skill" worth learning for a high school student? Should Fiona take time away from classroom studies to master this machine? Other skills, according to the popular view, are more general practices common to a variety of worksites. Students in a number of organizations, for instance, had to answer phones, thus developing a generalizable communications skill. But if skills are generalizable and easily transferred, and if they are important, then perhaps they can be more efficiently taught in school.

Over the last 15 years, many authors and organizations have tried to lay out specific lists of skills needed for the workplace that schools should teach. Perhaps the best known is contained in *What Work Requires of Schools*, a report of the Secretary's Commission on Achieving Necessary Skills (SCANS, 1991). Its authors propose the *fundamental skills* and *workplace competencies* required by the workplace of the future:

Foundations
Basic skills: reading, writing, arithmetic/mathematics, listening and speaking.
Thinking skills: creativity, decision-making, problem-solving, seeing things in the mind's eye, knowing how to learn, reasoning.
Personal qualities: responsibility, self-esteem, sociability, self-management, integrity/honesty.

Workplace competencies
Resources: identifies, organizes, plans, and allocates such resources as time, money, materials and facilities, and human resources.
Interpersonal: works with others as member of a team, teaches others new skills, serves clients/customers, exercises leadership, negotiates, and works with diversity.
Information: acquires, uses, organizes, maintains, interprets, and communicates information, including the use of computers to process it.
Systems: understands complex interrelationships, understands systems, monitors and corrects performance, and improves or designs systems.
Technology: works with a variety of technologies—selects them, applies them to tasks, maintains and troubleshoots equipment (see http://academicinnovations.com/ report.html).

A similar framework was proposed more recently by New Standards, a joint venture of the National Center on Education and the Economy (NCEE) and the Learning Research and Development Center (LRDC) at the University of Pittsburgh. The third volume of their report, *Performance Standards* (1997), describes a category of knowledge called *applied learning*:

> Applied learning focuses on the capabilities people need to be productive members of society, as individuals who apply the knowledge gained in school and elsewhere to analyze problems and propose solutions, to communicate effectively and coordinate action with others, and to use the tools of the information-age workplace. It connects the work students do in school with the demands of the twenty-first century workplace (p. 106).

The five performance standards related to applied learning are: problem-solving; communication tools and techniques; information tools and techniques; learning and self-management tools and techniques; and tools and techniques for working with others. Each standard describes several activities that students should engage in to meet it. Problem-solving, for instance, means that the student designs a product, service, or system; improves a system; and/or plans and organizes an event or activity (p. 108). The standards are described in terms broad enough to accommodate a wide range of activities, but the authors illustrate each one with specific cases.

The Lyceum Group, an educational consulting firm, markets yet another skills taxonomy to schools and businesses. Developed by ACT (formerly American College Testing) through an analysis of the common work tasks, the Work Keys system "identifies and measures generic, teachable, transferable skills that are the basis for effective performance in the workplace" (Lyceum Group 1998, www.fyi.net/~lyceum/TheWorkSkills-Metric.htm): applied academic skills, people and interpersonal skills, and problem-solving skills.

These various frameworks and others (see, for example, Hamilton, 1990; Stern et al., 1995) differ at the margins, or in the specific categories of skills they find crucial to workplace performance. But they share the general commonsense conception of skills described earlier. They assume that a learner *acquires* a skill in one way or another (direct instruction, observation, trial and error), and then *has* it; it may be used in performing specific tasks in the site where it was acquired, or generalized and applied in a variety of other settings. This vision of skill also seems to be embedded in the School-to-Work Opportunities Act of 1994. As the SCANS, New Standards and Work Keys schemes describe them, the work-related skills are intuitively sensible, appealing, and worthwhile.

But there is a school of thought in the sociology and psychology of work that finds this straightforward view of skills misleading and simplistic. "Like so many commonsense concepts, skill proves on reflection to be a complex and ambiguous idea" (Attewell, 1990). Attewell identifies several perspectives that call into question the commonsense notion that skills are an objective set of attributes that can be acquired by the individual and easily applied in many different settings.

For example, situated cognition theorists, according to Attewell, argue that when tasks are abstracted from the settings in which they are used so that they can be analyzed in laboratory studies, the tasks cease to resemble skills in the real world. These theorists point out that subjects who perform poorly in laboratory tests often perform the "same" skills adeptly in natural settings; thus, skills are highly grounded, situated in the specific contexts of their use, and so much so that they may cease to be the property of any one worker but rather reside in the interactive work of the group (Attewell, 1990, pp. 424–425). Ethnomethodologists reject the conception of skills as stable, unitary, and transferable, and insist instead that all human activity is an ongoing interactional accomplishment, a "complex coordination of perception, movement and decision, a myriad of choices, and a multitude of skills" (Attewell, p. 429). In this view, even skills regarded as simple—riding a bicycle, installing a component on an assembly line—turn out to be complicated performances. Kusterer (1978), for example, documented the extensive and largely unseen skills used by supposedly unskilled workers like bank tellers and factory laborers. More straightforward approaches to skill overlook the importance of these skills and the difficulty of learning them.

Stasz and Kaganoff's research (1997) can help us to define some of the learning that students do in the workplace. They found three broad categories of skills articulated in the literature: (1) Technical skills and competencies, which include mastering procedures; understanding fundamental principles and concepts underlying procedures; building a capacity for analytical judgment; and attaining computer literacy. (2) Generic workplace skills, which include problem-solving, communications, and teamwork. (3) Personal and social skills, which include good work attitudes and motivations, initiative, following orders, and a broad understanding of the organization (structure, rules and norms, interdepartmental relations, and customer relations). Although this framework is similar to the SCANS list, Stasz and Kaganoff emphasize that even "generic" skills often cannot be defined in the abstract, and that a significant component of any set of skills is specific to the context in which those skills are used.

Vallas (1990) reviews some of the ambiguities and disputes surrounding the skill idea. "When educational psychologists and human capital theorists use the concept of skill," he notes, "they typically have in mind the properties of the worker rather than the job"; sociologists, on the other hand, tend to focus on the requirements of jobs (p. 380). Vallas generally asserts that studies of skills need clearer definitions, and a more concrete link between skills and technology, status and learning. Spenner (1990) also reports conflict and confusion in the study of skills around such issues as the origins of skill and the mechanisms by which skills are valued (pp. 400–401). He notes disagreement over the extent to which skill is socially constructed and defined. These problems reveal the difficulty of reaching consensus on what student-workers need to learn and know as they perform tasks.

Darrah's work (1994; 1996) is perhaps the most powerful critique of a straightforward view of skills, especially for the purposes of this chapter. He criticizes the conception of skills that characterizes the plethora of "future workplace skills reports," such as SCANS. These reports analyze work by "decomposing jobs or people into constituent characteristics that are somehow necessary for the work to be performed" (pp. 5–6). The assumption that managers and educators can break jobs into sets of required skills and reconstitute them in tasks underlies both the design of work processes and the skills training efforts in businesses and schools. The problem, Darrah argues, is that this model severely misrepresents the way work actually gets done.

Darrah's (1996) book describes the work systems in two companies, a manufacturer of computer workstations and a maker of high-tech wire and cable. He demonstrates that his field data undermine four basic tenets of the dominant conception of skills: the notion that workers and jobs can be decomposed into "bundles of attributes (i.e., skills), thereby reducing them to discrete components"; the belief that "the skills identified are required in an obvious way, and . . . that if they were lacking the work would not get done"; the isolation of "workers and jobs from the larger context in which they are embedded," treating workplaces as mere backdrops for the application of skills; and the belief that workplace skills can be studied by the uncomplicated descriptive methods of positivist science (pp. 11–12).

The close observation of the two companies, Kramden Computers and Calhoun Wire and Cable, Darrah argues, reveals those tenets to be largely false, or at least problematic. The way workers do their jobs reflects their social identities as well as bundles of skills. It also involves their active construction of situations and actions, rather than their clear-cut application of algorithmic procedures and generalized skills. They do not simply do what is required of them, but they think problems through; improvise sometimes idiosyncratic strategies and solutions; evade certain aspects of their tasks and redefine others; and collaborate with others in unexpected, unofficial, and even forbidden ways. They take the whole organizational context into account as they work, not just the immediate demands of their tasks. The image suggested by the common view of skill requirements is that workers carry around with them tool chests filled with job-specific skills; as they encounter particular tasks, they haul out the skill-sets demanded by those tasks and use them to perform the specific operations expected by the work-process designers. That picture, Darrah shows at great length, is just not accurate (see also Keller & Keller, 1993; Kusterer, 1978; Pilcher, 1984).

These differences in the conception of skills have profound implications for the best means of preparing students to be effective adults both in the workplace and the community. If we cannot reliably identify and transmit sets of particular skills that can be used in particular situations, then we need to create ways of helping students manage their lives in workplaces more effectively. We may be able to teach them A, B, and C in a classroom, but there may be important skills such as D and E that we have not identified. And, we may not have been effective in teaching students how to use A, B, and C in real settings. At the same time, just having an experience in a workplace is no guarantee that a student will either learn necessary skills or learn how to use them. These are issues that we address in Chapters 9 and 10, the sections on pedagogy for work-based learning.

One other concept might help us in the analysis of the practical learning done by interns: *expertise*. Even though no one argues that high school and community college interns should be expected to become full-blown experts in the fields they occupy, the notion of expertise does identify the dimensions along which the students can grow, the direction in which they should be heading. There is abundant literature (see, for example, Chi et al., 1988; Hoffman, 1992) examining the distinctions between experts and novices in a variety of activity settings. Glaser and Chi (1988) review some of the key characteristics of experts' performance: they excel mainly in their own domains; they perceive large meaningful patterns ("chunks") in their areas; they are faster than novices, and solve problems with few errors; they have superior short-term and long-term memory; they see and represent a problem at a more principled level; they analyze problems qualitatively rather than simply apply algorithms; and they have strong self-monitoring skills (pp. xvii–xx).

Bereiter and Scardamalia (1993) argue for a slightly different conception of expertise, focused not on the traits of experts but on the process of performing skillful activities. One problem with the research on expertise, they suggest, is that it is based on the contrast between experts and novices, rather than between experts and experienced nonexperts. What distinguishes experts from nonexperts, they argue, is not just technique and not just knowledge, but their approach to problems: The expert addresses problems whereas the experienced nonexpert carries out practiced routines; the expert continually pushes the envelope in the field, trying to rethink the constitutive problems of the job, whereas the nonexpert constricts the problem to conform to the available routines, to what he is already accustomed to doing (p. 11).

Interestingly, then, expertise can be seen as having both individual and social aspects: The expert individual finds personally effective and rewarding ways of living at the edge of her competence; and the organization may have "a culture that encourages and sustains expert-like endeavors" (p. 20). This point has implications for work-based learning: The issue for interns is not so much whether they acquire the vast fund of domain-specific knowledge that marks them as experts, as whether they learn to go about their work expansively, with the inquisitive, restructuring, risk-taking attitude of the expert, or narrowly, with the routine, unquestioning attitude of the nonexpert.

Looking at the Cases

These conceptions of skill and expertise give us a handle on investigating the popular claim about work-based learning and practical skills. We take a somewhat eclectic (some would say contradictory) approach to this enterprise: We look at the data from field studies of work-based learning through a variety of lenses, ranging from the checklist format of SCANS and Work Keys to the more interpretive, flexible conceptions of Darrah and Bereiter. The questions of academic skills and personal development are addressed in other chapters.

In this section we will review our observational data on the student interns, asking such questions as these:

What kinds of local, site-specific skills and procedures did they display?

Did they acquire the kinds of generalized skills described in the SCANS (1991) list or the other frameworks for identifying work-related skills? Did they come to participate in communities of skilled practitioners in ways suggested by Darrah (1996)?

Did they move toward the sort of expertise described by Glaser and Chi (1988)?

Did they take part in the culture of expansive, learning-driven expertise portrayed by Bereiter and Scardamalia (1993)?

The evidence from our fieldnotes reveals a complex but largely encouraging picture. Clearly and unsurprisingly, many of our student-subjects did perform context-specific skills of various types. Some were quite simple and undemanding; others were complex and highly specialized. Some might be useful in other workplaces; others might not.

> Matthew, who interned in the postsurgical unit of a large urban hospital, made beds with the patients in them—a skill both manual and interpersonal.

> Fred, a student aide in a New England veterinary clinic, prepared packs of surgical instruments for routine neutering operations—a technical and manual procedural skill.

> Carola, a community college intern in the legal department of a municipal agency, started out filing case materials, but moved on to "digesting" court transcripts: pulling out specific information relevant to the lawyers' work—the first a low-level conceptual application skill, the latter a higher-level interpretive conceptual skill.

> Carmen, an intern in the accounting department of an advertising firm, reviewed and paid invoices in the accounts-payable process—an interpretive and procedural skill.

These sample skills can easily be described in terms of the framework in SCANS (1991). Clearly, the students were "mastering procedures": Putting together a surgical pack, for instance, required the student to sterilize and package a specific set of instruments; filing, which happened in many settings, involved checking the folder for the appropriate contents and then placing it in alphabetical order in the cabinets. Those examples were somewhat rote, demanding no real judgment, only recognition and step-following. Carola, on the other hand, did need to make substantive decisions in digesting transcripts: She had to have some conception of relevance about which items to pull out, which meant understanding something about the basic legal framework within which the work occurred; she had to know what the lawyers needed to know quickly and efficiently.

On some levels, the skills were very context-specific, unlikely to transfer to other arenas. When Fiona, a student-intern in the operating room of a hospital, set up an anesthesia machine, she followed steps very particular to that machine. Knowing how to "do the red cart" would be unlikely to help her, for instance, in setting up a computer-assisted loom in a textile factory. On the other hand, one could argue that there is a general sense of orderliness, precision, and diligence that transfers from the red cart to the loom.

But generalizability can also be assessed in terms of the SCANS framework. For instance, one category of fundamental skills in that scheme relates to thinking: creativity, decision-making, problem-solving, seeing things in the mind's eye, learning to learn, reasoning. Accepting for the moment that experiencing those activities in one context inevitably transfers to experience in another context (for a discussion of the controversy around that assumption, see Perkins & Salomon, 1989), we can say that some of our subjects did engage in those kinds of cognitive activity, and thus might be said to have developed those generalized skills:

> Maureen, a teacher's assistant in a 5th-grade music class, had to improvise ways to evaluate a number of students in a limited period of time; she had to think through the application of broad criteria to the specifics of kids' performances.

> José, who worked as an assistant to the manager in the housekeeping department of a hotel, had to set priorities in deciding what information and messages to relay to his boss.

On the other hand, some other students had very little opportunity to think creatively or to solve real problems. Rather, they were expected to follow established routines in performing tasks: filing personnel folders according to required systems; walking physical therapy patients back and forth as directed by the lead physical therapist; processing checks in the payroll office of a university. Of course, as Kusterer (1978) showed in his study of bank tellers, even jobs that look (and are officially defined as) unskilled sometimes require specialized knowledge and problem-solving practices, especially when the algorithmic procedures run into snags. But it is hard to argue that these glitches provided substantial educational opportunity for the interns.

Another general category of skills, according to several of the schemes, includes personal and social skills: displaying good work attitudes; taking initiative; following orders; participating effectively in teamwork; understanding the organization. Certainly the field researchers witnessed many scenes (sometimes during tasks, often during down time) in which student-interns engaged in context-appropriate interactions with colleagues, superiors, and clients.

> Fred, in the animal clinic, spent much of his time searching for tasks he could perform, since his supervisor often left him to his own devices: he would answer phones, replenish pet food, vacuum the floor. The vet appreciated this initiative.

> Matthew, a hospital intern, displayed considerable sensitivity to the feelings and needs of patients as he washed them and delivered their meals. He also once carried on a lengthy, friendly conversation with a medical resident about careers and schooling.

> José, who was assigned to the manager in the hotel housekeeping department, came to treat the maids and janitors as a manager would: with some degree of authority and control. At the same time, he was good at following his boss's orders.

Many students formed friendly and productive working relationships with their colleagues and supervisors, and the limited number who dealt with customers or patients seemed generally capable of courtesy and attentiveness. Moreover, they had many occasions to display responsibility: appearing on time, following through on task demands, keeping themselves under control in potentially difficult situations. This demand for responsible behavior in an authentic work setting might be one of the strongest elements of the skills learning in work-based learning. It may also lead to the frequent claim by student-interns that "they treated me like an adult."

SCANS (1991) also specifies various workplace competencies related to resources, interpersonal relations, information, systems, and technology (see p. 3). Although some of the subjects did encounter opportunities to use some of those skills, another lesson is clear: Merely being in the workplace does not guarantee that a student-intern will engage them. For instance, although most students could probably identify resources used in the work process, very few had occasion to organize, plan, or allocate money, time, materials, or human resources. As low-status persons in the organizational hierarchy, the interns typically worked within resource decisions made by others. Sometimes those decisions were visible to the students; often they were not, and the work system simply appeared as a given. Of course, this condition is to be expected of young student-workers, and does not necessarily imply that the learning experience was less than solid.

All the interns acquired and used information of one sort or another, and thus to some extent satisfied the SCANS standards; but not all were expected to organize, maintain, interpret, and communicate it. In the advertising firm accounting office, Carmen processed a great deal of information about cash flow, expense accounts, and vendor payments. The system she used for that activity was essentially given to her: She maintained it, but she did not invent new categories, reconstruct procedures, or communicate her findings other than through spreadsheets and checks. She did sometimes have to interpret data, for example, when she was processing expense accounts. Ali and Abdul, two community college interns doing computer networking in a banking firm, clearly had high-level information-processing demands not only in relation to the technology but to the users as well.

Not all students used information to a significant degree. Matthew, in the post-op ward of the hospital, was more like an extra pair of hands than an information processor. But a number did. José had to turn raw data into a communicable and useful message: He conducted an inventory of the hotel rooms and organized the data in a way that his supervisor could report to higher levels of management. On the whole, though, the typical student-intern handled information on a moderately low level: taking it in, processing it, and passing it along in rather mechanical and prescribed ways. Again, however, one could reasonably argue that this form of information-use was appropriate—and educational—for these young workers.

SCANS also called for competence in understanding, monitoring, designing, and improving systems. Our subjects did not do that very much. Rob, who worked in the physical therapy department of a hospital, did create a bulletin-board tool for tracking the arrival and departure of patients—but this incident is the only one in the data that shows a student taking the initiative to improve a system. More often, the interns appeared to take the system as given, and worked within it. Whether they understood those systems fully is hard to determine, because they could work effectively in their limited roles without necessarily encountering the broad sweep of system features and processes. Maureen, the music teacher's aide, probably knew how a middle school works, since she had been through one. But the four students working at a large urban hospital each had a very narrow perspective on the organization as a whole; their work rarely put them in contact with other components of the system. Even within their subsystems (departments), their knowledge was circumscribed. Matthew, for instance, saw a number of different medical personnel in his ward—RNs; LPNs; PAs; surgeons and other physicians of various specialties; orderlies; volunteers; social workers, and so forth—but he could identify only some of them for the researcher.

As for learning about technologies, the students often worked with unusual and complex tools: computers (spreadsheets, word processors, specialized data systems); anesthesia machines; walkers, canes, and other therapeutic devices; veterinary instruments, and so on. They did not select the tools, but did sometimes maintain and troubleshoot them. Clearly, they got a feel for the ways in which particular technologies are used in the workplace—and thus met the SCANS criteria at some level. Whether they understood the functions of those machines in the larger context, or the details of their internal operations, or the general meaning of technology in the work organization is another question.

If we move from the checklist analysis of SCANS to the more activity-oriented, constructivist stance of Darrah, the core question shifts from "did students learn A, B, and C?" to "did they come to participate in communities of skilled practitioners?" From this perspective, the issue is not whether they acquired and applied discrete skills, but whether they engaged in situated practices (Lave & Wenger, 1991) with other members. On this count, the data suggest a largely positive picture, with a few less-desirable instances.

On the negative end of the spectrum, a few interns were essentially isolated from the core activity systems in their workplaces. Irina, for instance, was assigned to the clerical operation of a foreign consulate. But her clerical skills were quite weak, and so her supervisor rarely gave her any meaningful work; instead, the student spent much of her time teaching herself how to use a word processor. Her only functional tasks involved preparing lists of companies doing business with the home country. She virtually never took part in—or even witnessed—the real work of the consulate. Similarly, Shin-Kap, a disabled student interning in the office of a community orchestra, was isolated from the musical and managerial work of the organization. These students could hardly be said to have participated in communities of skilled practitioners.

On the other end of the scale, some of the students became virtually full-scale members of their work communities, functioning in the same way as full-time veterans. Carmen, for instance, participated fully in the accounting staff of the advertising firm. Her skills were rudimentary, but not inappropriate for a neophyte worker. She was assigned the same kinds of tasks as other accountants; and she interacted with her colleagues and her supervisor in almost the same status. She was reluctant to become enmeshed in the social network of the office, but for reasons that had more to do with cultural style than with her membership in that community of practice. Fiona, who worked in the operating room with anesthesia machines, was clearly a legitimate participant (Lave & Wenger, 1991) in that community, in terms of both her performance of functional work and her interaction with her colleagues.

The status of these students might properly be described as peripheral: Fiona was an assistant to the anesthesiology technician; Fred was an aide in the veterinary clinic; Maureen was the equivalent of a student teacher in the music classroom. But they still had plenty of occasions to read situations, to draw on the collective expertise of their colleagues, and to identify and solve problems. This experience in its own right constituted an educational opportunity different from what they encountered in school. Carrying on in this emergent, interactive environment represents, as Darrah (1996) shows, an important form of skilled activity.

The interns' experiences have to be analyzed on a case by case basis, however. The degree of marginality of their participation varied from site to site. Some, as we have seen, were deeply enmeshed in the community whereas others were not at all. Most commonly, students were somewhere in between these extremes. Maria, who filed personnel materials in the human resources office of a large consulting firm, was certainly a full member of the filing-room community; but she was completely isolated from the rest of the organization, and never took part in the larger community of practice. Carola, in the legal department of a metropolitan transit system, did get to collaborate extensively with other paralegals on digesting transcripts, but she had no substantive interaction with lawyers.

In general, the observations of more than 25 students in their workplaces suggest that they often became increasingly involved in their communities of practice, but in a limited sense: They tended to have somewhat marginal roles; they tended to take on tasks for which the organization had prescribed procedures, rather than open-ended problems to solve; they struck up good working relations with their colleagues, and took part in standard office socializing. They used some low- and medium-level skills in the context of work activities, but did not often get even to the point that Darrah's computer assemblers did.

The educational question, of course, is whether that degree of participation constitutes a learning experience that is both worthwhile and generally unavailable in schools. Even though the students were in marginal roles in their organizations, most of them did have occasion to observe the larger community of practice, to interact with people in a functional system in ways not found in classrooms, and, in the process, to build some rudimentary skills. There are pedagogical issues related to this question—we will address them in Chapters 9 and 10—but our sense is that the foundation of the experience was solid and educationally beneficial.

Similarly, the data on the interns' development of expertise are mixed. Most commonly, the tasks they undertook could not really be said to lead to expertise in the way chess and computer programming do: Delivering meals to hospital patients, filing personnel folders, and cleaning pet cages are simple enough that, although one can imagine making mistakes, one can hardly picture being an expert. On the other hand, some students took on work in which one could improve significantly: managing the assignment of housekeepers in a large hotel; digesting court transcripts for lawyers; testing fecal samples for parasites. Given the limited amount of time interns had to build their expertise even in these roles, it is safe to say that few of them moved past the status of novice (Chi et al., 1988). But they did get better. Carmen, for example, began to memorize a list of vendors; this made her far quicker and more accurate in her processing of the advertising firm invoices. José had to conduct inventories of several hundred hotel rooms; by the end of the assignment, he could check out a room far more efficiently than he had at the beginning. The students were generally not experts, but they were headed in that direction.

The more interesting question related to expertise, however, comes from Bereiter and Scardamalia (1993): Did the students get to participate in an expansive workplace culture of learning-driven expertise, or were they led to solve problems only by using available routines? The short-term goal here, the one appropriate for a single-semester internship as opposed to a years-long career, is to instill in the students a frame of mind that leads them to push the envelope, to ask questions, and to keep learning at the margins of their competence. By this standard, once again, many internships were effective, but some were not.

The isolated workers, such as Maria in the consulting firm filing room, and Irina in the consulate, were not encouraged to expand their range of competence or to question the official procedures they were charged with carrying out. Even some of the medical settings, where skills were somewhat more complex, leaned toward routine performances: Fiona had to go through the same steps in setting up the anesthesia machine; Rob handled physical therapy patients in basically the same way every time. They could get better at these activities—faster, more accurate, more capable of handling snags; but they were not generally encouraged to reconstrue them, to take on new challenges without preparation, to stretch themselves.

Some of the settings, on the other hand, displayed signs of the culture of expertise that Bereiter favors. Even though Fred, in the animal clinic, did not directly perform many complex tasks, he did watch other members of the community do that. On top of the routine work (the neuterings, the vaccinations), the office was a learning environment, an arena where people generally tried individually and collectively to do things better. Similarly, there was room for improvisation in the music classroom, so Maureen could experiment with practices at the margins of her ability and could watch her supervising teacher doing things she had not seen before.

As was the case for learning in general (Chapter 2), for reinforcement of academic learning (Chapter 5), and for the learning of skills (earlier in this chapter), the point about the development of expertise is that it always depends on the situation. Some students do move toward extensive skills development and toward the expansive form of expertise that we have discussed. Others, clearly, do not. Work-based learning programs are not ipso facto guaranteed to provide these kinds of experiences. Under the right conditions, however, they can. Moreover, that experience of expertise appears more likely to occur in work settings than in classrooms.

Learning About Careers

Another claim made for work-based learning is that it provides opportunities for career exploration and planning (see, for example, Urquiola et al., 1997). Many students and educators make the intuitively plausible assertion that a key benefit of an internship is "trying out" a career option. Among our subjects, for instance, several students told the researchers explicitly that they had chosen their field placements because they planned to go into that career path: Fred wanted to be a veterinarian; Rob hoped to become a physical therapist; Carmen certainly aimed at a career in accounting. In roughly 350 hours of experience in a small animal hospital, Fred certainly got a strong feel for the work veterinarians do: the routine as well as the exciting, the managerial as well as the medical. One might ask whether he could have gotten just as rich an understanding of that career option if he had spent 35 hours in the clinic rather than 350; clearly, though, he learned a lot about this field of endeavor.

But the question of career-related learning through work-based experience is more complicated than these obvious comments suggest. Given the conception of learning theory outlined in Chapter 2, one cannot glibly assume that if you spend some time in a setting where people engage in Career A, you will inevitably learn a good deal about Career A. To learn extensively about the career, you need to participate in activities where knowledge about it is in use. Knowledge about a career includes more than understanding what, say, a veterinarian does from day to day, although that is clearly part of it. Career knowledge also includes such things as: entry requirements and processes; organizational settings for the work; working conditions; rewards (including compensation) and dissatisfactions; career paths and possibilities for advancement and success; degrees of autonomy and control; government or union regulations. For our purposes, we need to determine whether student-interns actually engage those sorts of knowledge in the workplace.

The issue of career exploration also slides inexorably into the domain of developmental theory, which is addressed in Chapter 7 in this book. Much of the significant literature on career development (Arthur et al., 1989; Blustein & Noumair, 1996; Super, 1957; Walsh & Osipow, 1988) focuses on the interplay between career decisions and self or identity, concepts beyond the scope of this section. What we can focus on here is the question of whether and how direct workplace experience might entail knowledge relevant to a student's consideration of career possibilities.

Phillips and Pazienza (1988) report a classic formulation of what one needs in order to make a wise occupational choice: (1) A clear understanding of oneself (aptitudes, abilities, interests, etc.). (2) "Knowledge of the requirements and conditions of success, advantages and disadvantages, compensation, opportunities, and prospects in different lines of work." (3) the capacity to reason effectively about the relationship between those two sets of facts (p. 2). The immediate issue, then, is whether work experience contributes to that foundation.

Note that this question and the observations that follow are only about the direct work-experience component of work-based learning programs.

That is, for now we are not looking systematically at the school-based elements of the program, to see how they shape students' thinking about careers. That shortcoming is quite serious, because it may be that the classroom activities in which work-based learning students examine their internship experiences are crucial in their decision-making. But here, we are just asking whether the work per se provides opportunities for career exploration.

Once again, it depends. The constructivist, participatory conception of learning described in Chapter 2 suggests that we need to analyze what students actually *do* in the workplace, to see what career-related knowledge they actively engage. Fred's experience in the animal clinic clearly gave him a good deal of information about the work activities of veterinarians and their staffs: He saw them performing operations, giving shots, talking with pet owners, maintaining their records, carrying on off-task conversations with assistants. He answered phones, and thus encountered the first point of contact between vets and their clients. He helped with filing, and therefore became familiar with some of the bureaucratic and organizational demands of the profession. He interviewed the doctors and technicians about how they got into the careers, their educational paths, and their levels of satisfaction. Moreover, he gave a presentation at his school on the question of what it takes to become a veterinarian. It seems clear that Fred learned a great deal about at least the small-town, small-practice version of the veterinary career.

After an initial period of mundane filing in the legal department of a municipal agency, Carola moved into an activity more consistent with the career of a paralegal: She constructed brief summaries of court transcripts for the attorneys. She also performed less-interesting and less-challenging tasks: inventorying files, stacking folders, photocopying materials, and updating docket entries. But by the end of the term, she was even conducting paralegal research using a computerized database: "I had to go into West-Law for an attorney. I had to find out if the cases were 'good law,' if there was negative feedback or if the decision was reversed" (observation iiia6: 60–63). Although her exposure to the paralegal career was relatively brief and local, it had to give her a substantial body of knowledge relevant to her own decision-making.

If getting a feel for the work activities in a career was a goal of these internships, a number of them must be counted as effective. Most students witnessed a good deal of the natural life of various occupations: the accounting office, the physical therapy clinic, the hotel. By keeping their eyes open and asking occasional questions, the interns could learn a great deal about life on the ground. This is no small thing for students entering a phase of their lives when they will have to make some important decisions.

They need to know whether they find the environment appealing and rewarding, whether they think they have a knack for the work, and whether getting into the field is feasible.

On the other hand, the interns did not usually go much beyond the daily-life perspective on careers. To be sure, some of the students had occasional, informal, and usually brief conversations with colleagues and supervisors about their educational preparation and career paths: Fred formally interviewed his supervisor for a presentation he was to give at school on what it takes to be a veterinarian; Rob chatted with physical therapy assistants about their choices of school programs; Matthew had a long conversation one day with a resident about topics ranging from liver disease to the duration and expense of medical education. But in the course of their work, students did not generally witness or engage knowledge about the longitudinal aspects of occupations. They interacted with people at different stages of their careers, but there is not evidence that they thought systematically about those patterns.

Even the conversations with colleagues and supervisors contained limited information: about personal choices for schooling, for instance, but less about compensation, opportunities and barriers, the relative value of advancement strategies, or possible alternative fields. Rather than engaging in "true reasoning" on the relation between knowledge of oneself and knowledge of the career (Phillips & Pazienza, 1988), the interns heard personal narratives with limited generalizability spiced with occasional idiosyncratic advice: "I went to State University because they had a good program in PT; you ought to try to get in there, not the City Community College."

Again, the pedagogical issue is whether this exposure to the daily life of a career justifies the time and resources expended on work-based learning. In later chapters, we will identify some of the strategies that teachers can use to enhance the career learning back at school. Our impression here, though, is that the students' learning about the everyday realities of their potential careers, even though it could have been even better, was substantial, eye-opening, and greater than anything they could get just in classrooms.

Conclusion

Surely the claim that work-based learning students learn practical skills is true on at least some level and to some extent. We have seen evidence of skill development in virtually all of the categories in the SCANS framework and others—in *some* settings. Nearly every student-subject performed tasks that required specialized ability in the local environment: setting up an anesthesia machine in an operating room; teaching keyboard technique to a 5th grader; filling out the assignment sheet for hotel house-keepers. Some of those skills involved organizing and allocating resources; some involved using and maintaining technologies; some demanded complex forms of teamwork and interpersonal communication. We could find at least one example of each skill type in the data.

But we could also identify sites where many of those skills were *not* in use by interns. Few, as we showed in Chapter 5, engaged in much reading, writing, or quantitative reasoning—at least in the academic, school-like sense. Most played marginal roles in the collaborative network through which organizations accomplished their purposes. They often used the un-official kinds of know-how described by Kusterer (1978), overcoming minor glitches, doing work-arounds that made their jobs easier and more efficient. They also participated effectively in the communities of practice depicted by Darrah (1996), though most often in the legitimate-but-peripheral roles of assistants, gofers, and order-followers. Some got to use discretion and judgment: Carola in her summarizing transcripts; Jose in his interactions with housekeepers and engineers in the hotel; Maureen in her tutoring of young music students. Many did not. In terms of building practical skills, it is not safe to assume that direct work experience will meet all the educators' criteria, but it makes a good beginning.

Even when students performed complex tasks crucial to the local work process, and more when those tasks were marginal and fairly easy to master, a key question must be raised about the notion of situated learning in the workplace: How will participating in those skilled (or semiskilled) activities shape their participation in other settings? This is the *transfer* problem: Will the intern carry what she learns in one place into her encounters with another? This issue is too vast to review in detail here, but a few points are worth making.

Perkins and Salomon (1989) suggest that, contrary to the situated cognitionist's radical argument that cognitive skills are always context-bound, people do transfer knowledge-use from one setting to another—under certain conditions.

> Transfer to new problems does take place . . . (a) when learners are shown how problems resemble each other; (b) when learners' attention is directed to the underlying goal structure of comparable problems; (c) when the learners are familiar with the problem domains; (d) when examples are accompanied with rules, particularly when the latter are formulated by the learners themselves; and perhaps most importantly, (e) when learning takes place in a social context (e.g., reciprocal teaching), whereby justifications, principles and explanations are socially fostered, generated, and contrasted . . . [T]ransfer is possible, [but] it is very much a matter of how the knowledge and skill are acquired and how the individual, now facing a new situation, goes about trying to handle it (p. 22).

They identify two principal mechanisms by which such transfer can take place: the "low road" of extensive and varied practice leading to near automatic use of the skill, which then can be used in another setting (driving a car helps one drive a truck); and the "high road" of the learners' "deliberate mindful extraction of a principle" (p. 22). If neither of these conditions is met, then skills tend to become context-bound.

The issue for work-based learning, then, is whether these mechanisms operate in the experience of students at work or in the classroom. Our field data suggest that the work activities do *not* provide the kinds of clues and incentives that encourage students to generalize the meaning of their experience. In the work context, attention is usually focused on getting the necessary tasks done, not on extracting broader principles and insights from them. One might imagine Carola abstracting her transcript-digesting skills into the more generalized skill of systematic summarizing of complex texts. But nothing in her experience in the legal department encouraged or supported that effort. There might be some useful residue left over from her activity, skills that she could use, say, in her English literature class; but if Perkins and Salomon are right, that carryover would be greater if someone drew her attention to the connections.

Such attention-focusing and elaborating is a pedagogical matter more appropriate for the later chapters on teaching in and for the workplace. On the whole, it does not happen much in work settings. As we will show in Chapter 10, it might happen in the classroom. A number of schemes exist (see Hamilton, 1990; Simon et al., 1991; Steinberg, 1998) proposing ways for educators to squeeze the greatest possible transfer out of situated work experience.

The same point might be made about career learning through work experience. Clearly there are benefits of firsthand participation in a specific vocational setting, benefits that go beyond what students experience in school. The more generalized knowledge about careers—preparation, alternative paths, compensation and rewards, other choices—probably does not become part of the intern's activities in the workplace. Addressing those broader issues might properly be regarded as the function of the school-based complements to the work-based experience. Someone needs to make a point of raising those questions and making sure that students engage that knowledge. It does not happen as a naturally occurring element of the situated learning. But the career-learning gains from internship experience seem to us a solid benefit of work-based learning programs.

CHAPTER 7

Work-Based Learning and Youth Development

In the past several decades, the youth-development perspective has been advanced and refined by practitioners and researchers concerned with the challenges youth face in their transition to adulthood. The perspective has tended to focus on risky adolescent behaviors and their prevention (see Dryfoos, 1990, for an example of this approach), however, there has recently arisen a movement within the field criticizing this problem-orientation. The new perspective is that "Problem-free is not fully prepared."[1] Rather than defining and addressing youth only in terms of their delinquent behaviors, many youth advocates now maintain that the basic needs of youth should be specified and attended to as they progress through stages of development to adulthood (Public/Private Ventures, n.d.). Thus, in general, the youth-development field now focuses on "supporting or promoting, during the second decade of life, the positive developmental processes that are known or assumed to advance health and well-being" (Benson & Saito, n.d.). A multitude of lists of such processes and desired youth outcomes have been put forth, based on psychological theory and accumulated knowledge from practitioners (see Public/Private Ventures, n.d.).

We find that there is much in common between the current youth-development approach and the promise of work-based learning. In this chapter, we demonstrate how the unique opportunities and experiences

---

[1]This slogan is attributed to Karen Pittman. See MacDonald and Valdivieso, n.d.

137

available to youth through work-based learning can contribute to their general development. Even though in our limited observations of students at worksites, it would have been difficult for us to actually see youth development occurring, we could see in the observations and hear in the student interviews the kinds of things occurring—exploration of adult roles, the taking on of increased responsibility over time, and so on—that youth-development proponents believe are beneficial to and promote positive youth development. Thus, using literature from the youth-development field and elsewhere, and data from our own fieldwork, we demonstrate how work-based learning can provide what young people need for "full flourishing" (Baizerman, 1994).

Desired Developmental Outcomes for Youth

As noted, many lists of desirable youth outcomes have been elaborated. For example, Pittman, Irby, and Ferber (n.d.), in defining the broad tasks of adolescence, have specified "5 Cs": developing competence, confidence, character, connections, and contributions. To assist adolescents in achieving these outcomes, these authors list three key community inputs: consistent, caring, and competent people; safe, structured, stimulating places; and a full range of options for training, exploring, and contributing. Other researchers recommend that: Young people intentionally participate in their own development; young people have multiple opportunities in their daily lives to learn, grow and develop; young people have consistent, ongoing relationships with caring adults; and young people develop measurable areas of ability and skills and higher levels of thriving behaviors (as cited in MacDonald & Valdivieso, n.d.). Still other researchers have concluded that healthy youth development requires youth to have opportunities for active and self-directed learning that include exploration, reflection, and expression; as well as opportunities to take on new roles and responsibilities (Cahill & Pitts, 1997; Zeldin & Charner, 1996).

According to Cahill and Pitts (1997), older adolescents, in particular, need diversity in opportunities and expectations so that they can explore themselves and their environment, and begin to develop different goals and awareness of the pathways toward meeting those goals. Cahill and Pitts also identify what they call desired youth competencies, such as personal/social competence, cognitive/creative competence, and vocational competence, among others.

What is common to these and other schemes is the focus on providing youth with diverse opportunities and supports: opportunities for exploring different options and building new competencies, with adult support throughout. This perspective is supported by theories of psychological development, which have long maintained that development requires a stimulating environment that poses resolvable but genuine problems or conflicts (Kolhberg & Mayer, 1972; also see Dewey, 1938). By working through problems, change should occur in thinking about one's self and the world. Thus, it is challenging experiences that lead to development. Vygotsky (1978) uses the concept of "zone of proximal development" to differentiate between one's actual and one's potential levels of development; he argues that learning that results in development occurs only through problem-solving in interactions with more-capable others.

With this general agreement on the circumstances in which young people develop best, the next step, then, is to determine how and where to provide youth with these opportunities and supports. Although schooling is one of the institutions with primary responsibility for preparing youth for adulthood (along with the family), some argue that schools do not provide what young people need for positive development (Costello et al., n.d.). Schools tend to be rigid and bureaucratic, offering young people few opportunities for autonomous exploration or contribution toward decisions of importance (ibid.). Schools also tend to be age- and skill-segregated, possibly tempering potential development (Coleman, 1974). In the typical large high school, students may not have sustained, meaningful contact with adult teachers. And minimal contact with adults, or any more highly-skilled others, may thwart psychological development for youth.

As we have noted in previous chapters, there has been a great deal of research examining whether part-time work is beneficial or harmful to adolescents. Although much of the research focuses on the relationship between working and academic outcomes, there is also debate about the consequences of work for psychological or psychosocial development (see Greenberger & Steinberg, 1986; Mortimer et al., 1999; Mortimer & Johnson, 1997). Some researchers have criticized teenage work as causing young people to grow up too quickly; in developing positive adult characteristics, teens may also take on less-desirable adult behaviors such as drinking alcohol and smoking. The extent and nature of adult contact and supervision in young people's part-time jobs is also unclear. Youth workers are concentrated in food-service and retail work, and Greenberger (1988) has observed that in many youth workplaces, young people are supervised by others of similar ages. Thus the workplace, for many high school students, is likely to be yet another institution in which they have contact primarily with their peers.

One large study, based on self-report data, did find positive developmental consequences of working. As part of a longitudinal study of Minnesota 9th graders that was initiated in 1987 by Mortimer and her colleagues, the students and their parents were interviewed about their experiences of employment (Mortimer, Harley, & Aronson, 1999). In 1990, the students were asked about the benefits and problems of working, and their parents were asked to retrospectively assess their own work experiences. The students and their parents overwhelmingly thought of their work experiences as beneficial in terms of the development of desirable adult characteristics; they said they gained responsibility, independence, social skills, and money- and time-management skills. In addition, the parents were favorable about their own children's employment.

However, in reviewing the literature, the researchers (Mortimer, Harley, & Aronson, 1999) note that there is as yet no evidence that working positively affects adolescent self-concept or self-esteem. In certain cases the Minnesota data showed that work could improve young people's sense of efficacy. The authors conclude that the quality of work is important, that "there are meaningful variations along several work dimensions that affect psychosocial functioning. For teens, there are developmental benefits to working in jobs that provide opportunities for skill acquisition and utilization, helping others, and sharing decision making with supervisors. Under these circumstances, the teen's sense of efficacy increases" (Mortimer, Harley, & Aronson, 1999, p. 155).

The potential of school-organized work-based learning for youth development is that it addresses the problem of youth having limited experiences outside of school and with adults in general, yet offers an improvement on the work experiences that young people tend to already have. Young people in school-to-work initiatives report having beneficial connections with adults that they would not otherwise have (see Hughes, Bailey, & Mechur, 2001, for a review). Chapter 3 reported that, when high school seniors were asked to compare work experiences arranged through school with jobs they found on their own, they rated the school-sponsored experiences higher on several different dimensions (see Hershey et al, 1999; Kemple, Poglinco, & Snipes, 1999; Stern et al., 1995). In addition, our survey of employers participating in internship programs, discussed in Chapter 4, found that internships tended to be of higher quality where the interns were somewhat but not too far behind other workers, lending support to the zone of proximal development theory. Thus work-based learning can be a means of providing the range of diverse opportunities and experiences, along with supports from adults, that are believed to serve as the foundation for positive youth outcomes. In the next section we illustrate this point with examples from our cases. It explores the link between the youth-development approach of providing opportunities and supports, and concepts such as "possible selves" and "planful competence" from the psychology literature. We then discuss the potential for a positive process of youth development to contribute to youth's academic achievement, before concluding.

Opportunities and Supports in Work-Based Learning

In our observations of and interviews with youth in work-based learning, we found evidence that work-based learning presents youth with opportunities for new roles and new learning, as well as the support that comes from being a member of an adult community of practice (Wenger, 1998). Without internship programs, these young people would not likely have spent concentrated time and have had legitimate roles in such places as an advertising firm, a hospital, a hotel, the various corporate offices, and so on. And, while the students learned their new roles and tasks, the adults provided scaffolding (Bruner, 1981), which could gradually be removed as the students became capable of autonomous work.

In several of our cases, we heard from the young people how the internships, and particularly the adult support, helped them to grow. Paul, who had a summer internship at a major corporation, said:

> INTERN: Well, I've noticed that I've changed a lot by the way I talk, because I talk different to my friends and I talk different at work . . . So, now when I talk to my friends, they're like, why are you talking so different? I am like, it's not different, it's the way I am, now I am accustomed myself to work, the way I talk at work . . . and I think it's better for me, because it's like teaching me how to grow up and stuff.
>
> RESEARCHER: Teaching you how to grow up?
>
> INTERN: Yeah.
>
> RESEARCHER: In what ways?
>
> INTERN: Well . . . how can I put it? Well, not acting like childish no more . . . learning how to like . . . What I mean by childish is like . . . how to behave to people, how to behave for myself, how to act. Because I think if you saw me like five months ago, six months ago, I was kind of childish to the way I am now. So it has helped me.

These changes in his behavior made him feel good about himself. He gave his coworkers credit for this:

> INTERN: You know, I actually felt kind of good inside, to think, you know, these people appreciate what I am doing. So it makes me feel better, and it makes me like want to keep on working with them. But that's one of the main reasons why I want to stay, because I see that they appreciate me, that they know what I am doing. Even though it's not a lot, but they see that I am doing the best I can to help them.

For the young people, having adults trusting them to work autonomously in some cases contributed to improved self-concepts. For example, one of the students, Hiroshi, was given a placement at a large publications warehouse for an important brokerage firm. He was at first disappointed to be working in the warehouse as opposed to corporate headquarters, but in the end he said he had learned more than he had expected to. During one interview, Hiroshi related how his role had become more autonomous over time, attributing his advancement to the support of his adult coworkers:

> INTERN: No, today's better because today, Eli's out and Richard's out, so I have more things to do, and I have the chance of determining, to make decisions of what to do here and what to do there. So I feel really good about it, too. Who will do this and who will do that. Somebody pick this up, somebody do this, and somebody do that. You know.

> RESEARCHER: Yeah, because when Roz walked out of the office for a little bit, she said, "I'm going out for a break, I want you to hold down the fort." And so I was really intrigued by that, because it was just us two in there, so you had to answer the phones and just take care of anything else if something came up. So that's a lot of responsibility for you.

> INTERN: And sometimes I'm afraid of taking responsibility. But after this I think that I should be proud of taking responsibilities . . . I've been encouraged many times in here . . . they give me a chance to try, try it out to do this and that. So I can be a, like the helper around the office, who gets things done faster and more efficient.

By the end of the internship, this young man could see the ways in which he had benefited:

> INTERN: And I learn, I've been mature, more mature. Now I can handle a lot of problems without anybody. I can handle it myself. That's one thing that I'm proud of. Whatever problems come up I can just deal with them instead of getting help. I know how to deal with pressure like from work and, other pressure, I can deal with them better than before this internship. So I really gained a lot from this internship.

> INTERN: I'm not just an intern. I'm part of the family. So, that I really feel really good about.

From Hiroshi's words one can infer that the internship experience contributed to his positive self-concept. Ross and Broh (2000) contend there are two components to self-concept: self-esteem and sense of control. Hiroshi felt that he was valued by his adult coworkers, which contributed to his self-esteem, and he also felt himself to be an effective person in this working environment, which contributed to his sense of control.

Hamilton and Hamilton (1997), long-time advocates for and researchers of youth-apprenticeship programs, have also found that student participants in work-based learning emphasize that they learn how to act like adults, with growing self-confidence as part of the process. The Hamiltons use the term "personal competence" to refer to desirable developmental aspects such as self-confidence, initiative, motivation, commitment to continuous improvement, and career planning. The Hamiltons also stress the importance of adult engagement with the youth in bringing about these aspects.

We saw these processes occurring with other interns, as well. Sinda, who had an internship with a travel industry magazine publisher, said the following:

> Jane [her supervisor], you know, she is just great. She shows me what to do and when I am doing it wrong, how to do it. You know, she is very busy, but she still takes the time out to show me stuff and how to do it. And she lets me do a lot of technical stuff, and that shows me that she . . . she, you know, trusts me to take care of this stuff. So I guess that's what encourages me, that when somebody trusts you to take on a lot of stuff like that, they think that you're motivated to do it even better.

Catherine, who worked in a large investment bank's mutual funds department, said that the work she did made her feel good about herself: "It felt good in terms of the fact that I was *capable* of doing that. I just felt good about myself" and "I felt respected by other people because they realized what I'm capable of." One young intern, Fred, said about his coworkers, "They're all great, they respect me, they treat me as an adult instead of a child. They're all teachers. They're there for me, they will answer questions and show me how to do stuff." Work-based learning allows youth to explore new roles that come with new problems, yet ideally also provides support and attention by adults that enable the young people to shoulder new responsibilities rather than flounder. In taking on challenging work in an adult context, the interns felt proud that others were relying on them to complete it, which led to their own growth.

Hamilton and Hamilton (1997) also write of the social competence that apprentices can acquire. Social competence includes, for example, learning about the structure and purposes of the organization, the roles of people in the organization, and how to access information, and also encompasses professional norms, ethics, and communication skills. Our cases yield many examples of young people learning about adult interaction and workplace behavior. An unanticipated yet interesting finding was that students often seemed surprised at the social nature of work. Perhaps the serious nature of many programs' pre-internship preparation leads students to expect that workplaces are grim and formal. Yet while the youth do learn appropriate workplace demeanor, they also learn that personal relationships play a large role. On the negative side, the student at the animal hospital was surprised to find that adults talk behind one another's backs just the way teenagers do. But on the positive side, Catherine, the young woman interning at a large bank, found that she could talk to her boss about a personal problem that was affecting her work. She said that she appreciated this, and explained how her vision of "a boss" had evolved:

> INTERN: That was an experience in itself, because a lot of people are kind of intimidated or just not comfortable talking to their boss. It's like . . . oh my god, oh my god, you know, whatever. It shouldn't be like that. And I've learned that, of course it depends on the individuals, but you should still kind of try to be equals in a certain sense . . . So it's just that the way I see it, it's just that one of the team members has more responsibilities than you. And that's about it and they're there for *you* to help *you* as opposed to, kind of, kick you in the butt. (laughs)

> (Later in the interview) RESEARCHER: So, I wonder if anyone told you specifically that when you're working with a boss in a corporation, there isn't really a hierarchy, but there's a team, and so you work as team members?

> INTERN: No, no, I think that's a decision I've made. That's my perception of it. Because one of these days I plan to be a boss. And that's how I would like my company to run.

As a result of her internship experience, this young woman concluded about adults at the workplace:

> They're real people, they go out on the weekends, they can joke around, it's not all business suit and no heart.

These examples illustrate the ways in which these workplace experiences gave these youth opportunities for growth that they might not otherwise have had, with the adults at the workplaces providing a variety of types of support. Through work-based learning, students can come to know adults and gain an understanding of adult roles that they might not otherwise. Through an introduction to the social nature of work as well, young people can gain a sense of membership in a group unlike the family or groups at school.

Possible Selves

Marcus and Nurius (1986) use the concept of "possible selves" to describe the possibilities individuals imagine for themselves in the future: "An individual's repertoire of possible selves can be viewed as the cognitive manifestation of enduring goals, aspirations, motives, fears, and threats" (p. 954). This concept is relevant to our discussion in that participation in work-based learning, through allowing youth to come to know and try on different adult roles, quite likely broadens the range of possible selves youth can imagine. Young people in work-based learning may be able to envision more, in thinking "I could be. . . ." These possible selves are also likely to be professional and productive, given the types of settings our student-interns worked in. In addition, because work-based learning, as we have seen, can contribute to a youth's positive self-concept, that positive current view of the self can lead to imagining, and striving for, positive possible selves. Possible selves "provide the essential link between the self-concept and motivation" (p. 954) because "they function as incentives for future behavior" (p. 955).

Thus, through self-concepts and possible selves, adolescents define who they are and who they want to become in the future. Developing a sense of uniqueness also contributes to this process. As Costello and colleagues write, "Young people need to make their mark one way or another" (n.d., p. 191). The feeling of uniqueness can result from developing competence in new roles and new skills. Many of the student-interns we studied expressed a sense of being special by virtue of the internship experience they had. Several became very skilled in their place of work so that they found uniqueness in contrasting their way of completing tasks with that of others. For example, one young man who was interning in the physical therapy section of a hospital occasionally found the treatment of the patients (who were mostly elderly) by the therapists disturbing. In an interview, he critiqued the performance of a new therapist:

INTERN: You know what? I don't know if he was just nervous or shy, but, but the way he treated the patients? I don't think it was very . . . good.

RESEARCHER: Really? How?

INTERN: Because, like, when he was like, "Okay, let's go for a walk." You don't say that to the patient, you gotta be more enthusiastic, you know? Like, "Hey, you wanna get up and go for a walk?" And they say, "No." And then you, if they say no, you say, "Aw come on, you don't wanna just sit in that wheelchair the rest of your life" or, you know—You have to be encouraging, kind of.

A young female intern gained feelings of uniqueness by feeling that she had learned something that not just anyone could do:

INTERN: So I guess I feel like that's cool that I got to work with legal files, you know. And see how they are organized, you know. It's just not you have to put it a, b, c. You know it's really not that simple. You know, you have to put 'em in certain order. Like sometimes they'll have one company like "Salt 'n Pepper" but they can have like 15 different files on "Salt 'n Pepper" and you have to put 'em in a different order. And somebody that just came in probably wouldn't know how to do that. And I do.

For these and other students, their internship experiences gave them a sense of having knowledge that others did not commonly have. This sense of being good at something could certainly contribute to feelings of uniqueness as well as to a positive self-concept and imagination of possible selves.

The concept of finding vocation is related to that of possible selves in that finding vocation is the determination of which of the possible selves is most desired. Baizerman (1994), and Magnuson and Baizerman (1996), who have spent years interviewing youth for a project on vocation, work, and youth development, believe that "finding vocation" is an essential part of entering adulthood. Finding vocation involves discovering a direction in life that provides a sense of purpose and meaning. One may feel a "calling" and commitment to this purpose in the sense of wanting to make a contribution, so that self-transcendence may be a factor. Feelings of "it suits me" or a sense that "I must do this" may also be experienced. Finding vocation usually involves settling on a career or line of work, but it also includes taking pride in one's work and acquiring the knowledge and skills required to be successful. Thus, finding vocation is accompanied by a sense of purposefulness, what Clausen (1991) calls "planful competence." Planful competence refers to a thoughtful process of becoming committed to achieving one's ambitions. Studies of youth apprentices have found that the experience gave them career focus and direction, as well as knowledge of the steps needed to take to proceed toward the chosen career (Hamilton & Hamilton, 1997; Orr, 1996).

Our cases provide several examples of significant development of vocation during an internship experience. For example, Maureen was a high school senior in an intensive internship program at a comprehensive high school. Maureen was already a motivated, college-bound student; she had a high grade point average, and sufficient credits to have graduated a semester early. Instead, she decided to use the internship program to explore her interest and talent in music. She arranged an internship with the music teacher in a local middle school. At the beginning of the internship, she primarily observed the class. Later, she became more comfortable, interacting with the students and planning activities with the teacher. After several weeks, she expressed her desire to independently teach a lesson, and soon thereafter, did so. After a time, her supervisor told us that "She exuded confidence." By the time of our final interview with her, Maureen felt a real change in herself:

> INTERN: Before, my goals were I'd practice piano 4 hours a day, and I did a lot of work on my own. I played for people I wanted to play for and I did my homework and I hung out with my friends. There was just a lot of self-focus. And although I did things for other people, I mean that wasn't a real focus for me . . . it was more in improving myself so I could go on to do better things. As I was able to work through my internship, I realized that there's so many opportunities where I could be needed in the community, and where I can serve and help other people. And it has changed me so much and my outlook and my understandings of what I want to do with my life, or even in my self-esteem really, it's just gone up a lot. Before I thought I just had to be the best at whatever I was

doing and I wasn't good enough for anything. But now I just feel . . . I feel so happy that I can give to the kids that I teach. And before I was a little bit timid to take on private piano students, because I thought, "Oh, I can't . . . I don't want to mess them up or I don't want to be experimenting on kids." But through this internship and through other things I've been doing in the community, I have 10 private students right now, ranging in the ages from 4 to 32 . . . And, I just . . . I mean I love . . . I love my students so much. And I love teaching and I love being able to . . . I get this high when I'm teaching and being able to relay information. And I think the thing that really changed me the most was looking at the individual and making that initial connection of, hey we're both people and we both are human. And this is what I enjoy and this is what you enjoy and . . . and things in life connect. So once you can make that initial connection where the person trusts you . . . you can utilize that connection . . . And utilizing that connection you can teach. You can teach music. You can teach . . . whatever you're teaching. In my case it's teaching music or teaching about a composer's history or music theory or mastery of a piece. And once you've utilized that connection, hopefully, it is now up to the individual that you're teaching, that they will take the information that they have and connect that with the world around them. So, my big thing that I'm hung up on now is making connections . . . Between what I want to do . . . between me and my students and you know just the theory of connections . . . it just blows me away. 'Cause I just . . . when you find out something's true for you all of sudden you're just like . . . It's so true everywhere! . . . And it's just like I found this truth inside of me. And I don't know, I don't want to make it sound so spectacular, but that's what happened to me and I don't want to try sounding cheesy about it, but . . . That's how I feel.

Maureen's internship certainly had a positive effect on her development, in that it helped her to find her vocation. Maureen felt a meaning in her music teaching. She also felt a sense of higher purpose for her life. Maureen found her "authentic self" (Baizerman & Magnuson, n.d.). She did so not through independent or academic study but through involvement with the work world and with others. She began to understand that she could use her life to connect with, and make a contribution to, the lives of others.

Instances such as these are cause for optimism that there is, indeed, a relationship between work-based learning activity and development. Through fostering engagement in activities that connect youth with the adult world they are soon headed for, the experience can contribute to positive changes in a young person's sense of purpose, direction, and commitment in life.

Youth Development and Intellectual Development

If work-based learning can promote maturation and psychological development, what influence will it have on the student's intellectual development and academic learning? If increased maturity, focus, motivation, and sense of purpose generated by work-based learning can also transfer to the classroom, then experiences in the workplace can have an influence on academic achievement.

As discussed previously, many youth are disengaged from high school. In a recent Public Agenda survey of a national random sample of high school students, 85 percent said that they can't wait for the school day to end, 82 percent said the best thing about going to school is being with their friends, and 55 percent said that, when they get out of school, they won't need to know most of the things they are being taught (Johnson, Farkas, & Bers, 1997). Through student interviews, Steinberg has found evidence that lack of student engagement in schooling affects academic achievement (1996). His findings reinforce several education reform books written over a decade ago on issues of student malaise and "the shopping mall high school" (Powell, Farrar, & Cohen, 1985). Steinberg found that by high school, friends are generally a more important influence on students' school performance than their parents, and most students don't see doing well in high school as being very important. According to their own reports, between one-third and 40 percent of students say that when they are in class they neither try very hard nor pay attention.

Students do accept that they need an education for a successful future. The Public Agenda survey reports that most students view high school as an exercise in "getting by—doing as little as possible to get the grades they need" to get into college (Johnson, Farkas, & Bers, 1997, p. 11). The most common reason students give for trying hard in school (when they do) is not genuine interest in the material but the extrinsic motivation of getting good enough grades to be able to go college (Steinberg, 1996).

Can psychological development increase a student's engagement in school? College professors who teach adults (usually in night classes) as well as traditional-aged college students often observe that the adults are more engaged in their studies. Although adults certainly have circumstances that conflict with their schoolwork, they generally have much more purpose and direction. Although in a previous chapter we found only weak evidence for direct positive effects of work-based learning on academic achievement as traditionally measured, there is possibly a positive *indirect* relationship to the extent that work-based learning addresses students' disengagement in school. Indeed, in recent studies on students in school-to-work programs, of which work-based learning is usually a part, the students report that these programs make them more interested in school, and they have higher attendance and lower dropout rates than comparison students (Kemple, 1997; Kemple & Snipes, 2000; Linnehan, 1998; Stasz, 1999; Westchester Institute for Human Services Research, 1997).

In an analysis of national data (NELS), Ross and Broh (2000) found a relationship between having a sense of personal control and subsequent academic achievement for high school students. Having a sense of personal control in the 10th grade was significantly associated with high grades and test scores in the 12th grade. If participation in work-based learning leads to a high sense of personal control, then work-based learning could indirectly positively affect academic achievement. This type of potential relationship between work-based learning and academics should be the basis for future research.

Conclusions

The youth-development framework gives another way to think about the value of work-based learning for youth, in addition to the academic-achievement or career-development models. We contend that work-based learning shows significant potential for contributing to positive youth development, through entrée into the adult world with its opportunities for challenge (yet support) from new relationships with adults. These opportunities and supports may otherwise be absent from young people's school and work lives. With work-based learning, youth can potentially increase their competence in a variety of areas, improve their self-concepts, and envision possible selves. They might even find meaningful vocations.

This framework for examining the benefits of work-based learning may result in different kinds of policy prescriptions for good programs and advice given to students in pursuing their internship experiences. Instead of orienting students to the labor market by pointing out the practical paths to achieving a particular occupation or pointing out which occupations provide the most income and status, students might, for example, be encouraged to explore different work and community activities, asking themselves in each case what they learned about their interests and who they are as a person, and which experiences were the most worthwhile to them and why. We will take this issue up further in later chapters on pedagogy for work-based learning.

CHAPTER **8**

New Modes of Thought

As we have seen, the advocates of school-to-work programs (Steinberg, 1998; Stern et al., 1995) make many claims about what sorts of learning students can accomplish. In Chapter 5, we addressed the claim that work experience reinforces academic learning—and found mixed evidence for that claim. Other proponents (see Hamilton, 1990; Pauly et al., 1995) argue that students can explore and plan careers through school-to-work programs. We looked at that possibility in Chapter 6, and discovered some support for it. In the preceding chapter, we reviewed claims about the impact of work-based learning on adolescent development, and generally found that, although the issue is more complex than popular rhetoric suggests, the program has significant potential in that realm.

In this chapter we construct a claim of our own, beyond the three others we have examined already: that students in work-based learning programs learn to think in new ways not generally available to them in school classrooms. To develop and evaluate this claim, we draw on two kinds of literature: theoretical material about situated and distributed cognition, and our observations of interns supplemented by observations from two other empirical studies—Moore's (1981a & b) research on the School for External Learning, and Stasz and Kaganoff's (1997) analysis of three work-based learning programs in Los Angeles. As before, we test that claim against the available evidence from the observations, and explore its inherent logic. The theoretical literatures do not provide direct empirical support for the claim, since previous scholars have not looked specifically at work-based learning programs (though many have looked at apprenticeships; see, for example, Lave & Wenger, 1991). But combining their logic with our data may provide a strong warrant for our claim about new modes of thought.

Moreover, we suggest that the curious relationship between school and work creates a tension or dialectic that contributes to the student's learning. Being in a workplace as a student sets in motion a set of thought processes that cannot be matched by either straight classroom or straight work experience. Those new processes may constitute another value-added element of work-based learning programs.

Benefits of Contextualized Learning

There are a number of ways in which thinking in the workplace may differ significantly from thinking in the classroom. We mentioned Resnick's influential formulation of the distinction earlier, but there are other, more subtle analyses available. In this section, we present some of those frameworks and see how they apply to the data in the three studies. If, and to the extent that, these new modes of thought actually occur, school-to-work programs may provide a special benefit to students.

Problem-Formation

Scribner (1986), reporting on her studies of everyday thinking in a dairy plant, suggests several features of working intelligence that distinguish it from the intelligence used in schools. One is the opportunity—even the demand—to define as well as to solve problems in the work arena (also see Perkins, 1993, p. 99).

> Models of formal problem solving suggest that problems are "given" and that intellectual work consists of selecting and executing a series of steps that will lead to a solution; the initial problem may be decomposed into subproblems as part of the solution procedure, but its terms are fixed. By contrast the dairy studies suggest that expertise in practical problem solving frequently hinges on an apt formulation or redefinition of the initial problem (Scribner, 1986, p. 21).

Students in school are normally given a problem and expected to follow more-or-less standard, teacher-supplied procedures to solve it. In workplaces, by contrast, the problem space is frequently ambiguous and shifting; effective solutions often require making sense out of what is at issue. To be sure, as Scribner points out, many problems are, in fact, "preset by social-institutional objectives and technological conditions" (not to mention by workplace culture); "but even preset problems," she notes, "may be subjectively reconstituted" (p. 21). This sort of cognitive skill is not usually acquired by students until well into the college career, even into graduate school. Exposing high school students to the process of problem-formation in the workplace could conceivably alter their fundamental conception of thinking and learning, even in the classroom.

According to the evidence in our three studies, Scribner is correct in noting that problems in workplaces are often predetermined. Clear-cut tasks—cleaning up the operating room in a veterinary hospital, setting up the anesthesiology machine in a hospital, filing records in the legal office of a business—may not even constitute problems in the sense that Scribner implies: disruptions to the normal flow of productive work, snags that require thoughtful resolution before the work can continue. Often the dimensions of the problems that appear during task-work are quite simple.

> Fiona, a young woman assisting the anesthesiology technician in a hospital operating room, was charged with setting up a particular machine before procedures. One day she was having a little trouble pushing the cart. She asked her supervisor if some of the wheels were locked. Debby answered, "No." Fiona moved the cart back and forth and just figured the alignment was off. (observation viib1:32–35)

Sometimes the nature of the problem is deeply embedded in the work process.

> Carmen, an intern in the accounting office of an advertising agency, was directed to enter a batch of invoices into the computer system. First, she had to know the ID code for the vendor in order to enter the invoice into the system or look it up in the PFM system (Production File Maintenance System). . . . She couldn't type in the vendor name. Instead, she had to guess the code and hope that the name appeared within the 20 or so firms that appeared on the screen. (observation iva1)

The problem was determined by the computer system: Find the vendor code. She could improvise methods for solving the problem, but she couldn't reinvent the problem.

On the other hand, students did sometimes have occasion to define problems in their worksites. That might mean choosing a high-priority issue from among a number of options that were presented; or it might mean inventing a whole new realm of issues to work on.

> Maureen, a teacher's assistant in a 5th-grade music class, was supposed to assess members of the class on six elements of piano-playing. She played a duet with one boy, who seemed very excited by that process—and then very disappointed when she left him to assess other children. Seeing his disappointment as a problem, she eventually returned to spend a little more time with him. (observation xiiid2)

> Carl, a School of External Learning student interning in the office of a member of the city council, started the term by doing clerical work and answering phones. After watching what was being done in the office awhile and noting that the council member often had trouble finding material on specific bills, he decided to create a system for tracking the progress of legislation through the Council. His supervisor was thrilled (Moore, 1981b).

The degree to which student-interns could initiate new conceptions of problems varied widely across sites, depending on many factors; for example, the technical elements of the production process, the time pressures on the organization, the extent of power hierarchies. But clearly, some work-based learning students do have an opportunity to engage in problem definition or redefinition, often in ways they do not encounter in classrooms.

Flexible Modes of Solution

Scribner also claims that working intelligence is "marked by flexibility—solving the 'same problem' now one way, now another, each way finely fitted to the occasion" (1986, p. 22). Schools generally expect more algorithmic solution procedures: "add the figures in the ones column, carry over to the tens. . . ." Moreover, the contexts within which problems arise are predictable and few: tests, questions from the teacher or the book. Because work situations vary more than classroom ones, student-interns can develop not only a larger repertoire of solution skills but also the capacity to recognize subtle but important contextual differences that might make one approach more effective than another.

Again, work-based learning students often learn that different solutions are sometimes appropriate for the "same" problem.

> Matthew, who worked in the postsurgical care unit of the hospital in a big city, often had to make beds with the patients in them. Even though the technical demands of the work remained essentially constant, he interacted differently with the different patients, depending on a number of shifting factors: their moods, their sizes, their degrees of physical infirmity, even the time of the day. (observation viiic2)

> Heather, the School of External Learning history-museum tour guide, sometimes introduced classes to a set of artifacts (candlesticks, bedwarmers, hotirons) during the auditorium phase of the tour; she would ask questions to find out what the children knew already, then elaborate on their responses. Her style and content both varied substantially depending on their input, their enthusiasm (or lack of it), their questions, and their teacher's participation. As she got better at the job, her flexibility—her repertoire—increased (Moore, 1986).

This notion of the expanding repertoire of problem-solving tactics is highly consistent with the literature on the evolution of skill and expertise in the workplace (see, for example, Glaser et al., 1988). Work-based learning students tend to have more such opportunities than students in the classroom do because problem-solving methods in school tend to be more constrained by rules and conventions.

Using the Environment

Scribner's third claim about practical thinking is that it incorporates elements of the task environment into the problem-solving system. The worker does not simply solve the problem *in* the environment; she *uses* the context in her situated intellectual activities. As an example, Scribner describes the way dairy-plant preloaders (the people who assemble the products that will go out on the delivery trucks) use the visual characteristics of milk crates to perform quantitative operations; they *see* solutions to number problems in the appearance of crates rather than calculate them in their heads (Scribner, 1986, p. 23). Schools, on the other hand, normally treat the thinking process as acontextual, as unaffected by the environment (see Resnick, 1987). Students who learn to exploit the context in problem-solving enlarge their powers by adding tools, realizing complexity, and improvising relations. They develop the capacity to scan the environment for potential resources, to imagine alternative paths toward solutions, and to choose among those paths. They become more attentive to features of the situation that might play a role in their work. In the school classroom, they are more constrained in their use of the environment: During a test, looking something up in a textbook may be defined as cheating, as is talking with a classmate about alternative approaches. Thus, if students in work-based learning come to use their environments more effectively, this form of learning would constitute another value-added feature of the program.

Some workplaces, according to the observations, are, in fact, resource-rich environments that give student-interns a great deal of latitude in accomplishing cognitive, social and manual tasks.

> Roger, a School of External Learning apprentice in a master cabinetmaker's shop, had to saw pieces of lumber for a chest of drawers. Rather than measure each piece individually, he measured one carefully and then used it as a template for the others. Moreover, he learned to use the first board as a visual model for succeeding pieces, so they all had consistent grain patterns (Moore 1981b).

> Nell, who interned in the radiology department of a hospital, learned a code system called Soundex for filing X rays. This device helped her code patients' names and pull their charts. She could tell by looking at the shelves of file folders which ones required which kinds of work, because she recognized the color patterns in the files. (observation viiia2)

Effort-Saving

Finally, Scribner identifies effort-saving as a characteristic of practical thinking (1986, p. 25). Workers try to expend the least possible mental or physical energy in performing a task—and in so doing, they may refine their conceptions of problems and enlarge their repertoire of skills for handling them. Classroom problem-solving (especially on tests) may encourage speed, but one is not supposed to skip steps or devise shortcuts. Yet the ability to save effort, whether mental or physical, while still performing the task adequately, may demand a rather high level of expertise, something student-interns may come to understand in the workplace and take back to class. On the other hand, of course, this effort-saving process may decrease students' learning by embedding knowledge in the technology and allowing neophyte workers to perform tasks without understanding them fully (see Pea, 1993).

In the course of a one-semester or school-year-long internship, few students in the three studies got to the point where they could be regarded as experts in their positions. But some of them did learn certain functions well enough to devise ways to save time and effort.

> Carmen, the accounting intern, eventually memorized enough of the vendor codes to make it unnecessary to look them up in the computer database. This knowledge, though not complex, saved her considerable effort. (observation iva3)

> Carl, the city council member's intern, learned over time to handle constituent complaint calls more expeditiously and effectively. He developed an understanding of which city agencies handled which kinds of problems; he built relationships with key personnel at those agencies; he even memorized telephone numbers. As a result, when a resident of the council member's district called to report a tenant-landlord problem, for instance, he saved substantial time by immediately calling the right person in the housing department to resolve the dispute. He also needed less of his supervisor's time and advice (Moore, 1981b).

Forms of Representation

Another aspect of practical intelligence that may give learning advantages to work-based learning students might be the need to engage a variety of forms of representation. As Resnick (1987) points out, most school-based thought is essentially symbolic, rarely embedded in real-world activities. People at work, on the other hand, learn to represent their knowledge in varied ways depending on the fine details of the situation (Perkins, 1993). And they do it in ongoing ways, as demonstrated in Suchman and Trigg's (1993) analysis of two computer scientists working at a whiteboard on an artificial intelligence problem. Their marks on the board evolve in tandem with their collaborative understanding of the problem and its solution;

they create "concrete conceptual objects" (p. 160), which they can then manipulate and transform. Similarly, Keller and Keller (1993) show how an iron-craftsman shifts his representations of the activity as the physical object takes shape. This variability of representations enhances the problem-solving capabilities of an individual or team, but is not common among school-based thinkers.

> In the cabinetmaker's shop, apprentice woodworkers learned to apprehend the quality of a piece of furniture literally in their hands. They would run their fingers along the edge of a drawer, slide it in and out, lift it—all to reach a tactile-manual judgment about whether it was adequate. They developed a *feel* for the craft (Moore, 1981b).

> In the history museum, Heather had access to an unusual array of artifacts representing the actual historical processes she was telling students about. She could manipulate these objects in her discussions with schoolchildren, showing them (rather than explaining to them) how bedwarmers were made and used, or how carriages transported goods (Moore, 1986).

Cognitive Teamwork

Edwin Hutchins's (1993) study of navigation on a naval vessel demonstrates yet another aspect of situated cognition that may constitute a value-added form of work-based learning over classrooms: distributed thinking, or teamwork (also see Pea, 1993, p. 48; Perkins, 1993, p. 99, and Chapter 2 of this volume). "Looking at navigation as it is actually conducted aboard ships . . . brought home to me the extent to which cognitive accomplishments can be joint accomplishments, not attributable to any individual" (Hutchins, 1993, p. 35).

Hutchins describes the work activities of a team of sailors who collaborate in guiding a ship through a river and into a harbor. In the process, they share the cognitive and technical work in a way that turns them into a kind of collective mind. Different members of the team fix the ship's position by visual bearings, track its progress on a nautical chart, and keep the deck log. On the open sea, one person can actually perform all these tasks, but in the more time-pressured environment of the river, elements of the work have to be distributed and coordinated. What is particularly intriguing about Hutchins's example is that the distribution of labor perfectly represents the trajectory of learning for the navy quartermaster: By progressing gradually through the hierarchy of roles constituting the navigation team, the individual eventually becomes competent in the performance of the whole task.

This experiential participation in a complex form of distributed intelligence rarely appears in the school classroom, where tasks are almost always assigned to individuals rather than groups. In fact, in the more conventional classroom, students who work together on solving problems, especially in tests or on papers, are accused of cheating. In recent years, to be sure, more and more teachers have begun to use collaborative and team-based learning methods—but those approaches tend to be pedagogically driven interventions rather than naturally occurring functional processes.

Hutchins identifies the properties of work systems where this kind of learning can take place: Knowledge is distributed; tasks are broken down in such a way that peripheral participants can perform some of them; lines of communication and observation allow the novice access to expert performance; workers get quick feedback on their performance and an opportunity to correct errors. The activity system has flexibility and robustness; if it runs into trouble, it adapts by redistributing labor (pp. 48–52). Classrooms do not generally contain these features; workplaces sometimes do.

When interns can take part in such systems, they engage knowledge in ways different from their usual school-based thinking. They learn differently, by participating in a community of practice (Lave & Wenger, 1991; Wenger, 1998). According to the studies, that type of experience sometimes happens in work-based learning settings.

> Fiona, the operating-room assistant, participated in a complex community of practice during procedures, one that included highly specialized professionals like the surgeons, anesthesiologists, and nurses, as well as lower-level technicians and orderlies. Although she was not at all likely to take over any of the professional roles in the near future, she did have a tangible sense of taking part in a multifaceted team, where knowledge of different kinds was being used by different members, all for a common purpose. She could also watch and listen to the interactions among the physicians; she doubtless could not understand some of what they were saying or doing, but she could get the big picture. (observation viiib1)

> Similarly, the medical careers academy interns in Los Angeles functioned as members of research teams. They came to understand enough of the underlying science to see where their own contributions fit, and to have a general sense of what other members were doing (Stasz & Kaganoff, 1997).

There may be an educational downside to this distributed cognition process. As Pea (1993) argues, off-loading cognitive work onto other participants or tools may involve a trade-off between giving the newcomer access to an activity and limiting her understanding of its intellectual foundations. Fiona did participate in the surgical team—but she comprehended only a very small range of the knowledge-in-use in the operation. On the other hand, the medical careers students in Los Angeles occupied roles that, though peripheral, gave them opportunities to learn substantially about the research process. The difference between effective placements and those that are more constrained, apparently, has to do with the possibilities for role expansion: the anesthesiology technician can go only so far toward a broader function in the surgical team; but the research assistant is on a path toward becoming a full-fledged researcher.

Executive Functions

In his discussion of distributed cognition in a "person-plus" system, Perkins (1993) argues that all cognitive organisms have an executive function, "routines that do the often nonroutine job of making choices, operating at decision points to explore the consequences of options and select a path of action" (p. 96). This executive function, like other elements of cognition, can be distributed in a number of ways. In schools, the teacher and the text generally make key decisions about the course of the activity—in Bernstein's (1975) terms, these interactions are strongly "framed"—and students are expected to follow along. The learner does not exercise much discretion or power in the work.

In the workplace, however, the executive functions can be distributed in more variable ways. The worker-learner can sometimes exercise a degree of autonomy rare in classrooms, and can make important decisions about what to do next.

> Carl's work on the bill-tracking system was completely autonomous on his part. He not only decided on his own to move into that domain, but he also managed his time so he could continue to perform his constituent-service functions while designing the new system (Moore, 1981b).

The distribution of the executive function can also shift over time as the learner becomes more capable of taking on aspects of the work activity.

> When Heather started interning as a tour guide in the museum, her supervisor and the veteran tour guides decided when she was ready to undertake specific tasks, like the artifacts cart. As she gained expertise, she made decisions more and more on her own: about when to shift the topic of discussion in the lecture hall; about when she needed to do additional research on a particular historical issue; about what style of speech she should use during the walk through the exhibits (Moore, 1986).

> Students in a school-based enterprise in Los Angeles made decisions, sometimes individually and sometimes as a team, about strategies and tactics for marketing their salad dressing to local stores and distributors. Teachers gave them coaching support, but the students themselves gradually assumed more and more of that decision-making function (Stasz & Kaganoff, 1997).

On the other hand, student-interns in some sites did *not* exercise the executive function. As Perkins argues (p. 99), total learner autonomy is not always a wise pedagogical choice; sometimes the learner does not know enough to make sensible decisions about what to do next, and learns more if some authority (teacher, supervisor) makes those decisions. Ideally, as in Heather's case, the learner gets that function back as her knowledge and skill increase. But "the catch, in much educational practice, is that the student never gets back much autonomy at all" (Perkins, 1993, p. 99). Linda, a curriculum firm intern in the School of External Learning study (Moore, 1986), became less likely over time to decide what to do; her supervisors had to assign her very specific tasks, then assess them as she finished them up. Fiona's work in the anesthesiology department was driven primarily by routines; she did not always have to be told what to do, but she did not really make activity-shaping decisions on her own.

On the whole, though, it might be fair to say that researchers in these three studies saw students performing the executive functions in the workplace more frequently than they would have in the classroom, where teachers commonly control the flow of activity.

Higher-Order Thinking

Perkins (1993) also raises the intriguing question of how higher-order knowledge is distributed in thinking-learning situations. By higher-order knowledge, he means "problem-solving strategies and patterns of justification, explanation and inquiry characteristic of the discipline" (or, one might add, of the community of practice)—heuristics and strategic thinking. "This higher-order knowledge not only informs the construction of understandings of content-level knowledge but also provides grist for the executive function" (p. 101).

Perkins goes on to argue that, although higher-order knowledge is sometimes off-loaded onto machines (expert systems, for example), "By and large, [it] should be in the person (or distributed among the minds of participating persons) rather than physically downloaded" (p. 104). This preference reflects the fact that higher-order knowledge is referenced more or less continuously in complex activities, and is fairly stable and compact.

The evidence on whether this aspect of situated cognition represents a benefit of work-based learning over classroom learning is rather ambiguous. Given the relatively low status of most high-school interns and the high degree of division of cognitive labor in their workplaces, it may be that many students do not participate in the use of higher-order knowledge on the heuristic or strategic plane. Many of the students in the studies performed tasks that were marginal to the main activity, and thus did not engage the issues of justification, explanation, or inquiry. In the curriculum firm, for instance, Linda calculated reading levels for new texts; but not only did she not have to justify or explain that activity, she was not even sure what the work was for (Moore, 1986). Fred, in the veterinary hospital, was told why he was expected to do certain pickup chores (filling feed dishes, cleaning up after operations), but did not have to explain them himself. Even Carmen, in the accounting office, basically carried out the operations she was assigned; she did not have to think through their function in the larger activity system—she may have, but that cognitive work had no particular function in the office.

On the other hand, some of the interns participated more often in the use of higher-order knowledge than is common in schools. Carl, in the city council member's office, used highly sophisticated, strategic knowledge about legislative process and political dynamics. Museum tour guide Heather engaged in high-level thinking about historical inquiry, about the behavior of schoolchildren, and about educational practice. Ali and Abdul, computer-networking technicians in a banking firm, were floating troubleshooters, and often had to think through matters of strategy. This sort of experience, when it happens, clearly represents a value-added dimension of work-based learning. The issue, of course, is whether it happens enough.

Understanding Social Relations

Another form of thinking and learning that students encounter in workplaces more than in schools centers on their understanding of the character of social relations. Clearly, the variety of relations is greater at work than in classrooms. Simply by virtue of having to interact with people in multiple ways—as coworker, as subordinate, as producer of goods, and provider of services—the intern experiences more complex interactions. Moreover, she generally has to think about those relations in new ways, as well, since they have practical and immediate consequences.

Simon et al. (1991), in discussing the value of work-based learning, focus in part on the way that work can "be understood as a particular wage-labor exchange constituted on historical grounds with respect to the social and technical relations of production" (p. 8). Students who directly experience those relations can begin to explore not only existing forms, but their histories and possible changes in them. They can inquire into factors like social class, gender, race and ethnicity, power and authority. They can search out the implicit rules and conventions of social interaction in their setting, the workplace culture. The nature of work life is not an academic abstraction to interns, but a living reality, open to interrogation and action.

> Matthew, a student placed in the postsurgical unit of a large hospital, had occasion to deal with very different kinds of people in different conditions: nurses,

physicians, administrators, patients. Sometimes he had to take orders; sometimes he engaged in casual conversation; sometimes he witnessed political
machinations among staff. He gradually developed a more subtle understanding of the complex relations among people in his department, shaped by
power, by expertise, by need. (case viiic)

Carmen, the IEE subject working in the accounting department of an advertising firm, made a serious error one day. An immigrant from Eastern Europe,
where such mistakes can be disastrous for a worker, she apologized so profusely
and so frequently to her supervisor that he finally lost patience and told her to
stop. In the process, she learned something not only about her own situation
but about the nature of authority in American workplaces. (observation iva3)

Thus, work-based learning clearly teaches students more about social
relations, organizational dynamics, and workplace cultures than any
classroom could. How they process that learning, how they bring it to
consciousness, of course, is a pedagogical matter. But the opportunity is
certainly there.

Diverse Modes of Thought

Finally, student-interns may benefit from exposure to different modes of
thought, or "ways of experiencing, interpreting, and expressing our understanding of ourselves and the world (which shape) how claims are justified
and how causes are attributed" (Olson, 1996, pp. 1–2). Other terms are
used to denote the same general phenomenon: discourses (Cherryholmes,
1991); learning styles (Kolb, 1984); genres (Bruner, 1996, p. 98). Generally,
they suggest that the specifics of talk, action, and thought in a situation
may be shaped by a broad worldview or perspective, and that a style suited
to one cultural setting may not be appropriate for another. Different societies and different institutions display a bias toward particular modes of
thought—they privilege them differently (Olson, 1996, p. 9).

Typically, schools favor a mode of thought that goes by several names:
the scientific, the paradigmatic, the explanatory. It treats the world of
phenomena as objective, impersonal, knowable through rigorous inquiry.
It seeks to remove personal experience, emotion and bias from claims
about truth. It tends toward the linear, the systematic, the verifiable, the
decontextualized. Most often, it involves deductive, propositional reasoning (Bruner, 1996). In a certain cognitive realm, this mode of thought
functions quite well, and is well worth learning.

But there are other modes, as well, that merit attention. Science is not
the only path to knowledge. "The deep issue for the student of cognition,"
Bruner writes, "is how the meaning seeker proceeds in getting to a final
formulation. We get trapped by the ideals of science when we insist on an
exclusive role for well-formed computation, verifiability and truth condi-

tionality" (1996, p. 100). He begins to distinguish some of these other modes, though the lines between them are fuzzy; in fact, more than one may operate in a given cognitive event. One is Jonathan Edwards's *interpretive* mode, as distinct from Isaac Newton's *explanatory* mode. Another is the *actional* mode: the form of meaning-making "concerned with relating events, utterances, acts or whatever to the so-called arguments of action: who is the agent of what act toward what goal by what instrumentality in what setting with what constraints, etc." People think in this mode when they are trying to get things done. A third is the *normative* mode, which deals with "meanings relative to obligations, general standards, conformities and deviations." These are all distinct from the *propositional* mode, in which "meaning making is dominated by the formal necessities imposed by the rules of the symbolic, syntactic and conceptual systems that we use in achieving decontextualized meanings" (pp. 94–98).

Citing studies that show that everyday thinking does not conform to the scientific paradigm, Bruner goes on to distinguish that mode from the literary, the narrative, the story-based, the dramatic. This mode:

> "personalizes" meaning by anchoring it in what people do, feel, believe, hope for, and so on. It defines what is expectable and canonical and assures cultural solidarity through myths, legends, genres and the like. These nourish folk meanings. The propositional idealization of meanings is radically more impersonal. In the guise of truth, it seeks to transcend both the individuality of the listener and the nature of the occasion on which such meanings are told (p. 101).

Here, in fact, may be the greatest appeal of work-based learning to its participants, the reason it so often gets rave reviews from students, even when they cannot express very clearly what they have learned: Namely, it is narrative, dramatic, and personal. By contrast, school-based learning is decontextualized, propositional—*no fun!* Oatley (1996) makes a similar point:

> One of the features of reading narrative, as Aristotle pointed out, is that we ourselves are affected by emotions as the plans and actions of a protagonist meet vicissitudes ... The occurrence of such emotions, I take it, is evidence that a reader is personally connected to the story; one seldom hears about people experiencing emotions (except perhaps anxiety and exasperation) when reading scientific textbooks. When we identify with agents in a story, when we run their actions on our own planning processes, the emotions produced as the protagonist's actions meet with events in the story world happen to us (p. 130).

This deep engagement with the story, with the experience, allows a more powerful form of reasoning that Oatley calls *abduction*, the making of inferences and construction of hypotheses even in the absence of full information. Because this personal involvement, then, with its attendant emotions and less-constrained reasoning processes, tends to engage the intern with a wider range of styles of knowing than are available or appropriate in a school classroom, it may constitute another added value of work-based learning.

Students in the three studies had many opportunities to think in non-propositional, narrative, personally engaged modes—even in ostensibly scientific settings. When a technician in the animal clinic told a student named Fred about a veterinarian who did research on earmites by putting some in his own ears, the intern learned something about the scientific method—but not in the typical academic fashion. Instead, he got a picture of scientific inquiry as a distinctly human enterprise. Rob, who worked in the physical therapy department of a general hospital, interacted directly with a large group of patients who exhibited not only different medical conditions but vastly diverse personal reactions to them. Some were resistant, some cooperative; some were depressed, and some were optimistic.

> A white elderly woman, maybe in her late 70s, arrived. She kept making a loud, deep, gutteral noise. She kept yelling, "I can't do it, I can't do it, take me back, I can't do it!" M (a PT assistant) attended to her. In a commanding voice, M said, "We haven't asked you to do anything. Now, that's enough." But that didn't help matters. The patient got louder and louder and kept yelling, "I can't do it!" (observation viiid2: 104–108)

> (The PTs) took a patient through a walking exercise. She walked more slowly than the previous patient, but she also walked farther. As the patient went through her walking exercise, M asked her questions while D (the head PT) wrote down the answers in a report . . . When the patient finished her walking exercise she sat down in a wheelchair and Rob rolled her to the gymnasium. Rob asked the patient if she wanted a pillow; she said, "Yes." Rob put a pillow under her legs. Then he placed a blanket over her legs. (observation viiid2: 47–64)

The differences between these two patients, who might have had similar problems, taught Rob to think more subtly about the human side of health care. The experiences also aroused different emotional reactions (impatience in one case, sympathy in another), which the student had to process in some way.

Similarly, Maureen, an intern in a 5th-grade music class, came to understand the personal element of teaching when she discovered a boy who was upset that she wasn't paying enough attention to him. Solving this problem required a mode of thought attuned to issues other than finger positions, scales, and harmonics. Heather, a history-museum tour guide, experienced history in a more narrative form than she would have in school. She learned to tell stories to the children that engaged them in the lives of colonial people, rather than just in the dates of events; and in her post-tour chats with other guides, she told stories that merged history with her experiences with the children.

Of course, this personal quality may or may not make work-based learning worthwhile as a pedagogical practice. On the positive side, it engages students in the meaning-making process, and is thus more conducive to learning than is being bored or alienated. On the negative side, it runs the risk of superficiality and taken-for-grantedness. Whether that is good enough for a school-based program is a huge social and political question. We need to ask what learners and teachers *do* with the narratives they experience. If they take them at face value, if they leave them at the level of folk theory, if they do not interrogate them, then we might well decide that the experiences, though potentially valuable in their own right, do not need school sponsorship. These are issues we will take up in a later section on pedagogy for work-based learning.

The School-Work Dialectic

There is another sense in which work-based experience may add learning value in a way that neither straight work nor straight classroom experience can do. The intern stands in a curious and unusual position relative to both these settings: student-worker. To overstate the case: As a worker, she is supposed to be competent in the performance of some productive activity; she is supposed to know what she is doing. As a student, on the other hand, she is, by definition, incompetent, in need of some kind of learning. The tension between those two roles, if it is exploited by effective pedagogical strategies, can be tremendously educational.

All new workers face a learning curve of some degree of steepness, and almost all work organizations recognize that fact. There is a period of initiation into the new setting, sometimes brief and sometimes lengthy, sometimes formally supported and sometimes not. But the underlying assumption is always that the worker's primary function in the organization is not to learn but to produce. A newcomer strives toward that status as competent: She pays attention to what is going on, she tries to make sense of new challenges and procedures, she works at building expertise on whatever tasks she is assigned. Often her focus is narrowly on those tasks, rather than on the larger context. Sometimes she asks questions or seeks help; sometimes she conceals her lack of knowledge and skill in the service of maintaining her status as a worker.

A student, on the other hand, is assumed to need to be taught things. Schools do not always encourage questions, but they anticipate what those might be and organize curricula around them. The student's work is learning, not producing (except in the sense that writing papers and taking tests is a form of production). Her competence lies in displaying that learning at appropriate times and in appropriate forms, not in having mastered it at the beginning. (Indeed, teachers do not know what to do with students who already know what the course is to teach them.)

But the intern stands at the intersection of these two roles, and thereby sets in motion a powerful dynamic: asking unusual questions in and about the workplace. The student part of the role gives the individual warrant to be less than competent, to ask questions, to make mistakes and to explore the big picture. The worker part of the role injects the intern into a meaningful community of practice, an authentic activity system in which actions and knowledge-use have real consequences.

The contradiction between the two parts of the intern role can produce a learning dialectic, a compelling impulse to answer the questions, to make sense, to build that competence. The student can ask questions more broadly than the new worker can: not just "How do I do this?" but "What does this mean? Why do we do it this way?" This expansive process can lead to the kinds of educative experiences that Dewey (1938) described. The problem-solving process has greater intensity and scope than it would be in the classroom alone, because the work entails more kinds of problems with more kinds of possible solutions involving more participants in more kinds of personal and organizational relationships; and it is greater than it would be in the workplace alone, because it entails more kinds of questions about more kinds of phenomena using different kinds of standards of verification.

There is a risk, of course, that this dialectic will fail to develop in any specific situation. Since the power of everyday life is overwhelming, and since people tend to work at integrating themselves fully into whatever context they find themselves in, the student may begin to view the work experience only through the lens of the new worker. Since the supervisor at work is concerned primarily with the student's productive role as worker, she may neglect the learning dialectic and focus on the production process. Finally, since the school-based educator is not on the scene and may not have a clear idea of how to exploit the work experience in the classroom, the tougher questions may never get asked and the larger insights may not be reached.

Matthew, the post-op assistant in the general hospital, tended to keep his eye on the immediate tasks in the ward: making beds, delivering food, moving patients. But sometimes he got into conversations with nurses or doctors in which he inquired into the larger meaning of the institution and the career possibilities in it. Similarly, Fred spent most of his time at the animal clinic cleaning the exam room, preparing neuter packs, and answering phones, but he also talked with the researcher about long-range vocational plans and about connections between the internship and his AP

Biology class. The dialectic did not always work: Some students gave almost no sign of looking at the bigger picture. But sometimes it did.

It is worth recalling that these special learning benefits of workplace experience are potential, not inevitable. As the theories of learning sketched earlier in this book suggest, what makes all the difference is the specific experience of the specific student in the specific activity in the specific organization. Whether these possibilities are realized always depends on the intersection of all those elements of the situation. Making sure that they are, in fact, realized constitutes the core pedagogical challenge for proponents of work-based education.

Conclusion

In general, the evidence from our studies suggests that there is a reasonable empirical foundation for the claim that student-interns learn to engage in modes of thought that they might not experience in school classrooms. Not always, but sometimes, they have the opportunity to define as well as solve problems; they can approach problems flexibly, using a variety of strategies and tactics depending on the situation; they can use elements of the environment to conduct their work. Moreover, they sometimes learn to represent problem spaces in a variety of ways, not just abstract and symbolic but material and social. Perhaps most important, they learn to participate in teams, solving problems in concert with other workers. On rarer but still available occasions, they perform cognitive tasks that could be called executive functions or that entail higher-order thought.

Again, these value-added features of work-based learning are not inevitable; they do not occur in every placement experience. But when they do, they constitute a clear benefit above and beyond classroom-based learning. Even the educational innovations like learning communities, problem-based learning, and active learning, all derived from the same basic constructivist theory that we support, cannot hope to achieve the same degree of complexity, intensity, and authenticity that work experience can. On the other hand, as we will discuss in the chapters on pedagogy, learning in the workplace may be less efficient, less incremental, and less accountable than teacher-controlled processes. Exploiting the benefits and minimizing the pitfalls, of course, represents the greatest challenge for advocates of work-based learning.

Here is one final irony in the litany of claims about work-based learning: Although we acknowledged in Chapter 5 that the academic reinforcement argument is perhaps the weakest of the four, the new modes of thought claim may circle back on the earlier one to change its terms. That is, although it is unlikely that any form of work-based learning will improve students' scores on standardized tests (test-taking is a unique context in its own right, with no obvious corollaries in the work world), it is entirely possible that engaging in the expansive, challenging, and varied forms of cognitive activity available in work-based learning could turn interns into better students back at school. The higher-order thinking and executive functions, the problem-constituting processes, and the expert flexibility demanded by many work experiences are precisely those mental skills that advanced graduate students need. High school and community college students who acquire these capacities may really be ahead of the game in later schooling; they may be capable of conducting academic inquiry in a way their school-bound classmates cannot. They may be better at asking questions, at searching for resources, at employing diverse strategies for getting their work done, at teaming up with others to solve problems, at recognizing the social as well as the technical dimensions of issues. Work-based learning students could end up being better students as well as better workers. This possibility is completely speculative at this point—we collected no data on students' performance in school after their work placements ended. But the logic of the learning dynamic is certainly plausible, and worth investigating in future studies.

CHAPTER **9**

Pedagogical Strategies for Work-Based Learning

The previous chapters of this book examined the various claims that have been made for the value of work-based learning, and found varying degrees of support for them. These claims might be thought of as referring to the curriculum of experience, the kinds of things one learns or the ways in which one develops as a function of participating in work activities. In this and the next chapter, we explore the different ways this curriculum is organized and enhanced; that is, we investigate the pedagogy of work-based learning.

As Munby and his colleagues (2000) have found in their extensive research on cooperative eduction in Canada, a workplace has a curriculum much as a school does. Whereas the main characteristic of the school curriculum is the orderly sequencing of instruction, a workplace curriculum is driven by the purposes of that particular organization. The purpose of school is learning and the purpose of much work is not learning; however, the learning that does occur at workplaces has an authentic quality in that it serves real world, specific goals.

In work-based learning, students learn both in the workplace and in the classroom. Indeed, as we have just argued, the dialectic between the two domains of experience can produce a powerful educational dynamic. Because of this dual situation, we split our pedagogical analysis into two parts. This chapter focuses on the naturally occurring pedagogy of work organizations, the kinds of strategies and tactics used by supervisors and coworkers to induct newcomers (in our case, student-interns) into the knowledge of the workplace. Chapter 10 will survey the methods used by school programs and personnel to ensure that students' work experience leads to learning, and will offer some hints for improving the quality of those practices.

Pedagogy is normally defined as a conscious set of principles and strategies used by teachers in instructing their students; the term is usually applied only to school-based practices. We suggest that pedagogy can be discovered in any social context where knowledge is distributed and used. In a place such as a worksite, participants use various kinds of knowledge to structure their relationships, their use of resources (social, informational, and material), and their activities, in a concerted effort to achieve certain shared purposes. Pedagogy can be defined as the social organization of the social activities, organizational structures, and cultural practices by which newcomers, such as student-interns, come to encounter and engage that knowledge. The process of becoming involved in the knowledge-use in a community of practice, as Lave and Wenger (1991) argue, is learning; pedagogy is the social organization of that process.

Pedagogy is thus situated in the social context, and as such, occurs naturally as part of the environment. Sometimes those processes are *intentional* in their effect on learning: People organize aspects of their activities explicitly to ensure that knowledge is appropriately and effectively distributed. Depending on whether they are in a workplace, a classroom, or a household, people might refer to this element of work as on-the-job training, instruction, or self-development, but for that moment, the learning is the central purpose of the work activity. In the workplace, of course, the longer-range goal is to enhance the quality and efficiency of the production process; but for the time being, someone wants someone to learn something. On the other hand, the pedagogical features of work may be *incidental*, a by-product of activity the primary purpose of which is *not* someone's learning. People at work sometimes learn simply by virtue of taking part in the practices of their colleagues. In the process of doing the work, they encounter new information and ideas, they reorganize their conception of certain phenomena, and they reconstrue their strategies for problems and challenges. Our definition of pedagogy includes both the intentional and the incidental, whether in the workplace or in the classroom.

One way that has been proposed to ensure learning in the workplace is to have the adults at the worksites actually teaching the student-interns. As Stasz and Kaganoff (1997) point out, "It is curious that educators and the public often express concern when teachers can teach with emergency credentials or with little formal knowledge of the subject matter, but seem oblivious to the qualifications of adults who teach students at work" (p. 77). These authors recommend providing appropriate training to interns' supervisors and monitoring their performance as teachers. Hamilton and Hamilton (1997) also emphasize that "clear teaching roles and responsibilities" should be assigned to worksite coaches and mentors (p. 40).

As discussed in Chapter 4, many programs are having success in recruiting employer participants, but it is probably overly optimistic to think that requiring employers to undergo training and monitoring won't lead to a mass exodus from the programs. Yet school personnel can examine workplaces, oversee internships, and create classroom-based assignments and activities; they can give attention to pedagogy for work-based learning to ensure that it is educational.

This chapter lays out a framework through which a school-based, work-based learning educator might analyze the situated pedagogy of a particular work context (including, for that matter, a classroom). That analysis should contribute to a number of decisions and practices: choosing and developing work placements for interns; consulting with the work-based supervisor to maximize the student's on-site learning; monitoring and evaluating the internship experience; and, perhaps most important, determining when it might be necessary to complement the direct work experience with some sort of pedagogical intervention back at school. There are good reasons, in other words, for the school-based educator to examine the way learning happens naturally in a particular setting.

To lay out this analytic process, first we identify the phases of work activity through which members engage various elements of the knowledge-in-use. Then we suggest some of the factors that shape the particular learning process. Finally, we classify certain pedagogical strategies and tactics that appear in real-world worksites. The fieldnotes from three of our intern observations will illustrate the potential utility of this framework, demonstrating the insights that can be gained through this kind of investigation.

The Task Analysis Framework

Much of our basic approach to the analysis of situated pedagogy has emerged from an earlier study of interns at the School for External Learning, a big-city alternative school that gives students experience in a broad array of workplaces (Moore, 1981a, 1981b, 1986). Our approach has been refined and expanded as a result of more recent work at the Institute on Education and the Economy (Berryman & Bailey, 1992), Harvard University (Perkins, 1993), and RAND (Stasz & Kaganoff, 1997). The fundamental premise of this framework is that participants in an activity system socially organize the process through which knowledge is defined, distributed, and used. The framework identifies the particular elements of that process that are worth noting, and suggests relationships among them.

The core of the newcomer's induction into the use of situated knowledge is her participation in the various work activities in the environment. That participation can be described as moving through several phases, focusing on the way specific tasks are set up, performed, and assessed. Thus, the first stage in the analysis of situated pedagogy is to locate the work tasks that the focal person engages in, and then to determine how those tasks are established, accomplished, and processed.

1. *Establishing.* First, the person has to discover the terms of the task: What needs to be done, how the work should be performed, and the criteria by which performance will be judged. The establishing phase may vary on several dimensions: Who initiates it (the worker herself, a colleague or supervisor, a client or customer); when it happens relative to the work itself; how explicit it is in terms of directions and criteria; and what resources (information or materials) are provided.

2. *Accomplishing.* Next, the person has to carry out the task, using the information and directions provided earlier, as well as devising new knowledge in the process. There are several components of this phase: Who takes part (the newcomer alone, or a set of colleagues and/or supervisors); timing (how long the work can take, and whether it is done in one interrupted period or intermittently); the relations among the participants (the distribution of power and status, and the division of labor); and the resources used in the performance of the task.

3. *Processing.* Finally, the worker may get feedback on the performance of the task, and may have an opportunity to rethink strategy and tactics. This information helps her determine how well she did the work and consider how she might do it differently in the future. Again, there are several variables in this element of the episode: Who provides the feedback or structures the rethinking (the worker herself, a colleague, a supervisor, or a client or customer); the timing of the processing (during the work, intermittently, or in a post-task event); and the form and channel of the feedback (verbally or in writing; formal or informal).

In the course of these three phases of the task episode, the worker might gain access to a number of forms of knowledge-in-use: about the elements of the work, about the way it is organized in the environment, about the nature of expert performance. To understand the pedagogical features of the situation, we need to look at the process by which the student's participation in that knowledge is organized.

Factors Shaping Pedagogy

The specific texture of the pedagogical process in any given situation will vary depending on a number of general factors. (See Moore, 1981b for an earlier version of this framework.) A new worker might get a lot of explicit instruction, or she might be left to figure out the skill on her own; other people might be readily available if she needs help, or there may be no other resources. Hypothetically, certain kinds of tasks might call for certain forms of pedagogy. The school-based educator conducting a comprehensive analysis of the process should examine these variables (see Table 9.1).

1. *Features of the work.* The way a newcomer gets to participate depends partly on the nature of the work itself. The tasks may be explored along two basic dimensions: Sociocognitive demands refer to the specific kinds of knowledge and skills the worker needs in order to perform the work competently (see Chapter 6 for a list of the forms of knowledge used in the workplace), and include both internal thinking processes as well as interaction and social skills. Pragmatics refers to the impact the task has on the larger work process, on the organization, and on the relative prestige or status of the worker.

2. *Access characteristics of the knowledge.* Perkins (1993) suggests another important aspect of the pedagogical features of a situation (although he does not use that term): the "access characteristics of the system—what knowledge it includes access to, via representations that afford what access to information, by way of what retrieval paths for accessing the information, and with what access to further constructions based on that knowledge" (p. 91). Pedagogical strategies will vary depending on what kinds of knowledge are available, how they are represented, what it takes to get access to them, and what participants can do with them to formulate further knowledge. Partly, the issue is the location of the knowledge: in heads, in documents, in tools, in practices; and partly the issue is who can gain access to it and what they must do to achieve that access. These questions are partly technical (what you have to be able to do, to read, to understand) and partly political (who is allowed access, and who is not).

    Another scheme for describing the knowledge features of the workplace is Basil Bernstein's (1975) concepts of classification and frame. Both the division of knowledge into categories (classification) and the determination of who controls access to that knowledge (frame) are socially defined and politically enforced. A workplace in which classification is weak—in which knowledge is lumped into broad, amorphous, and permeable types—is a very different learning environment from one in which knowledge is strongly segmented into neatly constructed categories. And one in which high-level managers maintain a monopoly control over access to knowledge, as in a Taylorist operation, is very different from one in which anyone can choose to learn anything.

3. *Features of the work context.* Another category of factors shaping the situated pedagogy relates to the organizational context within which the work proceeds. How knowledge is distributed—how people learn—varies depending on such elements as the social organization, the workplace culture, and the production process. The social organization refers to the nature and extent of hierarchy and the distribution and use of power within the organization. An organization with highly segmented roles, in which each status is responsible for a limited range of work and, therefore, knowledge, is a very different learning environment from one in which there is only one generalized status (tour guide, for instance) and everyone does roughly the same things, using roughly the same knowledge.

    Workplace culture refers to the beliefs and practices shared by participants in the organization around concepts like production, status, and learning (Applebaum, 1984; Hamada & Sibley, 1994). An organization in which members compete with one another for limited rewards, for instance, provides learning opportunities very different from those in a place where people see themselves as collaborating in a common enterprise. The production process refers to the social and technical organization of the process by which work gets done, including the division of labor, the use of tools and practices, and the technical steps in production. An assembly-line process, for instance, gives each participant far less exposure to production knowledge than does a multiskilled work team.

4. *Features of the larger environment.* Things happening outside the immediate organizational context may also affect the distribution of knowledge-use inside. These aspects of the broader environment include: market conditions, such as the extent of competition among organizations in the same niche; regulations, such as the imposition of work rules, licensing procedures, and other directives on the operations of the organization by government, unions, or other bodies (Appelbaum & Batt, 1994); and technology, the pace and nature of change in the technologies used in the organization (e.g., the creation of new computer systems or professional practices), and the difficulty of mastering these new tools.

Table 9.1 Factors Shaping Pedagogy: Workplace Factors That Help to Determine the Potential for Learning by an Intern

Factors	More Learning	Less Learning
Sociocognitive demands	The intern's tasks require knowledge and skill	The intern's tasks are not challenging
Social-interactional demands	The intern has heavy contact with others of varying statuses and roles	The intern has little contact with others
Pragmatics	The intern's tasks are important to the organization	The intern's tasks are peripheral to the organization
Access characteristics	Access to the knowledge of the workplace is available to the intern	Access to the knowledge of the workplace is unavailable
Classification	Weak: less division of workplace knowledge	Strong: workplace knowledge is highly segmented
Frame	Weak: access to the knowledge of the workplace is not controlled	Strong: access is highly controlled
Social organization	Workplace roles are not highly segmented or hierarchical	Workplace roles are highly segmented and hierarchical
Workplace culture	Workers believe in collaboration and learning	Workers are status-oriented and competitive, and the intern is given low status
Production process	Less division of labor; work teams are used	High division of labor; Tayloristic

Fred: The Veterinary Clinic

On a country road in New England, an 18-year-old high-school student named Fred interned in a small animal hospital. Two veterinarians share the practice, and they employ several technician-assistants. Most of their work is with dogs, cats, and other small pets, and covers the usual gamut of services: spaying and neutering, vaccinations, treatment of various illnesses, and occasional surgeries. Fred's role in the animal hospital included a number of peripheral functions: filing patient records; cleaning the examination and operating rooms after treatments; cleaning the cages and feeding the animals; sterilizing surgical instruments; restocking equipment in the supply closet; making call-backs to the owners of recently treated pets to check on their condition; mailing out vaccination reminders; and answering the telephones.

In general, the sociocognitive demands of Fred's work were minimal; he did not need to use very much technical knowledge or skill, and he rarely encountered a snag that required problem-solving. Sterilizing the surgical instruments and filling syringes with rabies vaccine demanded a degree of care and familiarity with a specific procedure, but were not hard to master. Doing the call-backs required some communication skills, which Fred recognized he needed practice in. At one point, Fred tested fecal samples for worms and other conditions; his judgment had to be confirmed by a technician. At another time, an assistant told him to inject some fluid into a cat, and then left the room; Fred had to guess how to insert the needle. But most of the work could be mastered very quickly. The pragmatic features of the work were not very compelling; the tasks needed to be done, but were not at the core of the organization's mission. Rather, the work represented what might be called the odds and ends of clinic maintenance. Nor did the chores give Fred much status within the work group; although he was treated in a perfectly friendly and respectful fashion, he was clearly at the bottom of the hierarchy.

The social means by which Fred's tasks were established, accomplished, and processed reflected their rather mundane and routine character. More often than not, the student himself undertook the chores without explicit instructions: when a surgery was completed, he cleaned up; when a phone rang, he answered it; when records piled up, he filed them. He initiated each instance of the chores simply by recognizing that it needed to be done and taking action. Most of his tasks were established early on as a part of his routine. His supervisors had originally asked him to do the work, but after awhile, they did not need to tell him each time. They had shown him how to do each piece—prepare a "neuter pack" for the spaying operations, wash the towels, clean the operating area—and then left him to his own devices. This perfunctory instruction reflected the rather low-demand, low-status character of the tasks.

The accomplishing phase of Fred's work generally involved solo activity: cleaning up after the doctors and assistants had left the surgery, preparing neuter packs, filing. On occasion, he worked with another member of the staff: putting away large boxes of supplies and pet food, testing fecal samples. Sometimes he assisted in more complex activities, as when he helped a technician get a cat ready for an X ray. The resources necessary for carrying out the tasks were nearly always available, and the procedures were clear and generally unproblematic.

Fred seldom got explicit processing for the tasks he performed. Rarely did anyone tell him that he had done something well or poorly, or how he could do it differently. That absence points again to the routine and low-complexity character of the work; there was not much he could do wrong. In one unusual episode when he carried out a somewhat complicated and risky task, the job was established quickly and with little instruction, accomplished by guesswork, but processed somewhat more fully:

> L (a technician) then called out to Fred from the other room; she needed his help with the cat, which was lying on a table. She handed Fred a needle which was attached to an IV bag . . . and told him to stick the needle in the cat. She pointed out the fluid level in the bag and told Fred the amount the cat needed. Then she ran off. Fred seemed surprised; he looked at L as she ran off, and said he wasn't sure where to stick the needle. But L was already in the next room. So he grabbed some skin at the nape of the cat's neck, and slid the needle under the skin. He stood there for several minutes as he watched the fluid level in the bag. Finally (the vet) came over to check on what he was doing and Fred said something about inserting the needle subcutaneously, was that right? (The vet) said that was indeed right. She looked at the fluid bag and asked Fred at what level it had started. He replied, and she said he could adjust it so that the fluid dripped out more quickly. (IEE, observation xiiia3: 269–280)

The researcher wrote in her fieldnotes, "In this situation, all the employees were so busy that Fred was spontaneously given a task that someone else would have normally performed, and that he had never done before. At first he was shaken a bit, but he performed the task correctly" (pp. 282–284). Luckily, the vet managed to process the last stage of the work, so she could confirm Fred's work and even suggest how he might do it differently the next time. The fact that she did that testifies to the unusual importance of this task. Not much needed to be said about the quality of his performance on routine tasks.

Fred's participation in the stock of knowledge in the animal hospital was rather marginal, low-demand, low-intensity, low-prestige, and it is not difficult to understand why. The organizational structure, despite the small size of the work group, was highly segmented. The doctors clearly maintained a monopoly over the core elements of the knowledge-in-use. Partly the strong classification and frame reflected the cognitive and technical complexity of that knowledge: One needs a good deal of understanding of science and a strong grasp of technical procedures and materials to do the work of a veterinarian. Some of the technicians had intermediate levels of knowledge in those regards, but the student-intern certainly did not enter with that expertise and could not be expected to develop it quickly enough to perform functional tasks in the medical domain. Partly the division of labor was driven by government regulations, particularly by licensing requirements for people who provide professional health care to animals. And partly it was a function of the traditional culture of medical workplaces, in which doctors have long enjoyed high status and power.

José: Hotel Housekeeping Office

A student in a travel and tourism academy in a big-city high school interned as an assistant to the manager of the housekeeping staff in a large hotel. The staff comprises three types of workers: room attendants, housemen, and engineers. Room attendants clean guestrooms, while housemen and engineers perform various upkeep and repair jobs. The manager of the department is responsible for assigning jobs to all three groups, for supervising their work, and for inspecting the condition of the hotel rooms and common areas.

José's specific tasks included aspects of all those functions. He spent much of the first day of observations in the office, answering telephone calls from guests and housekeepers.

> When he picks up the phone, he says, "Good morning, housekeeping, this is José." Then he writes down what the other person says. If it's a guest making a request for a particular item (ironing board, hair dryer), he has a form to fill out. Then he has to look around for a room attendant, or call one, and ask them to deliver the item. If there is a problem with a lightbulb or something like that, he has to convey the message to the engineers or the housemen. He showed me an archaic-looking machine with lots of different keys. He showed me how to type in the room number, and then "need" and then "bulb." This machine then transmits that message to the front desk or to the engineers, depending on where it is sent. J also has to write down everything in the log book; he said he is supposed to do that first, before even carrying out the task. (observation xvia1: 94–103)

He also took calls from housekeepers reporting that specific rooms were ready; he entered the information in a customized computer program, so the front desk could know what was available. Some of the calls were non-routine: A guest wanted matches, and no one could find any; a man not affiliated with the hotel was seen in a hallway with a bell cart, and security had to be called. Twice during the study, José was assigned to inspect the hallways of the hotel, making note of stains, broken ice machines, and other problems. On several days he had to inspect the guestrooms for maintenance needs, so his manager could submit a comprehensive report to the higher-ups.

In general, chores were established by Mr. M or another supervisor acting in his place. Frequently—as with the hall and room inspections—José accomplished the work by himself; sometimes he collaborated with other subordinates in the office. The processing came in several ways. First, Mr. M occasionally commented specifically about José's performance, or suggested new ways of doing things. Second, José sometimes witnessed Mr. M's feedback to other members of the staff, which was often harsh. Third, Mr. M and José talked about standards in work, with the former showing the latter both the norms and the underlying ideology: hard work is necessary and good, and frontline workers tend to fall short of the standards of excellence and need to be closely monitored. Moreover, José heard Mr. M compliment his diligence and skill, noting that several other interns had not made the grade in that respect.

On the surface, these tasks appear to be rather mundane and lacking in educational substance. But the work stood at the hub of a complex system, giving José exposure to a significant array of knowledge: about the structure of operations in a large organization (the relations among housekeeping, the front desk, purchasing and receiving, and higher management); about power dynamics in a hierarchy; about disparate workplace norms and cultures; about business applications in computers (spreadsheets, communications systems); about the strategies and tactics of management in a largely blue-collar operation.

The sociocognitive demands of José's work went beyond the obvious ability to answer phones, fill out charts, and find carpet stains. Since the demands on his boss were constant, José had to learn how to decide when to interrupt him and when not to, which required an evolving sense of priorities among apparent emergencies, and also called for a fairly subtle sense of the relations among different operations in the hotel. If one guest wants matches and another needs a wheelchair, while someone has reported an intruder in the hallway, and three housekeepers are waiting for their assignments, what do you do first? Moreover, some of the inspection work required a degree of judgment: How badly does a lampshade need to be stained before you write it up for replacement? How do you decide that question: on the basis of guest complaints or of maintenance costs and corporate profits? Thus, on a sociocognitive level, the knowledge-in-use was complex but not beyond the grasp of an intelligent teenager (as the veterinary and medical knowledge was).

Finally, the social-skill demands of the job were fairly complex. José's phone contact with guests, some of them annoyed about problems in their rooms, had to be conducted with some tact (although the fieldnotes indicate that he was not strong at this skill in the early days). He was also placed in an intermediate position in the staff, between his manager and the maintenance staff. He had to read situations so as to know how to act with housekeepers, with front-desk people, with his boss. (Again, he was sometimes abrupt in this interaction; he could have used some feedback on employee relations.) This process involved his developing an identity as a member of management, and taking on the demeanor and values of that role. For instance, he frequently mentioned that the housekeepers tended to slack off, and suggested that they had to be supervised closely so they would do their jobs; in that stance, he adopted a management perspective.

The pragmatics of the work relate to the last point. In some respects, housekeeping seems to be a low-prestige element of the operation. It is actually one of the most important in a hotel, as it has to be done well if the customers are to be satisfied. The managerial tasks associated with house-keeping—assignments, supervision, inspection—are also crucial, if less visible to the guests. In addition, within the staff there is a clear hierarchy, from the room cleaners upward through the engineers to the managers. To the extent that José could position himself as affiliated with management, his status in the organization rose, despite his being an intern and a high school student. Thus, on a pragmatic level, the work was central to the business, and exposed the student to reasonably intense contact with a broad spectrum of activities and roles. It also enabled José to develop an identification with a community of practice in the organization: management, and thus to deepen his involvement and heighten his motivation.

What factors shaped the hotel housekeeping operation as a learning environment? The culture of the workplace, tied up in the history of the hotel industry, included a clear distinction between managers and workers, and an entrenched conception of their respective roles and characters. The fact that, even as an intern, José was affiliated with the manager of the office gave him immediate entry into the knowledge-use system. Organizationally, the hotel was very hierarchical, but José's position gave him functional access to quite a range of activities. He had occasion to interact meaningfully with room attendants, housemen, and engineers; with front-desk and other hotel employees; and even with guests. Mr. M seemed dedicated to inducting José into the management mentality so that he could off-load some of his work onto the student.

Fiona: The Hospital Operating Room

One of the students in an urban medical careers academy worked for the anesthesiology technicians in a general hospital. The basic function of the team was to prepare, run, and clean the machines used to administer anesthesia during surgeries. The larger community of practice, of course, included a considerable variety of participants: the surgeons; the anesthesiologists; the operating room (OR) nurses; the anesthesiology technicians, and the orderlies. Knowledge-use in this environment covered a lot of territory: highly specialized medical knowledge about disease and dysfunction in the human body, and about how to treat those problems; the procedures for performing given operations (sequence of actions, along with the use of tools needed for each); the functions and appearances of the various implements (scalpels, retractors, etc.) used in the operations; the social hierarchy and power relations among the players (the lead role of the surgeon, the subordinate role of the technicians; the subteams within the whole group, and so on).

Of course, Fiona's actual sphere of experience was narrower than this general picture suggests. The role of the anesthesia technicians fell into two major phases: between the operations and during them. Much of the work involved preparing the carts and machines: moving them to the correct place; stocking them with the necessary tubes, connectors, and other materials; checking them to make sure they were functioning properly. During an operation the techs had to keep the machines working. And afterward, they had to clean up the equipment and ready it for the next cycle.

> Fiona reported to OR#5 because she heard the request for a "turnover" over the intercom. A patient was inside the room . . . Fiona and M [a technician] worked on the anesthesia machine and the red cart . . . Fiona returned to the workroom to get supplies for the red cart. Then she quickly walked back to OR#5 to put the supplies into the cart. M told Fiona that she could fill the fluorine; Fiona has done this task once before. She told M that D [her supervisor] told her to wear gloves. M looked at Fiona and said, "OK," but also said quietly that it wasn't really necessary, though she was wearing gloves herself . . . The fluorine was in a little bottle with a tube attached to it. Fiona attached the tube to the anesthesia machine, then pulled a lever; the liquid moved through the tube into a container connected to the machine. As the container filled, an indicator moved higher toward the top line. However, it didn't quite reach the top line as it was supposed to. Fiona kept moving the bottle up and down, and then switched the lever back and forth. When that didn't work, she asked M to help her. (observation viiib2: 245–267)

The sociocognitive demands of these activities were largely technical: maintaining and operating machinery. This knowledge was essentially of the what and how variety, not the why, the procedural rather than the substantive. That is, Fiona and her supervisors had to make sure the right things were available to the doctors and nurses—but they did not need to know what the surgeons actually did with the tools, or how the tools worked, or what the patient's condition was, or anything like that. The researcher asked Fiona several times what certain machines did, and she usually did not know. She did not need to know: She could do her job without comprehension (Bloom, 1956). On the other hand, the techs were enmeshed in a complex social system with arcane rules of interaction; they had to know how to treat the respective actors—doctors, nurses, patients, other techs—in an appropriate way.

The pragmatic features of the work were fairly simple: The tasks were essential to the smooth functioning of the surgical process, but not at its core. In the constellation of tasks constituting the whole activity system, tending the anesthesia machines was a minor, though necessary, element. A mistake by a tech could have been significant, even harmful to the patient. But her status in the overall team was low. Interestingly, there is no indication in the fieldnotes that the physicians ever acknowledged the presence of the technicians.

Clearly, though, Fiona learned a number of things during her work in the OR: to set up the anesthesiology carts; to tend them during operations; to conduct inventories and to restock the carts; to clean and maintain certain equipment. Over time, her repertoire seemed to increase: She handled more machines (pediatric carts and bloodwarmers as well as the basic "red cart"), and could explain them more clearly; she took more initiative in taking on responsibilities; she developed collegial relations with the full-time technicians and with some other staff. She did not, on the other hand, display any more specialized knowledge about the use of the equipment in the surgical process, or about the conditions of the patients or their treatments. She did come to participate more fully in the limited community of technicians, but not very much more in the larger community of the surgical team.

Pedagogical Strategies

In each workplace, how were the interns instructed on a day-to-day basis? How did they learn? We have defined *pedagogy* as the social organization of the process by which participants in an activity encounter and engage various new forms of knowledge—that is, by which they learn. In observations at our field sites, we discovered a number of basic pedagogical strategies, general approaches to the process of bringing newcomers into the social use of knowledge. Those strategies can be described and categorized according to certain parameters or dimensions:

- *Timing:* Did the learning activity occur before, during, or after the work? Was it front-loaded, on-the-job, or back-loaded?
- *Direction:* Who was in control of the learning activity—the supervisor, coworkers, or the learner? (See Bernstein, 1975, for his related concepts of classification and frame.)
- *Intent:* Was learning an explicit purpose of the activity, or was it an incidental by-product of the work?
- *Activity:* Was the learner passively receiving information and instruction, or actively participating in the work activity?

Given these variables, we can identify a few major types of pedagogical strategies that appeared in the worksites we visited. The following types are not mutually exclusive—more than one may occur in a given scene—but they represent basic choices about how to go about inducting newcomers into knowledge-use systems. *Front-loaded instruction*, for example, generally entails the supervisor giving explicit instructions to the newcomer before she actively engages in the work. That instruction can be cursory or extensive, verbal or written (or even multimedia); it does not demand active participation by the student, except in the sense that listening to a lecture or watching a video might be considered active. The content is designed by the supervisor or trainer, based on a rational analysis of the work tasks the intern will take on. *Front-loaded observation*, on the other hand, generally involves the newcomer watching what is going on in the work activity; she does not actively participate in the work, but can ask questions. It can be more or less explicit as a training episode: the supervisor might take the intern on a walk around the site, pointing things out and explaining basic processes; or the student might simply sit and watch before getting down to business. In the latter case, the student is in a sense in control of the curriculum: she can attend to whatever she wants.

On-the-job training is a strategy in which the necessary instruction is provided as the work activity progresses, with the active participation of the learner. In its more explicit version, OJT is controlled by the supervisor or coworker, who decides what is important to teach, demonstrates and explains processes and skills, and leads the intern through initial trials. The training might be provided at precisely the moment the skill is required (what some call *just-in-time training*), or in chunks as the work proceeds. Conversely, the training might simply be embedded in the work process, allowing the student to figure things out as she participates in the activity. We called this the *laissez-faire strategy* or, less formally, *sink or swim*: the learning is implicit in the activity, directed more by the ongoing work than by a conscious pedagogical choice by the supervisor. On occasion, a group of newcomers might figure things out together, in a type of self-instruction or peer problem-solving.

Finally, learning often occurs after the work activity is completed. This *back-loaded instruction* sometimes takes the form of debriefing, a consultation between the supervisor and the intern in which the latter can ask questions, venture interpretations, and clarify points, and the former can check to make sure the student understands what happened. The curriculum of this encounter, then, is directed by both parties, and is explicitly learning-driven. In other cases, the learner determines her own information needs and seeks resources and help, or coworkers volunteer feedback.

We use another kind of term to describe not so much the pedagogical strategy as the relationship between the supervisor (or senior worker) and the student-intern: *mentoring*. This relationship can be manifested before, during, and after the work activity. It goes beyond the supervisor offering advice, instruction, and feedback about the performance of specific tasks or roles. It extends to explaining the workplace culture, modeling appropriate and effective behavior, and supporting the student's learning and development. Mentor is somehow a more holistic relationship than supervisor, not just concerned with training to get the work done, but attentive to the learner's growth and well-being. Some programs misuse and weaken the term by referring to all the worksite adult participants as mentors. In reality, every intern has a supervisor, but only some get a mentor.

Pedagogical Tactics

Within each of these general strategies, we found a variety of specific tactics used to engage the newcomer in the situated use of knowledge. These tactics can appear at different phases of the task episode—establishing, accomplishing, and processing—and in different stages of the newcomer's learning trajectory. Which tactic is chosen at any given moment in the work-learning activity depends on the factors identified earlier.

Front-loaded instruction, for example, can take a number of forms. In *lecturing*, the veteran (supervisor, trainer, coworker) delivers extensive verbal information before the task episode begins, laying out a comprehensive picture of the activity and the knowledge and skill it demands. The veteran might also engage in *modeling and demonstrating*, performing the relevant tasks as the newcomer watches. The veteran might or might not provide a running verbal commentary ("here's what you do next, this is why . . ."), and the performance might be real or simulated. The trainer might put the newcomer through a *dry run*, asking her to try an off-task, simulated performance of the activity to get the hang of the process. Finally, some supervisors take the intern on a *tour* of the facility, pointing out work processes, personnel and technologies, and giving an overview of the organization.

On-the-job pedagogies happen while the work is going on, and take several shapes. Merely *giving orders* to the intern, telling her to perform a particular task and how to do it, constitutes an implicit form of instruction, in that the goal is to accomplish the work; the intern actually learning something might be a by-product. Sometimes the student is simply *helping out*, taking an auxiliary role in the work activity while the veteran does most of it, but watching the whole operation. In *coaching*, the student takes primary responsibility for performing the task, but the supervisor-veteran gives simultaneous feedback and advice from the sidelines ("no, no, faster; good, that worked").

In other cases, the on-the-job learning is not controlled by the supervisor, but emerged in the process of the work itself. For instance, *trial and error* represents a pedagogical tactic in which the newcomer tries out various solutions to problems (sometimes in collaboration with other workers), checks to see how they worked out, and adjusts her performance depending on the outcomes. At almost any stage of the activity, the learner can initiate *questions and answers (Q&A)*, seeking information and guidance while the work proceeds; sometimes the veterans are amenable to those questions, and sometimes they are not. Finally, another tactic embedded in the work process is *practice*, the opportunity to learn simply by performing the same task over and over again, coming closer and closer to the ideal level of skill and knowledge.

Several pedagogical tactics appear after the work activity is completed, in the back-loading phase. The most obvious is the *supervisory session*, where the boss provides formal feedback and instruction for the next episode. He can put the intern through *checking and testing*, quizzing her about task knowledge; he can *remind* her of elements of the work, or give her *readings*. In extreme cases, he can *discipline* the new worker, passing on important messages about the boundaries of acceptable behavior. Less formally, the supervisor and other veterans can give *critical feedback* to the intern, telling her what she has done wrong in the work. Some of that feedback looks like *teasing* or even *hazing:* sometimes embarrassing jokes or rituals often carrying implicit messages about work practices and customs. Sometimes it takes the form of *storytelling*, narratives about past events or personalities that somehow manifest significant knowledge about the organization and the work.

This list is hardly exhaustive—any more than a list of classroom teaching techniques could be exhaustive—but it does suggest the variety of ways in which newcomers come to participate in the social stock of knowledge in a work environment. The social organization of the tactics varies in several ways: the relationship between the veteran and the learner may be more or less vertical, or more or less collaborative; the knowledge-encounter may be part of the ongoing work process or it may be separated from that activity; the neophyte may be given more or less open access to particular aspects of local lore, depending on the micropolitics of knowledge; the knowledge-in-use may be open to reorganization, or it may be strongly guarded by members resistant to change; the newcomer may be required to master the knowledge, or she may have to fight to get access to it. The possibilities are endless.

Again, the educator should keep an eye out for these various tactics when analyzing the intern's work situation. She may discover that an important form of knowledge is being made available to the student in an effective way or, conversely, that the student is being left in the dark because a teachable moment is being overlooked. In the latter case, she can either work with the supervisor to make sure the deficiency is corrected, or design an appropriate intervention back at school to broaden the student's learning.

Fred

As described earlier, Fred's tasks at the animal hospital were largely mundane and not likely to bring about substantial learning. The work was simple, and required only rudimentary front-loaded instruction to induct him into the necessary knowledge-use. On the other hand, Fred did have occasion to observe interesting and complex activities, and to ask questions about what was going on. In that sense and to that degree, the environment was educational for him. During the researcher's first observation, for instance, the intern watched and commented as the veterinarian amputated a cat's tail:

> Willy, another cat, was to have his tail removed. Fred explained to me that his tail was paralyzed and that he was also having trouble urinating on his own . . . The technician asked (the doctor) if he wanted Fred to hold the cat while they gave it the anesthesia, but Dr. D said no . . . Dr. D weighed the cat, and they gave him a shot while the tech held him down. It was a difficult task: The cat was hissing and moving around and obviously did not want to have a shot. Once they succeeded, the cat was out immediately. Dr. D and the tech placed the cat on the newly clean operating table and stuck a tube down its mouth. Then they discussed how much of its tail to shave, began shaving, and vacuumed up the hair. Then they began "expressing" the bladder, which Fred explained to me. . . . While the doctor and technician were performing these tasks, Fred remained at the sink just on the other side of the operating room, but he could see in the room perfectly . . . He told me in a matter-of-fact way what was going on at each moment . . . Fred asked the doctor if the purpose of a cat's tail is to help the cat balance. The technician replied that probably balance is one purpose, but cats seem to do fine without them. Fred continued with his running commentary, saying, "She's sterilizing the area" as the technician rubbed some liquid all over the cat's tail and behind. The tech corrected him, saying the area would be "aseptic," not sterile. . . . The doctor first made an incision all the way around the tail near its base, then began to cut deeper through the skin. . . . The tech checked the cat's heart rate. Fred asked, "How much of the tail is actually bone?" The doctor replied, "It's bone all the way down." The doctor continued to cut through skin and then bone . . . Fred suddenly left the room . . . he was getting a throwaway camera from his bag; he wanted to take a picture of the surgery. Dr. D and the tech posed with good humor. (observation xiiia1: 50–97)

This episode constituted one of the more fascinating experiences of Fred's internship, but also revealed some of the core pedagogy in the site. When Fred was not engaged in one of his routine tasks, he had the opportunity to watch procedures and activities carried out by the veterinarians and the technicians. The purpose of Fred's observing, it is important to note, was not to prepare him to perform any part of these tasks; he would never get to that stage of skill and knowledge, and would always remain a peripheral participant. In fact, the vet rejected the offer to have Fred merely hold the cat down. But there were several potentially educative elements to these scenes. Simply watching gave Fred some information. And he also asked occasional questions of the doctors and the technicians: What's the function of the tail? Is it bone all the way down? Later, as Fred observed a spaying operation, he asked the doctor if they could spay a dog in heat; she replied that it's actually easier then because the relevant organs are slightly enlarged. Off-task discussions like these provided a fair amount of interesting (if fragmented and episodic) information for the student.

Sometimes while Fred was observing an operation, the doctors quizzed Fred about aspects of their activity, even though he was not performing a function in it.

> Dr. V began to "test" Fred, asking him to explain to me what she was doing. She lifted something red out of the body cavity of the dog, and asked Fred what it was. Fred got the answer wrong. Dr. V said that she had tied off the blood supply to the two ovaries, and was now tying off the blood supply to the two parts of the uterus . . . Fred wondered aloud about the differences between human anatomy and dog anatomy. (observation xiiia3: 176–182)

This episode is an example of a testing/checking tactic, although it has the curious quality of being disconnected from the learner's functional participation in the activity.

A range of other tactics appear in the fieldnotes. Fred learned about the sterilization of surgical tools by helping out a technician; he prepared a neuter pack, and she prepped the autoclave and tossed the pack into it. Another technician taught him about examining slides by the show-and-tell method; she showed him the materials from a dog with leukemia and told him what he was seeing. She also engaged in storytelling, relating an incident in which another veterinarian did research on ear mites by putting some in his own ear. A number of casual, off-task conversations also carried information for Fred: one, for instance, was about asthma in dogs; in another, one of the doctors described working in a zoo. When Fred made comments about what was going on in surgery, the vets and technicians sometimes *corrected* him; for instance, he referred to "spongy tissue" that Dr. V told him was "fatty."

The pedagogy of work in this site, then, involved the student's engaging in a good deal of menial, peripheral support activities and very little of the core work of the clinic. But it also gave him a number of opportunities to observe and ask questions about the professionals' activities—though perhaps not in a systematic enough way to enable him to build a deep understanding of that work. Still, Fred learned much of what he wanted to learn in the clinic: essentially, what life is like for a small-town veterinarian. He developed a strong feel for the culture of the community of practice that he aspired to join.

José

On José's first day, he was taken on the tour; Mr. M, the supervisor, gave José and the other interns starting that day a complete tour of the hotel and introduced them to many of the staff. After that, Mr. M adopted a general pedagogical strategy of on-the-job training for José. He arranged to have the intern take on more and more functions, and to learn them as he did them. Sometimes José performed tasks that Mr. M would have done otherwise, thus freeing up the boss for other responsibilities. On other occasions, the student did work that was useful, but might not have been done if he had not taken it on.

The tactics involved in this process included most of the types mentioned previously. During the first observation, for instance, when José was answering the telephone in the housekeeping office, an assistant manager, R, was with him and provided coaching; sometimes he handed the problem off to her, but often he got advice from her and did the work himself.

> The phone rang again and J asked the person to hold while he asked R about special handicapped equipment. She said yes, get their room number, and he said into the phone, "Someone will be there shortly," and then hung up. The phone rang again, and he took some notes . . . For most of the incoming calls, J either handed the phone to R, or held his hand over the mouthpiece while he asked R what to do. (observation xv1a1: 139–152)

Earlier, Mr. M or R had most likely modeled the phone-answering task, as well as lectured him about the general procedures. Making the assistant available to José as a coach represented a form of scaffolding, since her support could be gradually phased out as his knowledge-use grew. Indeed, by the end of the term, José himself was coaching other interns who had not yet been introduced to this role.

Most often during the researcher's visits, José helped out, carrying out administrative tasks that Mr. M might have done. But the supervisor was not present all the time; often, the establishing phase was clear and simple enough to carry José through the accomplishing. On occasion, José worked with Mr. M in a way that educated José in some aspect of the management process and ideology. For instance, the intern reported that he and Mr. M had "taken wet rags and wiped down some of the walls, which had 'scared' the housemen, because it meant the boss was doing their job." This event taught José about both management tactics and ideology.

Functionally, the organization managed to make learning resources available to José on a timely basis: coaching from veterans; substantial tasks that required some problem-solving and some discretion; room to make mistakes and rectify them. Moreover, it provided adequate feedback (on some aspects of the work, at least; he did not develop interactional skills as much as he might have), so he could learn from each opportunity. Yet this is not to say that the internship experience was educationally perfect. On some occasions, José was shut out of certain meetings where he might have encountered a broader range of knowledge-in-use. On others, he did not get feedback that might have honed his performance. His identification with management and against workers raises a perplexing pedagogical issue: Would he have learned more by experiencing the workers' perspective on the organization as well as management's? How might that have happened?

Nonetheless, we can see that José's work experience, while engaging him in a series of superficially mundane tasks (checking hallways for carpet stains, printing out assignment sheets), also made him think about more complex issues about organizational processes, technical operations, and social relations. There was a good deal of grist for the learning mill in this placement.

Fiona

By what social means did Fiona learn during her experience? The general pedagogical strategies that her supervisors used were front-loaded instruction and on-the-job training. In the early days of her internship, her supervisor gave her a tour of the operating-room floor, showing her the spaces, the equipment, and the personnel that she would be encountering. She demonstrated important elements of the technicians' work: setting up the machines, checking them, running them. She had Fiona do a dry run of the process, practicing a couple of times to get the hang of it. Just-in-time instruction occurred later in the term, too, whenever Fiona was about to take responsibility for a new machine or function. One supervisor gave her a lecture, for instance, about a new piece of equipment:

> D [the supervisor] gave Fiona an orientation on the pediatric cart, which is smaller than the red cart used only for adults. She reviewed the medical instruments that Fiona should be familiar with. The pediatric cart had many of the same instruments as the red cart, but they were smaller. There was one item on the pediatric cart that was not found on the red cart: a STAT box. D emphasized that the STAT box contained medicine that expires. She also said that the pediatric cart must be signed out because of the STAT box, and told Fiona that it was not necessary to refill the STAT box medicine because there is a satellite pharmacy on site at the hospital . . . Fiona asked D, "Is the pediatric cart used for patients who are 12 years old and under?" D replied, "Yes." Fiona asked, "If an older child or adult is really tiny, is the pediatric cart used?" D answered, "Yes, one time we used it for a frail old lady." (observation viiib1: 198–207)

Once the intern had been oriented to the enterprise, the pedagogy shifted to various forms of on-the-job training. Some instruction was embedded in giving orders: "In the operating room, M told Fiona to attach a clean circuit to the anesthesiology machine, but to make sure that everything was turned off so the balloon did not inflate." Notice that this instruction carried two kinds of messages: What to do and why to do it, or what would happen if she did not do it correctly. Some knowledge was shared through disciplining: A nurse in the OR chastised the researcher for not wearing a surgical mask in a supposedly sterile field; Fiona, witnessing this event, picked up messages not only about proper procedure but about its importance.

Frequently, Fiona asked questions, probing for additional knowledge as she engaged a task, as during the pediatric cart lesson. But the most common tactic for engaging the intern in situated knowledge-use was helping out, assisting one of the regular techs in an actual chore. Repeated practice gave her many instances of each task to consider, so that she gradually came to master the entire sequence of activities.

On several occasions, one of the supervisors asked Fiona to observe an operation through a window from another room; he wanted her to see what was going on, but could not have her in the crowded operating theater. Interestingly, this same supervisor assigned her to some menial tasks that she had already learned; and he tended to hover around her in the early days, checking to make sure she was doing things correctly. In fact, Fiona mentioned the differences in teaching styles among the four technicians who oversaw her work. They varied substantially in the degree to which they were willing to let her take on new tasks, and to which they were prone to watching her carefully. This variation is an intriguing finding, actually, because it suggests that the choice of pedagogical strategies stems not only from the sociocognitive demands and pragmatic features of the tasks, or from the larger dynamics of the environment, but also from the more or less idiosyncratic styles of the supervisors—and, probably, the colleagues and the students themselves.

But the pedagogical strategies here were certainly shaped by the work and the context. First, the fact that Fiona did not engage much knowledge about medical and surgical processes and conditions, even about the chemistry and physiology of anesthesia, reflects some of the same factors that we saw in the animal hospital: Much of that knowledge is too advanced for a high-school student to learn and use; government regulations and licensing procedures limit the neophyte's access to specific activities; the strong classification and frame in the hospital set up social barriers that prevent newcomers from engaging the broader range of knowledge.

Second, the large size and complex organization of the environment contributed to the pedagogy. Fiona had direct and substantial contact with a limited set of actors in the hospital. The hierarchy was arranged so that her immediate supervisors, who were relatively low-level technicians themselves, were solely responsible for her training. The doctors, at the upper end of the social scale in the institution, could not be bothered by having to educate so lowly a figure as the intern. That is not to say they were disrespectful to her, but simply that their time and knowledge were demanded elsewhere. Therefore, much of the knowledge embedded in the full scope of activities in the operating room was not really accessible to Fiona. She was able to master certain technical procedures and mechanical operations, but she did not learn much about medicine, disease, surgery, chemistry, or any more expansive topics.

Conclusion

These case studies illustrate the complexity of analyzing situated pedagogy. The process by which neophytes in a workplace come to use new forms of knowledge is sometimes obvious, as in explicit teaching events (training sessions, workshops), and sometimes not. The social organization of knowledge-use more often serves the instrumental needs of the organization than it does the learning needs of the newcomers, but meeting those learning needs often improves the productivity of the organization. On the other hand, some organizations operate efficiently by compartmentalizing knowledge-use in a way that perpetuates the peripheral status of newcomers, and thwarts their learning. Determining the way work activities shape members' participation in knowledge-use is a subtle challenge.

These issues and dynamics deserve attention from educators responsible for placing, guiding, and evaluating work-based learners. Knowledge-rich organizations, such as hospitals and large corporations, do not always prove to be the most educational because they sometimes classify and frame the use of knowledge in ways that bar newcomers and other marginal players from growing participation in communities of practice. Work systems with weak classification and frame often afford interns greater access to that participation, and thus increase their learning. The framework sketched out in this chapter can be a tool for the educator who is trying to distinguish one type of learning environment from the other. Moreover, it offers a method for deciding when to intervene back at school with a pedagogical strategy designed to enhance the work-based learning, fill in the gaps, and exploit the teachable moments in the students' experiences.

A final point is that, in our field visits, we were told repeatedly by school-based personnel and by employers who provided internships that students need to take more responsibility for their own learning. We would encourage student-interns to assert themselves at the workplace, particularly with regard to asking questions and requesting challenging work.

CHAPTER 10

Pedagogy in the Classroom to Support Work-Based Learning

The conception of pedagogy presented in the last chapter can be used, we have argued, to analyze naturally occurring learning processes in the workplace, where education is not as high a priority as productivity. School-based teachers and internship coordinators can use the framework to consider what kinds of sites are appropriate for their student-interns. But we also believe that the same framework can be useful for the teachers' work back at school. The basic premise is that the educator needs to think about the kinds of knowledge she wants her students to participate in, and then to construct situations in which they can do that. The fundamental issue is this: What is being done and what can and *should* be done to guide, enhance, and assess the learning that occurs in the work-based component of a work-based learning program?

In this chapter, we go through several stages to address that question. First, we lay out a framework for identifying the purposes of the school-based component of a work-based learning program, and suggest two models of those purposes. Then we propose some essential principles that might underlie the effort to achieve those purposes. Next, we present some of the major strategies that we discovered in our research, approaches and devices used by various programs to structure interns' school-based learning. As we move through that review, we critique the practices in terms of the framework we have proposed, showing where they have been successful and where and how they might be improved.

The Purposes and Goals of School-Based Pedagogy
for Work-Based Learning

The question carried over from the preceding chapter is this: Under what circumstances, by what criteria, and to what end should school-based educators intervene in the naturally occurring work-based learning processes? If good learning happens in the course of the student-intern's experience at work, why not leave well enough alone? Why do anything back at school?

The general answer to that question was certainly implied by the analysis in the previous chapters: The claims advocates make for the benefits of work-based learning received mixed support from our field observations. We found that academic reinforcement did take place in some internships, but not in most, and that when it did, it was limited and episodic. The nature of academic reinforcement was further complicated by the discontinuities between knowledge-use in school and out (Resnick, 1987). The argument for practical skills was more solidly supported—but raised the question of whether highly specialized, situated skills are appropriate for student-interns. Similarly, although it was clear that interns got a feel for the daily life or culture of a possible occupational setting, their learning may have missed some important dimensions of career exploration. Many of them had experiences that could contribute to their personal development—to maturity, self-esteem, autonomy—but few got to process that development in a systematic way. Finally, even though we found many students engaging in modes of thought not typical in schools, there were two possible weaknesses there: a number of students did not appear to be participating in these new kinds of thinking and acting; and even those who did, had few opportunities to reflect on them in a way that would deepen and solidify the learning. The direct experiences in the workplace had many substantial educational benefits for many students, but more could certainly have been done to tease out additional important kinds of learning. In virtually every case, something valuable could (and sometimes did) happen back at school.

There is yet another general argument in favor of carefully designing a classroom component for a work-based learning program. It responds to an implication of the more radical version of situated cognition theory: that knowledge is context-bound, not transferable, and that what is learned in one situation will not be useful in another. If that were entirely the case, then work-based learning educators would have to justify their programs on the grounds that students were learning worthwhile things even though they could not apply them in contexts other than the workplaces where they learned them—and that would be a difficult case to make. Even if Fiona acquired complex and challenging knowledge about anesthesiology machines in her hospital internship, what good would that do if she could not use some of that knowledge in other situations? Unless she planned to make a career as an anesthesiology technician, chances are the specialized knowledge would be of limited value.

But a counterargument to situated learning theory stems from Perkins and Salomon's (1989) view on the transferability of skills (see Chapter 6). Perkins and Salomon identify the conditions under which people do transfer knowledge-use from one setting to another, and their insight provides a solid rationale for constructing pedagogical strategies for work-based learning. In particular, they observe that the transfer happens when students are encouraged to examine how problems are similar, as well as when students are encouraged to tease rules out of examples, and to generate and analyze justifications, principles, and explanations (p. 22). That is, knowledge learned and used in one context can become meaningful in another if the student-intern goes through a process of standing back from it, looking for its essential structure and content, and comparing it to knowledge used in other situations. Teachers in work-based learning programs can design strategies that engage students in just those forms of thinking and analysis.

Not only does that principle justify a specific approach to pedagogy for work-based learning, but it justifies the claim that a classroom component of such a program is worthwhile. The conditions for knowledge-transfer described by Perkins and Salomon are not likely to occur naturally in a workplace or internship site. Rather, they have to be created intentionally by someone who cares about the possibility of transfer, who does not want the learning to be permanently embedded in the context where it first happened: the school-based educator.

Answering the "why do anything?" question on a more specific level, however, demands a first step: a more fully developed conception of the purposes and principles driving such a program. Educators have to ask themselves what they hope students will gain from the work-based learning experience, both in the workplace and in school, and then tailor their pedagogical practices to those goals. Of course, the goals may differ across programs: One may focus on career exploration while another favors personal development. One may want to pursue the link between academic concepts and practical experience while another may want to prepare kids for specific vocations. The choice is up to the educators—but they need to make it explicitly and for good reasons.

The educational goals of a work-based learning program might center on any combination of the following categories, most of which are familiar from our earlier section on the claims:

1. *Cognitive growth.* In one way or another, the program may aim at building the student's capacity to think effectively and critically. That may mean, as some argue, academic reinforcement: the opportunity to practice, use, and deepen concepts and skills originally learned in school. That reinforcement can be centered on a specific discipline, such as biological science, or on more generic school-related skills, like reading and writing. Another form of cognitive growth that might constitute a program goal is embedded in our notion of new modes of thought: The opportunity to participate in problem-defining as well as problem-solving; in teamwork as well as individual effort; in diverse ways of representing the knowledge and connecting it to the environment.

    As we suggested in the earlier critique of advocates' claims, however, it is not enough to articulate learning goals in terms of broad categories like cognitive growth. One has to be more specific about the kinds of thinking that students ought to be performing.

2. *Building practical skills and knowledge of careers.* Another legitimate goal of work-based learning is to help students acquire various kinds of skills that will serve them well when they enter the work world full-time. Some of those skills may be generic, in the sense that they would be useful in a wide range of work activities and contexts. Others may be more specialized, suitable for students going into particular vocations: physical therapy, newspaper reporting, music teaching. Thus, the educators need to specify the kinds of skills that should be learned through the program.

    Moreover, learning about careers is an appropriate purpose of work-based learning. Again, though, the designers have to be more concrete about what kind and extent of career-related knowledge they want their students to engage. Is it sufficient to give an intern a feel for the everyday life of a person in a given occupation, or is it important to introduce other kinds of knowledge, such as information about compensation, career tracks, working conditions, and the like?

3. *Personal and social development.* Many of the teachers and students we interviewed for this study highlighted personal development as a key benefit of the program: the opportunity to become more mature, more responsible, more autonomous, and to build greater self-esteem. As we showed earlier, many students did, in fact, have experiences that would contribute to that sort of development. And many reported to us that they were thrilled to be "treated like an adult" by people at their internship sites. It is useful, we think, to make the distinction between personal develop-

ment and *social* development, at least as a way of focusing one's pedagogical goals. The latter term refers more to social skills like communication and teamwork (Hamilton & Hamilton, 1997), whereas the former denotes changes in personal character traits. All of these concepts need more precise definitions.

4. *Opportunities for reflection: two models.* One of the objectives of work-based learning is to teach young people the skills and knowledge that they will need to be effective on the job. But workplace experiences also offer students an opportunity to reflect on what they find on the job, to ask why it is the way that they have found it, and how it might be different. These opportunities have important implications for classroom teaching associated with work-based learning, because the nature of the reflection that students might make about their work experience will, to a large extent, be determined by the teacher's guidance. Working with the experiences that students have in the world, teachers not only have the opportunity to shape what students learn in the academic or vocational sense, but what sorts of workers, family members, and citizens they become—what kind of person they grow into. The way a teacher engages students in processing their work experiences will affect their relationships with other people and institutions, the attitude they take toward knowledge and learning, and their sense of themselves as actors in the world. Indeed, these types of influences are inescapable. Every experience, in and out of school, contributes to a student's evolving sense of herself and the social world. Structuring the experience in one way will tend toward one kind of sense; structuring it in another way will move toward another sense altogether—whether the teacher intends those effects or not.

We believe there are essentially two models of pedagogy for work-based learning. We present them here in a simplified form, for the purpose of heuristic clarity. Surely they are not mutually exclusive; one can simultaneously employ methods from both. We maintain that educators who are considering strategies for work-based learning, however, should be aware of the differences between the two models. In the absence of conscious thought about this, the tendency will be for the teacher to move toward the first model and lose the educational opportunities of the second.

We call the first model of work-based learning pedagogy functionalist, in part because it is to some extent compatible with the tradition of structural-functionalism in sociology (Parsons, 1954), and also because it sees work-based learning's core purpose as preparing students for certain functions in the economy (see Lave, 1988). The functionalist takes the structure of the workplace—the forms of knowledge, the requisite skills, the social relations—as given and stable. He believes that he can identify what a student needs to know and be able to do in order to function effectively in the workplace, and that proper teaching methods will make the student ready for the work role. That might mean imparting core job skills (see SCANS, 1991), or it might mean building in students such habits and values as punctuality, accountability, and deference to authority. This approach resonates in the traditional literature on vocational and cooperative education, and in some newer writings on work-based learning (see Urquiola et al., 1997).

The other model of work-based learning pedagogy is the *reflective* or *critical* approach. Reflective pedagogy regards the structures and practices of the workplace as socially constructed, as potentially flawed, as subject to questioning and reflection. By this standard, a goal of work-based learning is not simply to prepare the student for work, but to create the conditions and resources through which she can understand and reflect on the existing system, imagine alternatives, and become an active participant in the construction of her workplace and, indeed, her society. The reflective approach does not ignore or deny the value of learning functional skills and knowledge, indeed it builds on that knowledge. But the student ideally learns how to understand and analyze the circumstances in which she is working and thereby becomes better able to participate in changing or improving those circumstances. This approach, of course, has many precedents: Dewey, Freire, Habermas, Foucault, Giroux, Apple; it has been developed most extensively by Simon et al. (1991).

As we will show in a moment, these two models have different implications for the pedagogical process: during the student's preparation for the work experience, during the processing of that experience, and during the evaluation or assessment. The point that we want to stress here, though, is the importance of recognizing these alternative models while designing pedagogical strategies for work-based learning.

Principles for Work-Based Learning Pedagogy

Several strategic principles form a foundation for an effective pedagogy for work-based learning. The first, and perhaps the most important, is that reflection is an indispensable element of the learning process. No matter how rich, no matter how varied, no matter how challenging, the direct experience of work is not enough to achieve the educational goals of work-based learning. If the student-worker does not have the opportunity to step back from the experience, and to interrogate it from a variety of intellectual and social perspectives, then she will tend to be drawn inexorably into the unexamined, taken-for-granted view of the meaning of her experience. In any workplace culture, coworkers tend to share and enforce certain tacit assumptions about activities, roles, and values. In order to problematize those assumptions, to foster a critical perspective in the learner, the instructor must engage her in a rigorous and extensive process of reflection.

This assertion finds deep philosophical support in the tradition of pragmatism rooted in James and Dewey; theoretical support in the constructivist psychology of Vygotsky, Piaget, and Bruner; and in the interactionist sociology of Mead and Blumer. To cite just one specific precursor, John Dewey always argued that the educational enterprise had to include more than the primary experience, and had to involve the learner's careful reconstruction and rethinking of that experience, connecting it with what came before and contemplating what would come next (Dewey, 1910; 1933/ 1964). All of these schools of thought insist on the active participation of the learner in the construction of knowledge. The literature on teacher education similarly emphasizes reflection for student-teachers, including the consideration of issues both ethical and moral, as well as the broader social and historical context of the work (Hatton & Smith, 1995). Moreover, the principle of reflection is supported empirically by Schön (1990), Boud and Walker (1993), and especially by Eyler and Giles (1999), whose pioneering studies of college-level service-learning demonstrated powerfully that effects on academic and personal growth were most evident in programs that engaged students in specific and extended reflection.

This process of reflection is a natural place to exploit the curious dynamic that we described in an earlier chapter: the dialectic of the student-worker role. The tension between needing to know and not knowing, between being expected to be competent in the performance of a task and being, in fact, a neophyte, has the fruitful character of creating a whole series of teachable moments. The intern can ask questions that the "real" worker cannot—especially in the safe haven of the classroom back at school. Those questions can be more profound, more probing, more challenging to the status quo than anything allowed back at work. The educator designing pedagogical strategies for work-based learning, therefore, has to give careful thought to ways of pulling students into that critical inquiry, of getting them past the quotidian qualities of their work lives and into a more challenging, expansive mind-set.

In fact, the student-worker dialectic operates in both directions: Students can learn not only to analyze work experience through the lenses of academic concepts, but can critique those concepts from the perspective of their experiences. If Weber's theory of bureaucracy can help Rob understand the division of labor in the urban hospital, so can working in the hospital inform his thinking about the sociology of organizations. This possibility creates another challenge and opportunity for the work-based learning instructor, who needs to find ways of cross-fertilizing the students' thinking about academic concepts and practical experience. None of these insights come automatically, and none of the goals are achieved without intention and effort. Just as workers take the workplace culture for granted, students take for granted the nature of school-like thought; having them make the connection requires thought and planning.

That leads to our second principle of pedagogy for work-based learning: The teacher's role is not to disseminate knowledge, but to create the conditions under which students can construct their own. The goal should be to form a community of inquiry among interns so they can share the process of critiquing their experiences and their knowledge. The teacher cannot simply tell students about the meanings of their experiences, or about the applications of academic theory to their work organizations. Rather, she has to initiate a form of reflective or critical discourse (see, for example, Habermas, 1971; Moore, 1990), a probing conversational process in which students collaborate in interrogating their experiences, their ideas, their institutions.

This principle makes the design of pedagogical strategies far less linear than it might be for more traditional courses. There will inevitably be a good deal of serendipity and surprise in the progress of these discussions, issues that neither the students nor the instructor may have anticipated. The plan for the term, then, needs to be organized around a variety of ideas, problems, and resources, and must allow for flexible exploration of the different questions that may arise. That is not to say that the instructor cannot be ready with certain readings, certain questions, certain assignments—but she needs to be ready, as well, to go with the proverbial flow and adapt to the emergent interests and concerns of the students. The issues that arise will have meaning to the interns because they have an impact on life in the workplace, not just because they appear on the syllabus. The teacher must be prepared to exploit the teachable moments, to help students formulate their problems, and then explore them as fully as they need to.

Finally, we argue that the educator's role in the work-based learning program belongs primarily to the schoolteacher, not to the supervisor in the workplace. First, the sort of inquiry and reflection that we advocate— indeed, insist upon as a component of a high-quality work-based learning program—is not likely to occur naturally in the work setting, especially if the implications of that inquiry are critical. The core function of the workplace supervisor, then, ought to be to induct the student into the culture of the organization, to make sure she acquires the knowledge and skill to perform the tasks she is assigned, and to consult with her on improving her performance.

A second reason to locate the critical inquiry function in the teacher's role rather than the supervisor's is that, even if the latter were willing to accept that duty, it would take a great deal of time and energy to train him to do it. Pursuing this kind of reflection process is not something one does instinctively—it burrows beneath everyday consciousness—and so one needs help in learning to do it. That sort of training ought to be available for schoolteachers who run work-based learning programs, but is not likely to be feasible for workplace supervisors.

Forms of School-Based Pedagogy for Work-Based Learning

In this section, we review some of the pedagogical strategies that we witnessed in our study of the work-based learning programs, describing them as they appeared to us. More than that, however, we critique them according to the framework laid out in this chapter. We ask what kinds of goals they were attempting to accomplish; we determine the extent to which they subscribed to the principles we just proposed; and we suggest some ways the pedagogies might have been enhanced to achieve the goals of critical work-based learning.

As we have shown, the naturally occurring workplace pedagogy in the sites varied enormously, sometimes assuring a rich educational experience and sometimes not. Both Fred and José's placements offered opportunities for learning of all the different sorts listed at the beginning of this chapter. Fred, through becoming part of the daily routine of the animal hospital, was certainly engaged in career exploration, even though the hands-on work he carried out was mostly menial. José certainly acquired several new kinds of skills, and his work experience was full of opportunities for thinking and learning about complex issues such as organizational processes, technical operations, and social relations. What did their schools do to help them gain more from their internships?

In the many programs we studied, we found four commonly used school-based strategies for ensuring student learning in the workplace: journal writing; learning contracts or training plans; internship classes or seminars; and final papers, projects, or presentations. These methods appear in more-or-less detailed form in the literature on experiential education (see Inkster & Ross, 1995; Stanton & Ali, 1987; Sweitzer & King, 1999). We recommend that readers examine these sources. Our review here is empirically based, however, drawing on a synthesis of the observations we did in the programs.

Learning or Training Contracts and Plans

Some, but not all of the programs we studied created learning plans for the internships. Sometimes called learning contracts, sometimes called training plans, these documents are usually written outlines of what the students are expected to do and learn on the job. In a sense, they constitute the syllabus for the work experience. Some are generic, in the sense that the same outline is used for all students in all workplaces whereas some are constructed individually for each internship. They represent "contracts" when all three major parties to the arrangement—the student, the workplace supervisor, and the school-based instructor or coordinator—negotiate the terms and sign the agreement.

Plans vary widely in their degree of specificity and detail in the description of the work activities or responsibilities and in the articulation of learning goals. In one program we visited, the training plan lists the tasks to be accomplished weekly on checkoff sheets. In other cases, the plan itemizes the assignments the student will complete, but not necessarily with deadlines. Some plans include work the student must complete outside of the internship site (reading, writing, etc.), but most specify at least some of the activities the student will carry out at work. José's program did not use learning plans. Fred, on the other hand, was required to identify new learning goals every month; these were written on his monthly evaluation forms. As an example, one of his goals was to "learn how to deal with the public."

An urban alternative high school, where students earn most of their credits through internships, has been using Learning Experience Activities Packages (LEAPs) for over 20 years. The purpose of the LEAP is to list the objectives for the internship so they are clear to the student and the employer, and to provide a way for the student to document what he or she learns. LEAPs are tailored to each specific workplace by the internship coordinators. For example, the LEAP for students interning at the city's police department requires students to keep a journal that reflects on their experiences, write an organizational profile, read books about policework, interview three police officers, and research and write a final report. More detailed instructions are provided for each activity.

In a different state, the Financial Learning Academy uses assignment frameworks called Tool Boxes to provide a structure for learning at the worksites. In this program, which has a classroom in a local bank, students follow a finance-based curriculum while simultaneously accepting paid and unpaid projects in the bank and other area financial institutions. When a student begins a project, she is given Tool Box 1, which outlines what she can learn simply by observing activities in the workplace. For example:

> How do you see workers acting—toward their work, toward their fellow work-
> ers, toward customers—both telephone and walk-in . . . How do you see work-
> ers using their time—what do they read, write, time on phone. What are their
> scheduled hours. Lunch break how used . . . What skills and assignments do
> you see that workers have to do to complete their jobs: technical skills, inter-
> personal skills, customer-relation skills, accounting skills, filing skills, accuracy
> skills . . .

At the end of the second week of a project, the student must turn in a paper
with answers to these questions. She then receives Tool Box 2, the purpose
of which is to help her reflect on personal and technical skills. For example:

> Describe the project manager and employees you are working for and give
> titles. Tell what the department does. How does this department fit into the
> whole financial industry? What opportunities exist for advancement in this de-
> partment? Where do most employees in this department come from, how
> would you describe the interpersonal relations of this department? . . .

As a pedagogical device, the learning plan offers several potential benefits over the "mere" experience of work. First, in line with our insistence on
the active participation of the student in the learning process, it can enhance the student's sense of agency and ownership by taking seriously her
own construction of the meaning of the experience. Although staff of the
urban alternative school produce the LEAPs just as a teacher produces a
syllabus, in many programs the student negotiates the learning contract
with the school and the worksite. That means that she has to think through
her own goals and interests, and devise a sensible structure for pursuing
them that will be convincing to the two adults. In terms of the models for
reflection that we identified earlier, this substantial participation increases
the likelihood that the student will take a critical stance toward the experience, if only because she has a stake of her own in the process. Similarly, it
(usually) avoids putting the responsibility for constructing knowledge
solely on the faculty.

Moreover, the learning contract embodies the principle of reflection
that we proposed earlier. Unless the plan is completely boilerplate—a tem-
plate applied to every site (as it is on occasion)—writing it forces the students and teachers to think concretely and extensively about what learning
is available and what activities will generate it. Many of the forms are organized into terms not unlike the categories of goals we mentioned at the beginning of this chapter: technical skills, interpersonal skills, knowledge of
yourself, and so on.

Of course, the details of the reflection process matter. The kinds of goals
that are set in the learning contract make a big difference in the impact of

the agreement. The students in the Financial Learning Academy, for instance, were being exposed to an essentially functionalist curriculum in the Tool Boxes cited; the implication of the questions was that the students needed primarily to know who was who and what knowledge and skills they were using, and then adjust themselves to that norm. Fred's training plan for the animal hospital, similarly, may have stayed at a fairly descriptive level, identifying core skills and tasks but not uncovering their deeper meaning. The LEAPs, on the other hand, could have been interpreted (depending, again, on the details) as taking the students into the realm of critical inquiry, asking harder and more profound questions about the nature of policework in a big city: about crime and its causes; about the pros and cons of community policing; about racial profiling; and so on. One of the roles of the teacher in this process, we maintain, is to ensure that the learning plans transcend the standard model of "here's what you need to be an X"; that they delve into the questions of social and political relations, a complex understanding of underlying causes and dynamics, and a vision of possible and desirable alternatives.

Journals

Almost all of the programs we visited, including those of Fred and José, require students to keep journals of their work-based learning experience. Students are expected to write an entry for every day they are on the job, and teachers or internship coordinators periodically collect and read the journals. Programs differ with respect to specifying the content of the entries. Some ask that students only describe what they do every day; others want students to emphasize their feelings about what they do; and still others structure the journals around certain themes or questions.

On the most practical level, journals serve as a quality-control method for school personnel who do not have the time to actually visit the internship sites. By reading the journals regularly, staff members can monitor the students' activities and gain a sense of emerging problems. If a student repeatedly writes, "Today I did the same thing I did yesterday," then the teacher knows that it is time for a phone call or visit to the worksite supervisor. In the case of José, the journal seemed to serve this basic purpose, as his entries consisted of only two or three lines describing his tasks of the day. For example, this is all José wrote for one particular day (other than noting the researcher's visit):

> I spent the day at the (hotel) in the office. It was really busy. I was given some paperwork to do along with answering the phones, which never stopped ringing.

On a deeper level, journals can provoke reflection on the part of students, and serve as an outlet for the expression of thoughts or feelings that cannot be declared at the worksite. Fred wrote in his very first journal entry:

> The emotional part of the job will probably be the hardest to deal with. Once I begin to figure what procedures are high-risk and what's not. I figure once I understand these factors, I may feel more empathy toward the animal. I mean right now I feel for the animal but don't truly understand what's going on so there may be more to feel.

Several weeks later an animal was euthanized during his work time. He wrote:

> I almost lost it. I remembered seeing the dog a few days earlier and he was looking like he was getting better. Today he looked fine for an extremely old dog. It was very hard on everyone else there too, because they had known Harry longer than I. They managed to keep it together. I felt bad . . . It's a tough choice. When is the right time to put away something you really love? I am glad I wasn't there when he was put under. I am not ready for that. Not yet at least.

These words show that Fred was learning that jobs in veterinary medicine do have an emotional aspect to manage. The comments could also serve as a starting point for a classroom discussion on euthanasia, or program staff could urge Fred to discuss these issues with his colleagues.

We did hear from some students that they found journal-writing to be tedious and a burden. Some were very unsure of the point of the journals. Other students complained that they spent time on their journals but the teachers made no comments on them; for their part, the teachers argued that they did not want to be perceived as evaluating the journals, but wanted to validate the students' expressions.

Like the learning contract, the journal is a useful pedagogical device—especially if it is taken past the mere reporting of activity. It is a wonderful device for reflection, and provides space for unexpected insights and analyses. Even the bare level of describing what one does and how one feels about it takes one into a slightly more reflective frame of mind, and raises the possibility of deeper thinking. But we think that journals ought to offer a combination of opportunities and challenges for the student-intern: Describing complex work processes in fairly good detail (perhaps even using representational devices like flowcharts or organization charts); reporting one's responses or feelings related to those events; identifying emergent issues in the work, whether about social dynamics or organizational growth, or budgeting dilemmas and changes in the clientele. The journal can be regarded in a sense as an extended enterprise in self-ethnography, turning the student into a participant-observer in the workplace, and giving her the chance to analyze processes and relationships in great detail. Moreover, the journal can introduce the student to the utility of a number of forms of academic inquiry: history (ask about how the company has come to the point it has over the past 25 years); sociology (ask about gender relations in the workplace, or the distribution of power); psychology (inquire into issues of motivation and personality).

In our observation, the programs tend to stay on a fairly descriptive and personal-responsive level, rather than to encourage students into this extended form of analysis. We believe that they miss an opportunity from this pedagogical technique, that more can be made of the journal than typically is.

Internship Classes

Several programs require students involved in work-based learning to attend a class or seminar together. The focus of these classes ranges from general workplace issues to the students' particular experiences. At one of our sites, a weekly seminar was a regular component of the program. Students shared information with one another about their workplaces and experiences. They also wrote a weekly paper on an assigned topic; one topic was to compare two similar occupations. At the urban alternative high school, students also attend an internship seminar. During the class we observed, the teacher divided the students into pairs, where they shared their internship experiences and then performed an in-class writing exercise.

Fred went to a weekly internship seminar back at school. He described many of his observations to his classmates, who were particularly fascinated by the stories about the surgeries. He was also assigned books to read on veterinary medicine and writing exercises, the subject of which were often decided in the group discussions. This seminar clearly added educational value to his experience, and encouraged him to think about the work in ways he would not have otherwise. José, on the other hand, had a summer internship with no related class, and so he lacked the debriefing that Fred received. A concurrent seminar could have helped José think through the worker-management issues he was confronted with daily. For example, one day José was told by his supervisor to go to the second floor of the hotel to see if a worker was shampooing the carpeting there. When José arrived in the hallway, the worker yelled at him, saying, "They don't have to send a baby-sitter to watch me do my job!" In a later interview, José said:

> I did feel uncomfortable . . . That's why people didn't really like me much. 'Cause it's like, I am just a little kid, getting a high position. I understand, it must have made him feel very uncomfortable. I understand where they're coming from. I wouldn't want no 5-year-old kid to be my boss. (interview xvii2: 874–911)

José was mature enough to have some understanding of this situation, and the management-labor themes that were repeatedly evident during his internship, yet he did not have the opportunity to deconstruct these issues with teachers or other students in a structured and sustained way.

The seminars can function on a number of pedagogical levels. Even the mere reporting of day-to-day experiences shows students something about the variety of work contexts and issues. But teachers can design reasonable and extensive connections between the experience and the things kids are learning in school: They can lift concepts from social studies class (community, organization, family life) and have the students use them in analyzing their internships. They can borrow tools from classes in psychology as a device for figuring out why people act the way they do. They can raise questions from economics about why the students' various organizations are doing well or badly, and what impact those fortunes have on work life, productivity, and change.

Moreover, as Simon and his colleagues demonstrated so well in *Learning Work* (1991), the seminar can become an occasion for the critical discourse we described earlier in this chapter. In one class described in the book, a young woman interning at McDonald's asked a question arising from a sense of pique: "Why is it that the girls have to work the cash registers while the boys get to be in the back making the hamburgers and fries?" Putting aside the judgment about the relative merits of taking orders from throngs of customers and standing over a tub of hot grease, the teacher immediately turned the discussion toward the more pervasive question of sex segregation in the workplace. Several other students had related comments from their experiences in very different settings, and the instructor led them all to consider some very intriguing and difficult questions about why these patterns might exist and what might be done about them. The conversation was simultaneously abstract and concrete, theoretical and practical, rooted in experience but connected by ideas. Participating in such discourse must have given the students a greater sense of power in their work lives and in their learning. Teachable moments like that can be found in virtually every internship seminar session, because the abstractions (gender, race, power, change) are, in fact, meaningful primarily in the context of lived experience—and work-based learning students are having those lived experiences through which they can explore the ideas, and vice versa.

Final Papers, Projects, and Presentations

Finally, most of the programs we studied required students to complete and also sometimes present a final paper or project. Students in the Financial Learning Academy must present to their classmates their discoveries from the Tool Box activities. At another of our research sites, on "Graduation Challenge Day" students in the internship program turn in papers and make presentations about their placements to panels of teachers, parents, and employers. Presentations are rated according to three criteria: delivery, organization, and content. For each area, students can receive a grade of unsatisfactory, pass, or high-quality.

Fred's program required him to write a paper and make a presentation. His topic was veterinary medicine. He started by giving the purpose of his internship this way: "To see if I could handle the hardships of veterinary medicine." He described his first few weeks at the animal hospital, explaining how he became more confident in his performance over time. He described the tasks, the other workers, and some of the surgeries he observed. He then answered questions from the audience about the kinds of animals the hospital cared for, and about preventive animal health.

José's program required him only to complete two short papers: one on his supervisor, which was to be drawn from an interview; and the other on what he thought about his internship. The purpose of the first paper was for José to understand the education and qualifications for a career in the hotel industry, as well as to gain a good idea of a hotel employee's career path. The second paper served merely to encourage him to reflect on the experience—without any specific forms of analysis.

As in the case of all the other pedagogical tactics, the final assignment can be used more or less effectively, depending on how the instructor structures it and engages the student in some kind of thinking and acting. The examples we witnessed were clearly useful for getting the students to articulate what they had done and what they thought about it. But those strategies tended to be on a fairly reportorial and somewhat superficial level. Interns were not usually challenged to dig beneath the surface of their work or organization in the sense described by Simon. Nor were they asked to extrapolate from their situated experiences in the way suggested by Perkins and Salomon. That is not to say that the teaching methods were ineffective, merely that they did not take advantage of all of the learning possibilities.

Our analysis in Chapter 9 of Fred's workplace seemed to suggest that his internship was not as rich as José's, yet a look at the pedagogy back at school demonstrates that Fred's experience was not as deficient as one might have first thought. Fred set learning goals, attended a weekly seminar with a teacher and other student-interns, and wrote and presented a final paper on his experience. José clearly had more varied, complex, and responsible tasks at the hotel than Fred did at the animal hospital, but José lacked a structured way to reflect on his days at the workplace, or to share his internship with others. Clearly, a well-designed teaching strategy could have elicited a great deal of interesting and productive thought from both students. Neither school did as much as might have been possible.

Conclusion

The first important conclusion of this chapter is that work-based learning needs a school-based component. The naturally occurring learning process in the workplace can be strong, but it is also lacking in certain important respects. The social organization of knowledge-use in the workplace is driven far more often by the productive requirements of the institution than by the learning needs of the neophyte, even though meeting those learning needs often improves productivity. Moreover, many organizations compartmentalize knowledge-use in a way that blocks access to newcomers and perpetuates their marginal status. Almost invariably, there are kinds of knowledge-use in the workplace that cannot be fully tapped by interns. Some form of supplementary learning activity is therefore crucial.

Moreover, if the situated cognitionists are right and knowledge-use is embedded in specific contexts, then relying solely on the workplace experience is to confine the learning to specialized and only narrowly useful knowledge. Unless interns are placed in sites where they fully intend to spend their careers, nontransferable knowledge will not do them much good. If Perkins and Salomon are correct in their argument about the conditions for knowledge transfer, and if those conditions are not found naturally in work settings, then classroom activities will be the only way to make the transfer happen.

Not only is the workplace experience inadequate as the sole source of learning, but there is a great deal of philosophical and empirical support for the claim that reflection is a crucial part of the educational process. From Dewey's general conception of how we think, to Eyler and Giles's findings about service-learning, a great deal of literature insists that the learner needs an opportunity to step back from the experience and interrogate it, parse it, examine it through new lenses.

Accepting the premise that a classroom component is necessary in a work-based learning program, then we identify two major kinds of decisions that the school-based educators must make in designing an effective pedagogy. First, what kinds of learning do they want students to do: about science; about writing; about organizational dynamics; about themselves; about society; about career paths or practical skills? Whatever those knowledge goals are, they should drive the construction of the pedagogy. And, as we argued in our section on learning theory, that pedagogy should be designed to engage the learners in the use of whatever kind of knowledge is the goal: If you want students to learn about scientific concepts, you should not merely tell them about those concepts but rather should create ways for them to participate in the use of those concepts; if you want them to understand history, they have to act like historians. These knowledge goals should not be left on a level of generality that makes such participation meaningless. "Knowing all about city government" is not inevitably accomplished when you place a student in a city council member's office; nor does a student in a hospital learn all about "medicine." The goals and objectives must be specified more concretely, in terms that can be realized in situated activity—whether in the workplace or in the classroom. Both parts of the pedagogy are important.

The second decision faced by the work-based learning pedagogue is how to balance the teaching emphasis between the functionalist or critical approaches. The specific kinds of questions one raises, the kinds of activities one initiates, and the student behaviors one elicits will be influenced by this choice.

The actual teaching tactics will flow from the answers to these larger questions. Different techniques will tease out different kinds of learning from workplace and classroom experiences. They all rely to some extent on one or another form of reflection: of making the connections explicit, of exploring the deeper dynamics, of challenging the taken-for-granted assumptions. They make the learner transcend the particularities of the "mere" experience: elaborate it, flesh it out, critique it.

The devices we reviewed earlier—the learning contract, the journal, the seminar, the final assignment—all provide occasions for these sorts of reflection. They are not activities that the interns will encounter in their regular workplace activities. Instead, they represent forms of the essential classroom-based pedagogy for effective work-based learning.

CHAPTER 11

Conclusions

Education reform is a constant imperative. Too many students never finish high school; many who do have not learned the skills that they will need to be productive members of society and are not prepared for college-level work; and surveys suggest that the large majority of students are not enthusiastically engaged in school. This book has had two overarching themes. First, we asked what role work-based learning can play in efforts to address these problems. Second, we asked what policymakers and educators can do to strengthen the effectiveness of work-based learning as an educational strategy.

Work-based learning has been, for many decades, a fundamental component of the country's educational system. Graduate and professional education in almost all cases has significant experience requirements, and adults realize that much of what makes them effective, they learned on the job or in their communities. No one is considered an expert without significant experience—that is, without an extended period of learning on the job. But there is less consensus about the value of work-based learning for high school, and often even for college students. Work-based learning seems to be particularly at odds with education reform increasingly focused on achievement on standardized assessments that cover extensive curricula.

In the 1990s, the School-to-Work Opportunities Act gave work-based learning at the high school level a boost by making it a central component of a high-profile national education reform agenda. This definitely drew attention to the strategy and generated significant amounts of experimentation and research. Evidence suggests that the Act accounted for a significant growth of work-based learning activities, although much of that tended to involve less-intensive strategies such as job shadowing. But the push provided by the Act specifically has faded as the funding it provided expired in 2001.

Nevertheless, there are at least two reasons why we can expect the widespread continuation and perhaps even further growth of this educational strategy for secondary school students. First, work-based learning was already a significant educational phenomenon before the passage of the 1994 Act. Estimates suggest that during the mid-1990s, too early for the Act to have had a significant effect, between one-fifth and one-quarter of all high school students held an internship or apprenticeship by the time they were seniors. These conclusions are based on data from both the 1997 National Longitudinal Survey of Youth (Rivera-Batiz, 2000) and the Mathematica evaluation, presented by Haimson and Bellotti in Chapter 3 of this book. And as we pointed out in Chapter 4, one-quarter of all employers, and even more of the larger employers, have also provided students with internships. Therefore, hundreds of thousands of students and employers were already actively engaged in this educational approach.

Second, several education reform strategies that involve work-based learning continue to grow despite the conclusion of the School-to-Work Act. The career academies model provides the best example. Although there are variations of the model, in general, a career academy is a type of school-within-a-school that combines a small learning community structure, a college-preparatory curriculum with a career theme, and partnerships with employers who provide work-based learning. The first academy was started in 1969 in Philadelphia. During the 1990s, the number of academies grew rapidly so that by 2000, there were at least 1000 operating across the country. There are currently three major networks of academies, based in Philadelphia, New York, and California (which funds academies state-wide); academies are also becoming prevalent in Atlanta, Chicago, and Denver (Stern et al., 2000).

In addition, evidence is beginning to emerge that female and minority students are well-represented in work-based learning programs (see Chapter 3). There is suggestive evidence that the types of programs that typically emphasize work-based learning are effective at reducing the dropout rate and increasing engagement with school for at-risk students (Kemple & Snipes, 2000). These data might serve as additional rationales for continuing and expanding work-based learning.

We started this book with five broad objectives: clarifying the purposes of work-based learning; testing the claims of its advocates; specifying the mechanisms through which it works; exploring the on-the-job and the classroom pedagogy associated with work-based learning; and analyzing the characteristics of, and potential for, employer participation in this educational strategy. Now, after our analysis, where do we stand on these objectives?

The Purposes

Our first objective was to work toward a clarification of the purposes of work-based learning. Our analysis does suggest that work-based learning can have multiple objectives, but working through the thicket of claims and arguments, one consensus does emerge. Work-based learning is a crucial means of preparing young people for a particular occupation once they have chosen that occupation and once they have acquired some basic background knowledge. This is perhaps most common in graduate and professional education, where every novice worker undergoes some period of formal or informal on-the-job instruction as part of their education. Work-based learning as direct career preparation, even at the high school level, is probably not controversial as long as it is preparing a student for a job more or less immediately after high school and as long as it does not displace a basic high school academic education. But with growing skepticism that a high school degree is an adequate basic education over the long run, any work-based learning must at least leave room for preparation for post-secondary education.

Thus, the controversy has to do with the role of work-based learning as part of a basic secondary school preparation that may teach some career knowledge and skills, but also prepares students for a rigorous post-secondary education. What are the roles that work-based learning can play within this framework? Our perspective on this question is basically pragmatic: This educational strategy can play the roles for which it is found to be effective. We address this in the next sections.

The Claims of Advocates

So which of the various claims about work-based learning is supported by our empirical evidence? We identified four basic claims for the effects of work-based learning: academic reinforcement; career skills and exploration; youth development; and learning new modes of thought.

Academic reinforcement. Our analysis suggests that the evidence in favor of academic reinforcement is weaker than the evidence for the other claims. This is especially true if academic achievement is understood to be measured by success on tests of knowledge of a broad curriculum. Academic reinforcement does occur, but it was absent from many of the internships that we studied. Moreover, when it does occur, educators cannot expect it to reinforce a significant percentage of a particular curriculum. On the other hand, examination of the other claims does suggest that work-based learning may have an indirect positive influence on academic achievement.

Career exploration and skills. The second argument that we examined was that work-based learning promoted career exploration and taught career-related skills. We certainly observed this type of learning taking place in many internships. Interns did learn many skills that were useful and needed in the organizations in which they worked. We also observed students learning problem-solving and teamwork skills often referred to as SCANS skills. But if we have a more ambitious goal of giving young people experience as participants in a community of practice, then our results are more mixed. In many cases, even those students who became productive members of a work group remained at the margins of those communities of practice, and the skills they learned were not integrated into a broader understanding or sense of the organizations and occupations in which they were engaged. Most did not learn "all aspects of the industry," as the School-to-Work Opportunities Act mandated, but rather got fairly narrow perspectives on related careers.

Youth development. We were encouraged by our exploration of the youth-development potential of work-based learning. The interns we studied did have opportunities to take on responsibility, to develop an understanding of who they were and what interested them, and to feel a sense of accomplishment and expertise; they often reported with satisfaction that they were "treated like an adult." Of course this did not always happen, and indeed some internships were boring and restricted and may have been overall negative experiences for the youth. One of the main problems for this topic is the absence of good measures of development. This is an issue that the whole field of youth development will need to address; indeed, a recent article in that field argues that we need better ways of knowing and tracking when and how youth development occurs (MacDonald & Valdivieso, n.d.).

New modes of thought. Finally, we constructed our own claim for the benefits of work-based learning. And our evidence did provide a reasonable empirical foundation for the argument that interns can learn new modes of thought that are different from the types of approaches that would be most common in the classroom. Student-interns have the opportunity to define problems and to approach them flexibly, using a variety of strategies and tactics. They learn to use the social and physical environment to represent and address problems, and they learn to function in a group, solving problems in concert with others, calling on the knowledge and expertise of those around them: they get a sense of collective cognition. On rare occasions, they perform cognitive tasks that could be called executive functions or that entail higher-order thought. Again, these features of work-based learning are not inevitable, but when they do occur, they constitute a benefit above and beyond classroom-based learning. The tension between the student and worker roles is one of the features that sets work-based learning apart from classroom instruction.

If the new modes of thought argument is supported, then it might offer an indirect mechanism to improve student academic learning. We argued in Chapter 5 that work-based learning is probably not an efficient way (at least in the short-term) to raise student scores on standardized tests. (Test-taking is a unique context in its own right, with no obvious corollaries in the work world.) Nevertheless, it is entirely possible that gaining experience in the expansive, challenging, and varied forms of cognitive activity that we observed in some internships could make interns better students in the classroom. The experiences available in some internships may help students formulate questions, search for resources, employ diverse strategies, work effectively with groups to solve problems, and recognize the social dimensions of problems. We cannot test this hypothesis with our data since we did not collect performance data for students after their work placements, but the logic of the learning dynamic is plausible, and deserves further analysis.

The Mechanisms of Work-Based Learning

Another one of our broad objectives was to specify the mechanisms through which work-based learning would have the claimed effects on students. In our analysis, we have emphasized two concepts—engagement and reflection.

Engagement. The theory, developed in Chapter 2, that supports the practice of work-based learning, insists on the centrality of situated experience in learning. If a student is to learn about a concept, then he or she must experience that concept in practice. So if educators want students not only to learn ideas and skills, but also to learn to use them in authentic settings, then the theory supports the claim that work experience will engage students with that knowledge more effectively than will book-oriented, teacher-driven, abstract instruction. But this also tells us that whatever knowledge and skills may be present in a workplace, work-based learning will only teach those with which students are actively engaged.

Reflection. Reflection is also a crucial mechanism for the realization of the educational benefits of work-based learning. Reflection is the process through which students step back from their experience and consciously learn from that experience. This mechanism plays three important roles in the educational value-added of work-based learning.

First, it is the key to the transfer of knowledge. One reason to move education at least partly out of the school is that classroom-learned knowledge does not transfer easily. But by the same logic, one could argue that knowledge and skills learned in one workplace will only weakly (or not at all) transfer to other settings. Conscious reflection on those skills and experiences can strengthen that transfer.

Second, reflection promotes the coordination of academic learning with work experience. Through reflection, the student can use academic knowledge as it relates to experiences. Students can explore academic concepts relevant to their work—the underlying science, sociology, or economics of the activities in which they are engaged. This can go beyond any explicit academic knowledge they might need in their particular placement, but it maintains contact with the relevance and use of that knowledge.

Third, reflection gives students the opportunity to view the workplace and their own experience in it as the subject of inquiry, not just the location of learning. As we emphasized in Chapter 10, critical reflection on the internship allows the experience to be much more than something that prepares students to be effective workers in workplaces as they exist. Students can get below the surface of their experience and ask why workplaces are organized as they are, how they might be improved, and how the student may or may not become involved in those changes.

The Pedagogy of Work-Based Learning

One of the most important conclusions of this book is that presence in a workplace, by itself, does not necessarily result in educationally useful experiences. Similarly, educators do not believe that students will learn simply if material is made available to them. It is useful to think of two types of work-based learning pedagogy—in the workplace and in the classroom. These two areas also correspond to the concepts of engagement and reflection. On-the-job pedagogy promotes educationally productive engagement with the work experience, but it is the job of the classroom teacher working with interns to encourage meaningful reflection on the experience.

On-the-Job Pedagogy (Engagement)

To some extent, the characteristics of the workplace will determine the educational potential of the internship. If very little learning is taking place at the site, or if the jobs are explicitly designed to require few skills, then students will have little opportunity for interesting engagement in learning in their internship, although a skilled classroom teacher may still be able to use the experience for interesting reflection. Thus, work-based learning coordinators need to try to find worksites with greater opportunities for learning. For example, we argued in Chapter 3 that firms that are organized around so-called high-performance work principles appear to offer internships with greater learning potential.

But working in a learning-rich worksite does not guarantee that the intern will be engaged in the learning-rich aspects of that site. Students can be given tasks that isolate them from the interesting activities taking place around them. Coordinators who are aware of the circumstances in which their interns are working might be able to encourage employers to give the youth different work. Indeed we found one case in which one of the interns herself asked for, and received, a change of assignment. In Chapter 9, we also discussed the various tactics that supervisors and mentors can use on the job to promote the engagement and learning of interns. All of this suggests that a work-based learning program will be more valuable if the supervisors and skilled workers who interact with the interns are willing to participate in mentor training. But this may be a lot to ask, so site selection may be the coordinators' most important tool for improving on-the-job pedagogy.

Classroom Pedagogy (Reflection)

Teachers and coordinators have much more control over the classroom component than they do over the on-the-job pedagogy. For practical reasons, the classroom pedagogy often takes place in special seminars for work-based learning students. There is more chance that the regular classroom teachers will be involved if the whole school is organized around occupational themes or at least encourages all students to do internships. Building on the student's work experience, teachers can use the classroom to promote cognitive development; reinforce career exploration and skills; and encourage social and psychological development. Four strategies are most commonly used: learning contracts and plans; journals; internship classes; and final papers, projects, and presentations. We have reported on cases from our research in which the classroom component of a student's experience increased the educational value of the placements.

Teachers can follow two broad strategies that we referred to as *functionalist* or *critical/reflective*, although the two are not necessarily in conflict. The functionalist strategy is aimed at teaching the skills that are used and needed in the workplace—this prepares young people to function effectively on their jobs and in society. The critical perspective begins by taking the workplace and the social and political context in which it operates as a subject of inquiry and reflection. This approach can be used either to reinforce academic skills or to ask much deeper questions about the nature of work and the enterprises in which it takes place, the essence of the relationships within the workplace, and how and whether those things can or should be changed.

Our data suggest that most teachers and coordinators emphasize the functionalist strategy, and we agree that this is a crucial component of any work-based learning effort. At the same time, students whose teachers do not also use the critical/reflective strategy are missing an important opportunity for intellectual and personal growth and development. The reflective approach addresses one of the strongest criticisms of work-based learning—that it does not promote academic skills. The strategy allows teachers to use the work experience to raise the very types of issues that the students are addressing in their core academic subjects, particularly English, history, and social studies. In addition to providing opportunities to see applications of science and mathematics, the critical approach gives teachers an opportunity to explore the contexts in which math and science are used. And looking toward college, the critical model can be used to raise issues that students will be encountering in applied science, sociology, economics, psychology, business, environmental science, philosophy, and many other courses.

Employer Involvement

Our fifth and final broad objective was to analyze the participation of employers. We have spent most of the time in this book discussing the benefits of work-based learning, but the benefits must be measured against any costs. The effort and resources needed to recruit and work with employers are a significant component of the costs of this educational strategy. Moreover, the willingness of employers to provide internship slots and to cooperate with coordinators has a significant impact on the educational quality of these experiences. Reluctant employers are not likely to work hard at finding tasks that will increase the youths' learning opportunities or at assigning and perhaps training mentors who can teach and guide the interns.

Our research has shown that a large number of employers are already willing to provide internships. Moreover, the coordinators working in the programs we examined did not generally indicate that the growth of their programs was limited by problems of employer recruitment. Indeed, of the 12 programs that we studied intensively, three subsequently closed, but none closed because of a lack of employer partners. However, further research is needed on whether the current economic downturn has negatively affected employer participation in educational programs.

Although some employers do derive short-term benefits from interns, philanthropic motives are still the mainstay of employer participation. To expand the number of internships significantly beyond the current numbers may require reaching groups of employers who are not participating already because they do not respond to philanthropic arguments. We do have some tentative evidence that the nonparticipants are more concerned than the participants about the costs of internships. On the other hand, we also found that employers who had organized their firms around high-performance work principles were most likely to provide internships and that those internships tended to be of higher quality. This creates a more optimistic picture of the potential for employer participation if, as some researchers have concluded, employers are continuing to shift toward high-performance work organization. In any case, we have concluded that American employers could support a larger number of interns, especially if there is a consensus about the educational value of this strategy.

The evidence that we have presented in this book indicates that work-based learning can be a powerful pedagogy for a number of important educational purposes. But it is not good for everything. In particular, it is not an efficient short-term strategy for improving tests scores, although we suspect that, done right, it can strengthen academic performance. Like any educational strategy, it does not operate on its own. Indeed, operating an effective work-based learning program takes considerable work: recruiting employers; becoming familiar with the internship sites and the supervisors and mentors; and constructing teaching strategies that maximize the classroom-based learning complementary to the work-based experience. Our conclusion is that the potential benefits are worth the effort. Given that conclusion, what are the next steps for educators and policymakers? We turn to that question in the next and final section of the chapter.

Recommendations

We believe that work-based learning is worth pursuing and expanding. How does work-based learning best fit into the current context and goals for education reform? The national legislation and funding that promoted and supported work-based learning has expired. Should advocates and policymakers try to resurrect a national approach? We think that political reality dictates that this will not happen. The national context has shifted; other issues have replaced the focus on international competitiveness and preparing a technical workforce that motivated the support for the School-to-Work Opportunities Act. The direction of policy appears more than ever to be toward local decision-making and toward accountability. Yet work-based learning is not incompatible with either of these new priorities.

Local control does not work against the establishment of work-based learning programs; we have seen a diversity of approaches, developed locally, that are effective. And in any case, many states, in anticipation of the loss of the federal Act, passed legislation supporting their own version of work-based learning (Schmidt, 1999). Given this context, there is still a role for the federal government in promoting experimentation at the local level and in promoting research on the vast variety of initiatives operating across the country. Research should include refining how to conceptualize and measure the ways in which work-based learning promotes young people's psychological development. We have developed a concept called new modes of thought to refer to the ways in which young people engage in activities and problems at work that are different from the ways they do so at school, but further research is needed. Given the growing preoccupation with academic achievement measured by more-or-less traditional academic assessments, it makes sense to explore the value of the broad spectrum of nonacademic activities in which adolescents participate, including internships, service-learning, extracurricular activities, and even leisure. Finally, the federal government should also continue to support dissemination of information about best practices in work-based learning programs.

The federal government is now following in the footsteps of state governments that have recently demanded more in the way of accountability. Many states have developed new, high-stakes tests, and the No Child Left Behind Act has firmly established testing and accountability as federal policy. Hence any educational strategy needs to take account of the movement toward increased accountability. Yet we see no reason why work-based learning would conflict with that movement. Certainly we would not recommend that work-based learning replace a significant amount of classroom learning or that it substitute for classroom preparation for tests. Internships might be able to replace some electives, but participating in work-based learning must be consistent with taking a full complement of core academic courses.

There are a variety of strategies for minimizing the practical conflicts between academic studies and internships. Work-based learning may take time away from other activities that adolescents currently take part in, such as part-time jobs, but paid internships would be more valuable substitutes. Many schools that use the academy model schedule their internships in the summer. Alternatively, some schools use what are referred to as "senior options," in which all students have internships during the spring of their senior year. Finally, as we have outlined, teachers can use students' workplace experiences to support broader academic learning and exploration about themselves.

It is significant that the federal emphasis on accountability now includes a specific focus on low-achieving students. Some research suggests that at-risk students have the most to gain from an educational strategy involving work-based learning (Foothill Associates, 1997; Hanser & Stasz, 1999; Kemple & Snipes, 2000). We have witnessed how employer and community involvement with schools gives many at-risk youth opportunities they would not have otherwise had. For students who are not engaged in school, bringing work and school together, helping them to think about what they want to do in the future, and providing them with an opportunity to develop competence outside of school may help them refocus.

We have argued that employer recruitment is not the major barrier to expansion of work-based learning. Nevertheless, working with employers is difficult and time-consuming, if done well. We have articulated some suggestions for expanding the pool of employers in Chapters 2 and 3. More detailed sets of recommendations are also available (see Bailey, 1995; Hershey et al., 1999). Two important themes emerge from these recommendations. First, when possible, coordinators should try to work with local employer associations. This gives the schools access to larger numbers of employers. Furthermore, employer associations are one way in which individual employers can articulate a collective interest. The second main theme is that high-quality work-based learning must be built on individual relationships between coordinators or teachers and employers. The more the coordinator knows about the placement and can work with the employer, the greater the chances are that the placement will be educational (although this is not to say that internships cannot be useful without close coordination between school and each workplace). Managing internships is a difficult and time-consuming job and the effectiveness of coordinators will increase as they have time to get to know employers and build a network of contacts. Therefore, the job should not be an additional responsibility tacked on to a full teaching job and turnover should be discouraged.

These recommendations also have implications for professional development for both coordinators and worksite mentors. Some experience with and instruction for managing internships and coordinating work experience with classroom learning could be incorporated into the education of teachers and other educators. And to the extent that they can be convinced to participate, worksite supervisors and mentors could also benefit from instruction in how to work most effectively with interns. Chapters 9 and 10 provide material that could be part of such a curriculum.

The images we have offered in this book speak to the powerful potential of work-based learning: a young woman in Vermont moves from child to child in a 5th-grade music class, helping each one grasp the meaning of harmony and rhythm; a law-firm intern in New York pores over the transcripts of court testimony, digging out the most salient points for her lawyer-supervisors; a tourism-academy student inspecting the halls of a hotel finds himself the target of resentment from frontline housemen who object to his unearned managerial position. The first student experiences herself in new ways in relation to children, and discovers a calling in teaching. The second intern challenges herself to use new analytical and expressive skills, and is taken seriously by legal professionals. And the third begins to understand the complexities of power and status in a work organization, and to ask questions about where he stands in that system of relationships.

None of these experiences would likely be found in a classroom. Instead, they build new kinds of knowledge and skill; foster new ways of thinking and problem-solving; engage young people in new forms of social interaction; and give firsthand information about careers and industries. Of course, not all internships provide such powerful experiences—some, in fact, look pretty mundane: filing records in the back room of a corporate marketing department; making beds in an urban hospital; trying to learn a word-processing program in a foreign consulate.

The key issue, again, is what students make of these experiences, how supervisors and teachers help them reflect on their work to tease out new knowledge and insight. When that is done well, our studies show, work-based learning clearly adds value to the education of young people. It brings more adults into the education system and into the lives of young people. It engages them with the world outside of school in compelling ways, encourages them to develop new reserves of self-respect and social skill, and challenges them to use new knowledge in solving unfamiliar problems. These benefits strike us as good reasons for continuing and furthering work-based learning as an educational strategy.

Guidelines for Conducting Ethnography in Research on Work-Based Learning

DAVID THORNTON MOORE

The Question of Method: How to Find What We're Looking For

In these guidelines I propose a concrete set of suggestions for field researchers, trying to identify (a) what kinds of information you need to be looking for, and (b) some strategies and tactics for generating that information. I propose ways of collecting data about those questions. I address such issues as: gaining access to the site and establishing a relationship with the subjects; things to do in the very first days in a field site; methods of observing activities and interactions in the workplace; ways of asking questions of people; and techniques for organizing, storing, and retrieving data.

These suggestions are based partly on my own experience in conducting ethnographic observations in internship sites; partly on that of colleagues like Roger Simon (author of *Learning Work*, 1991) and Gitti Jordan (workplace anthropologist at the Institute for Research on Learning) and partly on such research methods texts as Schatzman and Strauss, *Field Research* (1973); Fetterman, *Ethnography: Step by Step* (1989); and Hammersley and Atkinson, *Ethnography: Principles in Practice* (1983).

How should you go about actually collecting and analyzing information that will reveal the nature of students' experiences in their internship sites? Obviously, we're talking about primarily *ethnographic methods*: ways of constructing an adequate account of the workplace cultures (social relations, activities, contexts; knowledge-in-use) and the induction of interns into those cultures. That means *participant-observation*: Watching what people do; asking them questions; collecting artifacts.

What follows are some suggestions regarding a number of key strategic and tactical issues you need to resolve in conducting the ethnography. It goes without saying that these suggestions are neither exhaustive nor static: You will run into problems that I haven't thought of here and things will change as you go. We'll worry about that later. . . .

Sampling

The first challenge is choosing sites and students for your sample of observations. Ethnography being a labor-intensive and time-consuming enterprise, you obviously can't conduct a huge number of case studies. Nor would it make sense for you to sample randomly from some existing universe. Rather, you might do a form of *purposive sampling*. The first stage in that process is to identify the dimensions of the phenomenon that you think might create interesting and important differences across students' experiences. Those dimensions might break down into major and minor categories:

1. Features of the students
    a. age: high school v. college; 15–18 v. 20–30
    b. previous work experience: worked; never worked
    c. general aptitude/skill level: high; medium; low
    d. gender
    e. race/ethnicity
2. Features of the worksites
    a. sector: public v. private; profit v. nonprofit
    b. type of work: service; technology; manufacturing; etc.
    c. size: large; medium; small
    d. experience with intern program: none; some; much

Even with this number of variables, you can't cover all the possible student-site types. Therefore, you will have to choose the dimensions that you think are most important: for example, gender, type of work, and sector. Since there are three fieldworkers and three schools, it might make sense to break the sample down something like this:

- 18 sites (6 per fieldworker).
- Each study two students from each of the three schools.
- Half of each researcher's subjects male, half female (ideally, one male and one female from each school).
- Half working in for-profit sector, half in not-for-profit sector.

- Try to choose subjects representing rough demographic breakdown in the schools (that is, by race and ethnicity).

Contact, Access, and Entry

Ideally, you will select the sample students and sites *before* the start of the internship cycle, before the students enter their placements. Once you have chosen them (through resource coordinators, internship directors, advisers, whatever), you need to contact both the student and the site supervisor for permission to conduct the study. These conversations are a form of *explanation* and *negotiation*.

Explaining the project to the subjects requires honesty but not exhaustiveness. You need to tell people what the project is about (understanding how interns learn in the workplace) and what it is *not* about (evaluating either party). You don't need to go into huge detail about the former; you probably need to be reassuring about the latter: Make it clear that nobody will be negatively affected by the findings of the study.

Negotiating the project is a matter of agreeing on the terms of the researcher's presence and actions on the site. You need to do that with both the student and the site supervisor, who will be your natural first contact at the workplace. Different people will have different degrees of willingness to let you hang out in various contexts. My sense is that your basic position should be that you will never go where people don't want you to be; but you'll have to exercise judgment: If they will only let you sit in the reception area, but never actually watch people working, then you might elect not to study that site. You will have to discuss such aspects of the study as:

- How much time you will be there each visit; how many visits; on what days.
- What situations you will be able to observe directly.
- Which people you will be able to talk with (interview, chat), and when.
- Whether any information is confidential and/or proprietary.
- Whether you will be able to collect artifacts like copies of memos or bulletins.
- How the data will be used: Will identities be concealed? Who will see the report? How will it be used?

Entry, the phase of the project when you actually start conducting the fieldwork, requires several forms of sensitivity. Understand that people (both the student and the regular workforce) are getting used to your presence, which is an odd and discomfiting thing. Be accommodating and friendly but as unobtrusive as you can manage without being weird about it. As you move along, realize that your explanations and negotiations will probably continue to some extent.

The early stages of establishing *rapport* with people are crucial to later data-gathering. In your initial interview with the student, since you are engaging in an intense form of dialogic interaction, you want to construct a friendly, inquisitive, sensitive relationship with the subject. But you don't want to make promises you can't keep: You won't be the student's advocate, or teacher, shrink, or pal—just a very interested, open-minded, nonjudgmental observer. In your relations with people who work at the site, you need to be clear about who you are and what you're doing; answer questions (but don't necessarily volunteer a lot of information that people are not asking for); do not get in their way, or take their time without their willing consent.

The Early Observations

In the first couple of visits to the worksite, you have to choose a *field of vision*, a scope of things to look at. One could focus very narrowly on the student and her work activities, but I suggest making an effort to get to know the workplace in broader terms. There are a few tactics that might be useful in that regard:

Draw a map. One of the first things you do should be to draw a sociophysical map of the work environment(s). Start with a floor plan: a simple line diagram of where things are within the walls. Include desks, partitions, doors, windows, copying machines, water coolers, reception areas, and so on. In a second pass at the map, indicate either or both: where major kinds of work get done; where major categories of people are located. Indicate on your physical map where people are and what goes on there. Later in the observation process, you may use the map as an *elicitation device*: sit down with the student or with some other worker, and ask questions about where things happen, what the space means.

Get the organizational chart. You need to get a mental picture of who all the players are in this environment. The organizational chart is one tool for doing that. Some organizations will have a prepared chart, showing the total hierarchy from CEO to line workers. You may start there—but understand that it usually does not represent reality perfectly; as with the map, you may use it as an elicitation device to ask people how the organization is actually structured (and what to make of the deviations from the official picture). In other places, there will be no such chart, and you will need to build one. Use knowledgeable members (probably *not* the intern) to help you construct it: Ask them to work with you on representing the structure of relations (roles, departments, hierarchies, reporting chains). They may also reveal their sense of the important figures in the organization: Who's really key to various kinds of activities.

Picture the work flow. Try to get a representation of some basic process flows—that is, charts that show the sequence of fundamental *activities* (like building a chest of drawers, or leading a museum tour, or writing a newspaper article): What do people do first, next, and finally? What results from each step in the process? You obviously won't be able to chart every single work activity; try to choose the few that (a) are central to the organization's functions, and/or (b) are engaged by the intern.

Diagram the day and week. The work flowcharts may not describe a linear sequence of time. Try to construct time-line charts that "chunk" the day: that show major context changes from time to time. For instance, the major chunks in a school day might be: (a) hanging out on the front steps before the bell rings (15 minutes); (b) homeroom (25 minutes); (c) morning classes (a series of 45-minute periods with 5-minute transitions in between); (d) lunch (30 minutes); (e) afternoon classes (another series of periods and transitions); (f) last-period activities (clubs, teams); (g) dismissal. Most workplaces have some kind of rhythmic pattern; you want to try to describe your subject's pattern in a time-line chart.

These various tools give you a more-or-less comprehensive representation of the organization: its members and their relations; its activities; its major contexts. With those in hand (they will, of course, be modified as you learn more), you can proceed to the meat of the observations.

Core Observations

During the core of the cycle, you will be observing the student-intern and other participants in the workplace. At your discretion, you may choose to pursue different strategies for conducting the observations; I think it's a good idea to use all or most of these at one time or another.

Student-oriented observations. Spend all of at least a couple of visits shadowing the student, watching and recording what she does. There are a number of questions that can guide your note-taking and questions during these sessions.

1. What kinds of *tasks* does the student undertake? What *activities* does she participate in?
   a. What are the *features* of those tasks?
      i. What are their logical-technical demands: What does one need to know and be able to do in order to complete them competently? How complex are they?
      ii. What are their *pragmatic* importance in the organization: How important are they in the production process? Do oth-

ers count on their being done? Does doing this work confer status or power on a person?

b. How are the tasks *established*?
  i. Who initiates them: the student, the supervisor, or a customer?
  ii. What is the student told about how to perform the task: coaching, instruction, reading guidelines, etc.? If the task requires some skill and/or knowledge that the student lacks, how does she get it? If it requires knowledge that the student *does* have, how is that fact determined?
  iii. What is the student told about the criteria defining good performance: quality, speed, etc?

c. How are the tasks *accomplished*?
  i. What does the student actually have to do?
  ii. Who else participates? In what capacity: supervisor, partner, or helper?
  iii. What sorts of resources do the student and others use? How are those resources made available? What's missing?

d. How are the tasks *processed*?
  i. What sort of feedback does the student get?
  ii. Who provides that feedback: the student, the supervisor, a coworker, or a customer?
  iii. Does the student have an opportunity to reflect on the performance, so it will be more effective the next time?

2. What kinds of *contexts* does the student participate in?
  a. What is the *level of intensity* of that participation?
  b. What *roles* does she play in each context: observer, helper, or performer?
  c. How does she get *access* to the contexts: supervisor invitation, coworker sponsorship, self-initiation, etc.?
  d. Are there contexts to which she cannot get access? What goes on in those?
  e. What happens in *off-task activities*: lunch, water-cooler conversations, etc.? Does the student have open access to these? Do people talk about work-related issues, skills, relationships?

In some cases, you will discover the answers to these questions simply by *watching* what the student does, with whom she interacts, and so on. At other times, you will need to *ask questions* to find the answers. Typically, you should wait for a break in the activity before posing the questions; but unless they are really disruptive, it is better to ask them as soon as you can rather than waiting until a much later time. You can simply say, "What were you doing here? How did you get assigned to that work? Where did you get such-and-such information?" Basically, though, your strategy in this element is simply to watch and listen.

Setting-oriented observations. At other times, you may choose to stay in one place or context and observe, regardless of whether the intern is present all or part of the time. The purpose here is to understand the structuring of a particular kind of event, so that you can grasp more easily the nature of work, relationships, and activities in the organization. For instance, you might want to sit in the reception area of a social agency for a couple of hours, and watch how clients are handled in that setting. Or you might want to sit in on a staff meeting, even if the intern isn't there, so you can witness the various players and their relationships in that scene, and hear formal declarations about what the organization is doing. You can ask various kinds of questions in these setting-oriented observations:

1. What *activities* are being carried out in this setting?
   a. Who are the *participants*?
   b. What *functions* are accomplished here?
   c. How is the activity organized in *time and space*?
   d. What *resources* (material, financial, informational) are being used?
2. How are activities *controlled*?
   a. Who is in charge? Who makes decisions?
   b. What implicit *rules* or customs are in effect?
3. What kinds of *knowledge* are being used here?
   a. By whom? Who has it, and who does not?
   b. Where do they get that knowledge?
   c. How do participants collaborate in knowledge-use?

Again, the basic tactic is watching and listening. You may occasionally ask questions, if the situation permits.

Process-oriented observation. Another strategy is to try to follow a complete activity from start to finish. The sequence may be represented in the process flowchart that you constructed earlier. It may take several days or weeks; or it may be completed in an hour. Tracking the evolution of the activity will help you answer certain kinds of questions:

1. How is the activity *initiated* or set in motion?
   a. *Who* initiates it? Who has that power, and who does not?
   b. *When* is it initiated: Is there a calendar or clock set off, an event, a decision?
   c. What happens when it starts: Do certain people congregate? What resources do they need at the beginning? What decisions have to be made?
2. What happens as the activity unfolds?
   a. Who gets involved? At what points? For what purposes?

    b. Can anything interrupt or derail the activity?

    c. Who controls the ongoing activity? How?

    d. What kinds of knowledge are used in the activity? By whom?

3.   How is the activity concluded?

    a. Who calls it finished? By what criteria?

    b. How is the activity evaluated or processed?

    c. What comes next?

You should, of course, pay attention to whether the intern is involved at any point in this process: When? For what purpose, or in what role? Under whose leadership or control? This analysis will help you understand the integration (or lack of it) of the intern into the ongoing activities of the site: as peripheral participant, as observer, as central actor. It will help you determine the nature of the relationships the intern has with others in the use of various forms of practical knowledge-use.

Eliciting sessions. As you conduct these various kinds of observations, you will, of course, ask pertinent questions of the participants, to try to answer the core issues you have laid out. But you may also choose to spend some of your time in focused *interviews*, in which you formally ask people questions about what you have been seeing. This kind of conversation will be most effective when you have a fair amount of data under your belt, and are capable of formulating questions that go to the heart of key issues related to the intern's learning. One way to do these interviews is to use some of your previously gathered information as *eliciting devices*.

For instance, you might ask members to elaborate, revise, or correct the *maps* and *process charts* that you constructed earlier. Finding a suitable off-time to sit down with the intern or some other person, you show her the map, and ask, "Is this right? How would you change this? What does this mean? Why is it done like that?"

You might also use your *observation notes* as elicitation devices (almost as you would if you were able to audiotape or videotape some scenes): Read a segment of your notes on a particular event, and ask questions like, "What was going on there? Why did so-and-so do such-and-such? Where did that practice come from? I saw something going on here; what did it mean?" You can also offer your own interpretations or hunches, and ask people if they think you are right: "I have a feeling Mr. A and Ms. C are competing for the boss's attention in this scene. Does that sound right to you?" You have to be careful about these expressions, because you can sound biased or stupid—but if your relationship with the respondent is solid, that may not be disastrous.

Given the fact that you will make, at best, five 4-hour visits to each internship site, I suspect that this list of strategies is long enough to keep you busy, and that doing these things will generate a great deal of data about the student's experience in the workplace.

Technical Hints: Taking and Recording Notes, Doing Interviews, Collecting Artifacts

Finally, let me say a few words about the technical elements of gathering data by these methods. I have been talking primarily about kinds of questions to ask. They certainly imply particular kinds of data-collecting techniques, but I want to clarify a couple of points about them.

Taking Notes

For the sake of consistency and the ease of comparing data on different sites from different fieldworkers, I suggest that you devise a common strategy for formatting your fieldnotes. You will develop personal styles in recording and observing, but it will help if the notes are at least laid out in one way. You may opt for another method, but let me propose one possibility.

Note-taking on-site. While you are actually doing the observations, you may choose to write brief notes to yourself either on 3 × 5 cards or on a writing tablet. Depending on the capacity of your memory (mine is a sieve!), you will need a greater or lesser quantity of notes. In general, you should write down enough so that, when you sit down immediately after the visit to flesh them out, you can remember what they mean; you want to use the on-site rough notes as reminders that help you reconstruct the scene or conversation in greater detail. You should take just enough notes for that purpose. Don't take so many that you are looking down and writing most of the time; just scribble a few key words, then get back to watching and listening. (This skill is common among newspaper reporters; look at their notepads.) And don't take notes at moments when members of the scene would find it distracting or annoying. Make sure you keep the rough sheets in order; number them so you can put them in sequence if you drop them all!

Writing the fieldnotes. As soon as possible after you leave the site, you should sit down and type out the notes in an elaborated format. The content of the notes will vary depending on the type of observation or interview you did. But I have found that it helps to organize the notes in a way suggested by Schatzman and Strauss. They divide fieldnotes into three principal categories:

1. ONs: Observational Notes
   a. Ground-level descriptions of what happened: "He said, she said. . . ."
   b. As close to a verbal videotape as possible: minimize the interpretation or judgment; just say what you saw and heard.
2. TNs: Theoretical Notes
   a. First-cut interpretations of things going on in the ONs: "I think there was a power struggle going on between A and B in this scene. Why would they be doing that?"

      b. Interspersed among the ONs, reflecting on specific events, relationships, etc.

  3. MNs: Methodological Notes

      a. Reminders to yourself to do something: "Don't forget to ask A about this event. . . . Be sure to get a copy of the memo. . . . Get permission to attend a staff meeting."

      b. May elaborate somewhat on the reasons for doing this extra thing.

The vast bulk of the notes, especially toward the beginning of your observations, will be ONs. As you begin to see patterns, formulate hunches, and generate more elaborate interpretations, you will do more and more TNs. MNs are always useful; be sure to follow through on them.

Format. If you choose this format, you will write separate sections for each type of note. It helps, too, to have a *hanging indent* format for each section, so you can clearly see where the ONs finish and the TNs start. For example:

ON: AG and her supervisor sat down in the office for a conversation about the work she had done on the booklet. First the supervisor read the opening page, and then she made a couple of critical comments. . . .

TN: This episode may represent a classic case of the teaching-at-work process. The supervisor had some clear criteria in mind, and laid them out to the student. . . .

Another point: You should *number the lines* in all your notes—this can be done automatically with a program like The Ethnograph; WordPerfect and Microsoft Word both have line-numbering features, as well. This way you can refer to segments of the notes clearly and consistently.

For the same reason, you should devise a way of *titling* the fieldnotes. One way would be to assign each site a Roman numeral, then give each field visit an Arabic number. So if County Hospital was site number 7, and the current notes were on the fifth visit, and you wanted to refer to lines 101–110 in that set, you would say vii: 7: 101–110.

The headings of the fieldnotes ought to be consistent, too, and should provide summary information about the context, including the people referred to in the notes (by initials); they might look like this:

Site #	vii: County Hospital
Visit #	7
Date	November 12, 1996
Time	9 A.M.–1 P.M.
By	Kathy Hughes
Overview	Observation of student working on a brochure

Cast: AM = intern
       BN = supervisor
       CS = director of planning
       DM = computer specialist . . .

Analytic Memos (AMs)

As your TNs accumulate, you may start seeing recurrent themes or problems in them. At that point, you can start writing Analytic Memos to yourself (and your colleagues): short (1–2 pp.) essays pulling together the several incidents and TNs relevant to a given problem. For instance, you may discover that the intern frequently gets frustrated because she's asked to do things that she's not prepared to do, and no one can help her; it would be worth writing a memo on Establishing Tasks, examining the way people in this organization do or do not collaborate, or the way knowledge is distributed to newcomers. As the team evolves, you may discover that you want to assign common AM themes to yourselves, to look at problems across sites. In that case, each researcher would draw on her several site experiences to analyze the phenomenon of interest, then compare notes with the others. You might find commonalities, or you might find marked differences. Here is where the sampling of sites and subjects might come in handy: You might discover, for instance, that female students in all sorts of sites keep having a similar experience, or that different kinds of settings treat older students differently.

Interviews

There will be several forms of interviews, ranging from spontaneous and informal to planned and formal. Some will be done during the observations on-site, and some will be done in the schools. Some will be recorded only in after-the-fact notes, like observations; some may be tape-recorded. The point here is not to insist on one and only one strategy, but to raise some issues that will help you decide which format is most useful and appropriate.

- What is the *purpose* of the interview? Are you trying to elicit extensive information about the organization's history or functioning? Are you simply trying to understand a person's reaction to a specific event?
- How much *time* is the interview likely to take? A two-minute chat is very different from an hour-long conversation.
- How *sensitive* or difficult is the material likely to be to the respondent? Is s/he likely to be uncomfortable talking about the subject?
- How important is it that you capture the respondent's *exact words*? Is it necessary only to get the gist of the talk?

- Are you going to try to *compare* this person's responses with someone else's?

Informal conversations done during site visits can simply be treated as segments of the fieldnotes. More formal conversations, especially those with preplanned questions (protocols), should be written separately. The format can be parallel to that for the fieldnotes, except with initials indicating the speaker (AM: student; KH: Kathy Hughes) rather than ON, TN and MN. The lines should be numbered, and the page should have a heading, something like this:

Site #	vii—County Hospital
Interview #	14—CD (supervisor)
Topic	Intern's responsibilities
Date	November 26, 1996

Storage

Fieldnotes, interview transcripts, and assorted artifacts (memos, brochures, organization charts, etc.) should be stored in hard copy in files: one section for each site, with fieldnotes in one file, interviews in a second, and other materials in a third.

Ideally, the notes will also be stored on computer disks, in a single format. I recommend looking into something like The Ethnograph, a software program for the storage, organization, and retrieval of qualitative data like fieldnotes and interview transcripts. At the very least, The Ethnograph creates a very useful format for the notes: 40-character-wide lines, each numbered, leaving room for comments in the margins as well as line references.

Analytic memos can be stored in another file, either within the section for a specific site or in a more general category, transcending sites, depending on its content.

You should start *indexing* fieldnotes and interview transcripts as soon as you can. That means identifying various sections as being *about* some particular issue or phenomenon. The Ethnograph actually works on the basis of a self-defined system of categories or codes, so each line may be assigned up to 12 codes; then when you want to retrieve all the segments of the various notes relevant to that category, the system simply pulls them up and prints them. If you don't want to do that computer-based coding, you can simply write categorical descriptions of the various notes, so you can retrieve them more efficiently than memory alone will allow.

There are bound to be more issues in your methods and strategies than I have covered here. I hope this guide orients you at least to some extent to the practices and problems of the ethnographer.

References

Academy for Educational Development (1995). *Academy of travel and tourism: 1993–4 evaluation report*. New York: Author.

Anderson, J. R., L. M. Reder, & H. A. Simon (1996, May). Situated learning and education. *Educational Researcher, 25*(4), 511.

Applebaum, H., Ed. (1984). *Work in market and industrial societies*. Albany, NY: SUNY Press.

Appelbaum, E., & R. Batt (1994). *The new American workplace: Transforming work systems in the United States*. Ithaca, NY: ILR Press.

Arthur, M. B., D. T. Hall, & B. S. Lawrence, Eds. (1989). *Handbook of career theory*. New York: Cambridge University Press.

Attewell, P. (1990). What is skill? *Work and Occupations, 17*, 422–448.

Bailey, T. R. (1993). Can youth apprenticeship thrive in the United States? *Educational Researcher, 22*, 4–10.

———, Ed. (1995a). *Learning to work: Employer involvement in school-to-work transition programs*. Washington, D.C.: The Brookings Institution.

——— (1995b). Incentives for employer participation in school-to-work programs. In T. R. Bailey, Ed., *Learning to work: Employer involvement in school-to-work transition programs* (pp. 14–25). Washington, D.C.: The Brookings Institution.

Bailey, T. R., & D. Merritt (1997a). *School-to-work for the college bound* (MDS-799). Berkeley: National Center for Research in Vocational Education, University of California at Berkeley.

——— (1997b). Industry skill standards and education reform. *American Journal of Education, 105*, 401–436.

Bailey, T. R., K. L. Hughes, & T. Barr (2000). Achieving scale and quality in school-to-work internships: Findings from two employer surveys. *Educational Evaluation and Policy Analysis, 22*(1), 41–64.

Baizerman, M. (1994, June). *The call of vocation, work, and healthy youth development*. Proposal to the Lilly Foundation. Minneapolis: University of Minnesota.

Baizerman, M., & D. Magnuson (n.d.). *What does it mean to build character?* St. Paul, MN: College of St. Catherine.

Bassi, L., & J. Ludwig (2000). School-to-work programs in the United States: A multifirm case study of training, benefits, and costs. *Industrial and Labor Relations Review, 53*, 219–239.

Behn, W. H., M. Carnoy, M. A. Carter, J. C. Crain, & H. M. Levin (1974, November). School is bad; Work is worse. *School Review*, 49–68.

Belenky, M. F., B. McV. Clinchy, N. R. Goldberger, & J. M. Tarule (1997). *Women's ways of knowing: The development of self, voice, and mind*. New York: Basic Books.

Benson, P. L., & R. N. Saito (n.d.). The scientific foundations of youth development. *Youth Development: Issues, Challenges, and Directions*, 125–148. Philadelphia: Public/Private Ventures.

Bereiter, C., & M. Scardamalia (1993). *Surpassing ourselves: An inquiry into the nature and implications of expertise*. Chicago: Open Court.

Bernstein, B. (1975). *Class, codes and control: Vol.3. Towards a theory of educational transmission*. London: Routledge & Kegan Paul.

Berryman, S. E., & T. R. Bailey (1992). *The double helix of education and the economy*. New York: Institute on Education and the Economy, Teachers College, Columbia University.

Bloom, B. (1956). *Taxonomy of educational objectives: The classification of educational goals— Handbook 1: The cognitive domain*. New York: Longman.

Blumer, H. (1969). *Symbolic interactionism*. Englewood Cliffs, NJ: Prentice-Hall.

Blustein, D. L., & D. A. Noumair (1996). Self and identity in career development: Implications for theory and practice. *Journal of Counseling and Development, 74*, 433–442.

Bottoms, G., & A. Presson (n.d.). *Work-based learning: Good news, bad news, and hope*. (Research Brief No. 7). Atlanta: Southern Regional Education Board.

Boud, D., R. Cohen, & D. Walker (1993). *Using experience for learning*. Buckingham, England: Society for Research into Higher Education and Open University Press.

Brown, A., M. J. Kane, & C. Long (1989). Analogical transfer in young children: Analogies as tools for communication and exposition. *Applied Cognitive Psychology, 3*, 275–293.

Brown, J. S., A. Collins, & P. Duguid (1989). Situated cognition and the culture of learning. *Educational Researcher, 18*, 32–42.

Bruner, J. S. (1966). *Toward a theory of instruction*. New York: W.W. Norton.

———— (1975). *Beyond the information given*. New York: Basic Books.

———— (1977). *The process of education*. Cambridge: Harvard University Press.

———— (1981). The social context of language acquisition. *Language and Communication, 1*, 155–178.

———— (1996). Frames for thinking: Ways of making meaning. In D. R. Olson & N. Torrance, Eds., *Modes of thought: Explorations in culture and cognition*. New York: Cambridge University Press.

Cahill, M., & L. Pitts (1997). *Strengthening youth employment prospects through youth development*. New York: Youth Development Institute, Fund for the City of New York.

Cappelli, P., D. Shapiro, & N. Shumanis (1998). *Employer participation in school-to-work programs*. University of Pennsylvania: National Center on the Educational Quality of the Workforce.

Chi, M. T. H., R. Glaser, & M. J. Farr (Eds.). (1988). *The nature of expertise*. Hillsdale, NJ: Lawrence Erlbaum Associates.

Cherryholmes, C. (1991). *Power and criticism*. New York: Teachers College Press.

Clausen, J. S. (1991). Adolescent competence and the shaping of the life course. *American Journal of Sociology, 96*, 805–842.

Cole, M., J. Gay, J. A. Glick, & D. W. Sharp (1971). *The cultural context of learning and thinking: An exploration in experimental anthropology*. New York: Basic Books.

Cole, M., L. Hood, & R. P. McDermott (1978). *Ecological niche-picking: Ecological invalidity as an axiom of experimental cognitive psychology*. New York: Rockefeller University.

Cole, M., & B. Means (1986). *Comparative studies of how people think*. Cambridge: Harvard University Press.

Coleman, J. S. (1974). *Youth: Transition to adulthood*. Report of the Panel on Youth of the President's Science Advisory Committee. Chicago: University of Chicago Press.

Commission on the Skills of the American Workforce (1990). *America's choice: High skills or low wages!* Rochester, NY: National Center on Education and the Economy.

Corson, W., & M. Silverberg (1994). *The school-to-work/youth apprenticeship demonstration: Preliminary findings*. Princeton, NJ: Mathematica Policy Research, Inc.

Costello, J., M. Toles, J. Spielberger, & J. Wynn (n.d.). History, ideology and structure shape the organizations that shape youth. *Youth development: Issues, challenges, and directions*, 185–232. Philadelphia: Public/Private Ventures.

Darrah, C. N. (1996). *Learning and work: An exploration in industrial ethnography*. New York: Garland Press.

———— (1994). Skill requirements at work: Rhetoric versus reality. *Work and Occupations, 21*, 64–85.

Dertouzos, M., R. Lester, & R. Solow (1989). *Made in America: Regaining the productive edge.* Cambridge: MIT Press.

Descartes, R. (1960). Discourse on method. In M. C. Beardsley, Ed., *The European philosophers from Descartes to Nietzsche.* New York: The Modern Library.

Dewey, J. (1910). *How we think.* Boston: D.C. Heath.

――― (1933/1964). Why reflective thinking must be an educational aim. In R. D. Archambault, Ed., *John Dewey on education: Selected writings* (pp. 212–228). Chicago: University of Chicago Press.

――― (1938). *Experience and education.* New York: Collier Books.

Dryfoos, J. G. (1990). *Adolescents at risk: Prevalence and prevention.* New York: Oxford University Press.

Durkheim, E. (1915). *The elementary forms of religious life.* New York: The Free Press.

Erikson, E. H. (1968). *Identity: Youth and crisis.* New York: W.W. Norton.

Eyler, J., & D. E. Giles Jr. (1999). *Where's the learning in service-learning?* San Francisco: Jossey-Bass.

Fetterman, D. M. (1989). *Ethnography: Step by step.* Newbury Park, CA: Sage Publications.

Finch, M. T., M. J. Shanahan, J. T. Mortimer, & S. Ryu (1991). Work experience and control orientation in adolescence. *American Sociological Review, 56,* 597–611.

Foothill Associates (1997, summer). *California partnership academies: 1995–6 evaluation report.* Nevada City, CA: Author.

Glaser, M., R. Chi, M. Farr, & R. Glaser, Eds. (1988). *The nature of expertise.* Hillsdale, NJ: Lawrence Erlbaum.

Glaser, R., & M. T. H. Chi (1988). Overview. In M. T. H. Chi, R. Glaser, & M. J. Farr, Eds., *The nature of expertise* (pp. xv–xxviii). Hillsdale, NJ: Lawrence Erlbaum Associates.

Goodenough, W. (1957). Cultural anthropology and linguistics. In P. L. Gavin, Ed., *Report on the 7th annual roundtable meetings on linguistics and language study* (pp. 167–173). Georgetown University Monograph Series on Language and Linguistics (Vol. 9). Washington, D.C.: Georgetown University.

Greenberger, E. (1988). Working in teenage America. In J. T. Mortimer & K. M. Borman, Eds., *Work experience and psychological development* (pp. 221–250). Boulder, CO: Westview Press.

Greenberger, E., & L. Steinberg (1986). *When teenagers work: The psychological and social costs of adolescent employment.* New York: Basic Books.

Grubb, W. N., Ed. (1995a). *Education through occupations in American high schools. Vol 1. Approaches to integrating academic and vocational education.* New York: Teachers College Press.

――― (1995b). *Education through occupations in American high schools. Vol 2. The challenges of implementing curriculum integration.* New York: Teachers College Press.

Habermas, J. (1971). *Knowledge and human interests* (J. J. Shapiro, Trans.). Boston: Beacon Press.

Hamada, T., & W. E. Sibley, Eds. (1994). *Anthropological perspectives on organizational culture.* Lanham, MD: University Press of America.

Hamilton, S. F. (1989). *Learning on the job: Apprentices in West Germany.* Paper prepared for the annual meetings of the American Educational Research Association, Boston.

――― (1990). *Apprenticeship for adulthood.* New York: Free Press.

Hamilton, M. A., & S. F. Hamilton (1997). *Learning well at work: Choices for quality.* Ithaca, NY: Cornell University Press.

Hammersley, M., & Atkinson, P. (1983). *Ethnography: Principles in practice.* New York: Tavistock Publications.

Hanks, W. F. (1991). Foreword. In J. Lave & E. Wenger, Eds., *Situated learning.* New York: Cambridge University Press.

Hanser, L., & C. Stasz (1999). *The effects of enrollment in the transportation career academy program on student outcomes.* Paper prepared for the 1999 meeting of the American Educational Research Association. Santa Monica, CA: RAND Corporation.

Hatton, N., & D. Smith (1995). Reflection in teacher education: Towards definition and implementation. *Teaching and Teacher Education, 11*(1), 33–49.

Herndon, J. (1971). *How to survive in your native land.* New York: Simon & Schuster.

Hershey, A. M., P. Hudis, M. Silverberg, & J. Haimson (1997, April). *Partners in progress: Early steps in creating school-to-work systems.* Washington, D.C.: U.S. Department of Education Planning and Evaluation Service.

Hershey, A. M., & M. Silverberg (1993). *Employer involvement in school-to-work transition programs: What can we really expect?* Princeton, NJ: Mathematica Policy Research, Inc.

Hershey, A. M., M. K. Silverberg, J. Haimson, P. Hudis, & R. Jackson (1999, February). *Expanding options for students: Report to Congress on the national evaluation of school-to-work implementation.* Princeton, NJ: Mathematica Policy Research, Inc.

Hoffman, R. R., Ed. (1992). *The psychology of expertise: Cognitive research and empirical AI.* New York: Springer-Verlag.

Hollenbeck, K. (1996). *An evaluation of the manufacturing technology partnership (MTP) program.* (Upjohn Institute Technical Report No. 96–007). Kalamazoo, MI: The W. E. Upjohn Institute for Employment Research.

Hughes, K. L. (1998). *Employer recruitment is not the problem: A study of school-to-work transition programs.* (IEE Working Paper No. 5). New York: Institute on Education and the Economy, Teachers College, Columbia University.

Hughes, K. L., T. R. Bailey, & M. J. Mechur (2001). *School-to-work: Making a difference in education. A research report to America.* New York: Institute on Education and the Economy, Teachers College, Columbia University.

Hutchins, E. (1993). Learning to navigate. In S. Chaiklin & J. Lave, Eds., *Understanding Practice: Perspectives on activity and context* (pp. 35–63). New York: Cambridge University Press.

Inkster, R. P., & R. G. Ross (1995). *The Internship as partnership: A handbook for campus-based coordinators and advisors.* Raleigh, NC: National Society for Experiential Education.

James, W. (1983). *Talks to teachers and students about psychology.* Cambridge: Harvard University Press.

Jobs for the Future (1994). *Revitalizing high schools: What the school-to-career movement can contribute.* Washington, D.C.: American Youth Policy Forum, Jobs for the Future and the National Association of Secondary School Principals.

Jobs for the Future and Academy for Educational Development (n.d.). *School-to-work and youth development: Identifying common ground. An agenda for action.* Boston: Jobs for the Future.

Johnson, J., S. Farkas, & A. Bers (1997). *Getting by: What American teenagers really think about their schools.* New York: Public Agenda.

Kazis, R., & S. Goldberger (1995). The role of employers: The integration of work-based learning. In W. N. Grubb, Ed., *Education through occupations in American high schools. Volume 2: The challenges of implementing curriculum integration* (pp. 171–190). New York: Teachers College Press.

Kegan, R. (1982). *The evolving self: Problem and process in human development.* Cambridge: Harvard University Press.

——— (1983). A neo-Piagetian approach to object relations. In B. Lee & G. G. Noam, Eds., *Developmental approaches to the self,* (pp. 267–308). New York: Plenum.

Keller, C., & J. D. Keller (1993). Thinking and acting with iron. In S. Chaiklin & J. Lave, Eds., *Understanding practice: Perspectives on activity and context* (pp.125–143). New York: Cambridge University Press.

Kemple, J. (1997). *Communities of support for students and teachers: Emerging findings from a 10-site evaluation.* New York: Manpower Demonstration Research Corporation.

Kemple, J. J., S. Poglinco, & J. C. Snipes (1999). *Career academies: Building career awareness and work-based learning activities through employer partnerships.* New York: Manpower Demonstration Research Corporation.

Kemple, J. & J. C. Snipes (2000). *Career academies: Impacts on students' engagement and performance in high school.* New York: Manpower Demonstration Research Corporation.

Klein, S. G. (1995). *Employer incentives to participate in a national school-to-work initiative.* A paper prepared for the National Assessment of Vocational Education. Berkeley, CA: MPR Associates, Inc.

Kleiner, B. & C. Chapman (2000, March). *Youth service-learning and community service among 6th-through 12th-grade students in the United States: 1996 and 1999.* (NCES 2000–028). Washington, DC: National Center for Education Statistics, Office of Educational Research and Improvement, U.S. Department of Education.

Kohlberg, L. (1981). *The meaning and measurement of moral development.* Worcester, MA: Clark University Heinz Warner Institute.

Kohlberg, L. & R. Mayer (1972). Development as the aim of education. *Harvard Educational Review, 42,* 449–496.

Kolb, D. (1984). *Experiential learning.* Englewood Cliffs, NJ: Prentice-Hall.

Kopp, H., R. Kazis, & A. Churchill (1995). *Promising practices: A study of ten school-to-career programs.* Executive Summary. Boston: Jobs for the Future.

Kusterer, K. (1978). *Know-how on the job: The important working knowledge of unskilled workers.* Boulder, CO: Westview Press.

Lave, J. (1988). *Cognition in practice.* New York: Cambridge University Press.

Lave, J., & E. Wenger (1991). *Situated learning: Legitimate peripheral participation.* New York: Cambridge University Press.

Lazerson, M., & W. N. Grubb (1974). *American education and vocationalism: A documentary history 1870–1970.* New York: Teachers College Press.

Lerman, R., & H. Pouncy (1990, fall). The compelling case for youth apprenticeships. *The Public Interest,* 62–77.

Levy-Bruhl, L. (1910/1966). *How natives think.* New York: Washington Square Press.

Linnehan, F. (2001). The relation of a work-based mentoring program to the academic performance and behavior of African-American students. *Journal of Vocational Behavior* 59(3), 310–325.

Locke, J. (1690/1996). *An essay concerning human understanding* (Rev. Ed.). New York: Hackett.

Luria, A. R. (1976). *Cognitive development: Its cultural and social foundations.* Cambridge, MA: Harvard University Press.

Lyceum Group (1998). *The work keys system.* Concord, MA: Author.

Lynn, I., & J. Wills (1994). *School lessons work lessons: Recruiting and sustaining employer involvement in school-to-work programs.* Washington, D.C.: Institute on Educational Leadership.

MacDonald, G. B., & R. Valdivieso (n.d.). Measuring deficits and assets: How we track youth development now, and how we should track it. *Youth Development: Issues, Challenges, and Directions,* 149–184. Philadelphia: Public/Private Ventures.

Magnuson, D., & M. Baizerman (1996). *The call to commitment: A report on YouthWorks Americorps.* St. Paul, MN: College of St. Catherine.

Magoon, A. J. (1977). Constructivist approaches in educational research. *Review of Educational Research, 47*(4), 651–693.

Marcus, H., & P. Nurius (1986). Possible selves. *American Psychologist, 41*(9), 954–969.

Marsh, H. W. (1991). Employment during high school: Character building or a subversion of academic goals? *Sociology of Education, 64,* 172–189.

Martin, J. (1992). *Cultures in organizations: Three perspectives.* New York: Oxford University Press.

Maxwell, N. L., & V. Rubin (1997). *The relative impact of a career academy on post-secondary work and education skills in urban, public high schools.* Hayward, CA: The Human Investment Research and Education Center.

Mead, M. (1928). *Coming of age in America.* New York: William Morrow.

Moore, D. T. (1981a). Discovering the pedagogy of experience. *Harvard Educational Review, 51*(2), 286–300.

———— (1981b). *The social organization of educational encounters in non-school settings.* Washington, D.C.: National Institute of Education.

———— (1986). Knowledge at work: An approach to learning by interns. In K. Borman & J. Reisman, Eds., *Becoming a worker* (pp. 116–139). Norwood, NJ: Ablex Publishing.

———— (1990). Experiential education as critical discourse. In J. Kendall (Ed.), *Combining service and learning: Vol. 1.* (pp.273–283). Raleigh, NC: National Society for Experiential Education.

———— (1994). Changing images of work and work organization. *Quarterly Newsletter of the National Society for Experiential Education.* Part 1: Fall 1994, Vol. 20, No. 1; Part 2: Winter 1995: Vol. 20, No. 2.

———— (1999). *Toward a theory of work-based learning.* (IEE Brief Number 23). New York: Institute on Education and the Economy, Teachers College, Columbia University.

Morest, V. S. (forthcoming). *Transferability of occupational two-year degrees and certificates.* New York: Community College Research Center, Teachers College, Columbia University.

Mortimer, J. T., & M. D. Finch (1986). The effects of part-time work on adolescent self-concept and achievement. In K. M. Borman & J. Reisman, Eds., *Becoming a worker* (pp. 66–89). Norwood, NJ: Ablex Publishing.

Mortimer, J. T., & C. Yamoor (1987). Interrelations and parallels of school and work as sources of psychological development. In R. G. Corwin, Ed., *Research in the sociology of education and socialization: Vol. 7* (pp. 221–246). Greenwich, CT: JAI Press.

Mortimer, J. T., & M. K. Johnson (1997). *Adolescent work and the transition to adulthood.* Paper presented at the 1997 Annual Meeting of the American Sociological Association, Toronto.

Mortimer, J.T., C. Harley, & P. J. Aronson (1999). How do prior experiences in the workplace set the stage for transitions to adulthood? In A. Booth, A. C. Crouter, & M. J. Shanahan, Eds., *Transitions to adulthood in a changing economy: No work, no family, no future?* (pp. 131–159). Westport, CT: Praeger.

Munby, H., P. Chin, & N. Hutchinson (2000, April). *Co-operative education, the curriculum, and "working knowledge."* Paper presented at the 1st Internationalization of Curriculum Conference, Baton Rouge, LA: Louisiana State University.

National Academy of Sciences (1998). *Protecting youth at work: Health, safety, and development of working children and adolescents in the United States.* Washington, D.C.: National Academy Press.

National Center for Education Statistics (1998). *Digest of education statistics 1997.* Table 382. Washington, D.C.: U.S. Department of Education.

National Commission on Excellence in Education (1983). *A nation at risk.* Washington, D.C.: U.S. Department of Education.

New Standards (1997). *Performance Standards: Volume 3—high school.* Washington D.C.: NCEE and LRDC.

Oatley, K. (1996). Inference in narrative and science. In D. R. Olson & N. Torrance, Eds., *Modes of thought: Explorations in culture and cognition* (pp. 123–140). New York: Cambridge University Press.

Office of Technology Assessment (1995). *Learning to work: Making the transition from school to work.* Washington, D.C.: GPO.

Olson, D. R. (1996). Introduction. In D. R. Olson & N. Torrance, Eds., *Modes of thought: Explorations in culture and cognition* (pp. 1–14). New York: Cambridge University Press.

Olson, L. (1997). *The school-to-work revolution: How employers and educators are joining forces to prepare tomorrow's skilled workforce.* Reading, MA: Addison-Wesley.

Orr, M. T. (1996). *Wisconsin youth apprenticeship program in printing: Evaluation, 1993–1994.* Boston: Jobs for the Future.

Osterman, P. (1980). *Getting started: The youth labor market.* Cambridge: MIT Press.

——— (1995). Involving employers in school-to-work programs. In T. R. Bailey, Ed., *Learning to work: Employer involvement in school-to-work transition programs* (pp. 75–87). Washington, D.C.: The Brookings Institution.

Parsons, T. (1954). *Essays in sociological theory.* New York: Free Press.

Pauly, E., H. Kopp, & J. Haimson (1995). *Home-grown lessons: Innovative programs linking work and school.* San Francisco: Jossey-Bass Publishers.

Pea, R. D. (1993). Practices of distributed intelligence and designs for education. In G. Salomon, Ed., *Distributed cognitions: Psychological and educational considerations* (pp. 47–87). New York: Cambridge University Press.

Perkins, D. N. (1993). Person-plus: A distributed view of thinking and learning. In G. Salomon, Ed., *Distributed cognitions: Psychological and educational considerations* (pp. 88–110). New York: Cambridge University Press.

Perkins, D. N., & G. Salomon (1989, January–February). Are cognitive skills context-bound? *Educational Researcher*,16–25.

Philadelphia, School District of (1998). *Learning plans—Rationale.* Philadelphia: Office of Education for Employment.

Phillips, S. D., & N. J. Pazienza (1988). History and theory of the assessment of career development and decision making. In W. B. Walsh & S. H. Osipow, Eds., *Career decision making* (pp. 1–31). Hillsdale, NJ: Lawrence Erlbaum Associates.

Piaget, J. (1967). *Six psychological studies.* New York: Random House.

Pilcher, W. W. (1984). The Portland Longshoreman. In H. Applebaum (Ed.), *Work in market and industrial societies* (pp. 120–129). Albany, NY: SUNY Press.

Pittman, K., M. Irby, & T. Ferber (n.d.). Unfinished business: Further reflections on a decade of promoting youth development. *Youth Development: Issues, Challenges, and Directions* (pp. 17–64). Philadelphia: Public/Private Ventures.

Plato (1984). Great dialogues of Plato. (W.H.D. Rouse, Trans.). New York: New American Library.

Powell, G., E. Farrar, & D. K. Cohen (1985). *The shopping mall high school: Winners and losers in the educational marketplace.* Boston: Houghton Mifflin.

Public/Private Ventures (n.d.). Introduction and Overview. *Youth development: Issues, challenges, and directions* (pp. 7–16). Philadelphia: Author.

Raizen, S. A. (1989). *Reforming education for work: A cognitive science perspective.* Berkeley: National Center for Research in Vocational Education, University of California at Berkeley.

Resnick, L. (1987). Learning in school and out. *Educational Researcher 16*(9), 13–20.

Resnick, L. B., J. M. Levine, & S. D. Teasley, Eds. (1991). *Perspectives on socially shared cognition.* Washington, D.C.: American Psychological Association.

Rivera-Batiz, F. L. (2000, December). *The impact of school-to-work programs on minority youth.* Paper presented for the national invitational conference, What Do We Know About School-to-Work: Research and Practice, Philadelphia: Temple University Center for Research in Human Development and Education.

Rogoff, B., & J. Lave, Eds. (1984). *Everyday cognition.* Cambridge: Harvard University Press.

Rosenbaum, J. (1997, August). *Unrealistic plans and misdirected efforts: Are community colleges getting the right message to high school students?* (Community College Research Center Brief No. 4). New York: Institute on Education and the Economy, Teachers College, Columbia University.

Ross, C. E., & B. A. Broh (2000). The roles of self-esteem and the sense of personal control in the academic achievement process. *Sociology of Education, 73*, 270–284.

Salomon, G. (1993a). Editor's introduction. In Salomon, G., Ed., *Distributed cognitions: Psychological and educational considerations.* New York: Cambridge University Press.

Salomon, G., Ed. (1993b). *Distributed cognitions: Psychological and educational considerations.* New York: Cambridge University Press.

Schatzman, L., & A. L. Strauss (1973). *Field research: Strategies for a natural sociology.* Englewood Cliffs, NJ: Prentice-Hall.

Schmidt, T. (1999, March). School-to-work: Past and future. *National Conference of State Legislators Legisbrief 7*(16). Washington, D.C.: National Conference of State Legislators.

Schneider, B. (1994). Thinking about an occupation: A new developmental and contextual perspective. In A. M. Pallas, Ed., *Research in Sociology of Education and Socialization, Vol. 10.* (pp. 239–259). Greenwich, CT: JAI Press.

Scribner, S. (1986). Thinking in action: Some characteristics of practical thought. In R. J. Sternberg & R. K. Wagner, Eds., *Practical intelligence: Nature and origins of competence in the everyday world* (pp. 13–30). New York: Cambridge University Press.

Schoenhals, M., Tienda, M., & Schneider, B. (1998). The educational and personal consequences of adolescent employment. *Social Forces, 77*(2), 723–762.

Schön, D. A. (1990). *Educating the reflective practitioner.* San Francisco: Jossey-Bass.

Secretary's Commission on Achieving Necessary Skills (SCANS) (1991). *What work requires of schools.* Washington, D.C.: U.S. Department of Labor.

Shapiro, D. (1999, January). *School-to-work partnerships and employer participation: Evidence on persistence and attrition from the National Employer Survey.* Philadelphia: Institute for Research on Higher Education, University of Pennsylvania.

Shapiro, D., & M. Iannozzi (1998, September). Benefits to bridging work and school. *Annals of the American Academy of Political and Social Science, 559*, 157–166.

Simon, R. I., D. Dippo, & A. Schenke (1991). *Learning work: A critical pedagogy of work education.* New York: Bergin and Garvey.

Skinner, B. F. (1965). *Science and human behavior.* New York: Free Press.

———— (1972). *Beyond freedom and dignity.* New York: Bantam.

Spenner, K. I. (1990). Skill: Meanings, methods and measures. *Work and Occupations, 17*(4), 399–421.

Spradley, J. P. (1972). *Culture and cognition: Rules, maps and plans.* San Francisco: Chandler.

Stanton, T., & K. Ali (1987). *The experienced hand: A student manual for making the most of an internship* (2nd Ed.). Cranston, RI: Carroll Press.

Stasz, C. (1999). *Students' perceptions of their work-based learning experiences: A comparison of four programs.* Paper prepared for the annual meeting of the American Educational Research Association, Montreal, Quebec.

Stasz, C., & D. J. Brewer (1998a). Work-based learning: Student perspectives on quality and links to school. *Educational Evaluation and Policy Analysis, 20*(1), 31–46.

———— (1998b). *Academic skills at work: Two perspectives.* (MDS-1193). Berkeley, CA: National Center for Research in Vocational Education.

Stasz, C., & T. Kaganoff (1997). *Learning how to learn at work: Lessons from three high school programs.* (MDS-916). Berkeley, CA: National Center for Research in Vocational Education. (RP-667). Santa Monica, CA: RAND Corporation.

Steinberg, A. (1998). *Real learning, real work: School-to-work as high-school reform.* New York: Routledge.

Steinberg, L. (1996). *Beyond the classroom: Why school reform has failed and what parents need to do.* New York: Simon & Schuster.

Stern, D., McMillion, M., & C. Hopkins (1990). *Work experience for students in high school and college.* Berkeley, CA: National Center for Research in Vocational Education.

Stern, D. (1992). *School-to-work programs and services in secondary schools and two-year public post-secondary institutions: Findings from the National Assessment of Vocational Education Survey.* Berkeley, CA: School of Education, University of California.

Stern, D. (1995). Employer options for participation in school-to-work programs. In T. R. Bailey, Ed., *Learning to work: Employer involvement in school-to-work transition programs* (pp. 45–55). Washington, D.C.: The Brookings Institution.

Stern, D., N. Finkelstein, J. R. Stone III, J. Latting, & C. Dornsife (1995). *School-to-work: Research on programs in the United States.* Washington, D.C.: Falmer Press.

Stern, D., J. Stone III, C. Hopkins, M. McMillion, & R. Crain (1994). *School-based enterprise: Productive learning in American high schools.* San Francisco: Jossey-Bass.

Stern, D., N. Finkelstein, M. Urquiola, & H. Cagampang (1997). What difference does it make if school and work are connected? Evidence on co-operative education in the United States. *Economics of Education Review, 16*(3), 213–229.

Stern, D., & D. Briggs (1999). *Competition or complementary between work and school: Some insights from high school students.* Paper prepared for the annual meeting of the American Educational Research Association, Montreal, Quebec.

Stern, D., & D. Briggs (2001). Does paid employment help or hinder performance in secondary school? Insights from U.S. high school students. *Journal of Education and Work 14*(3), 355–372.

Stern, D., D. Dayton, & M. Raby (2000, October). *Career academies: Building blocks for reconstructing American high schools.* Manuscript. Berkeley: University of California.

Sternberg, R. J. (1986). Introduction: The nature and scope of practical intelligence. In R. J. Sternberg & R. K. Wagner (Eds.), *Practical intelligence: Nature and origins of competence in the everyday world* (pp. 1–12). New York: Cambridge University Press.

Stone, J. R. III, & J. T. Mortimer (1998). The effect of adolescent employment on vocational development: Public and educational policy implications. *Journal of Vocational Behavior, 53,* 184–214.

Suchman, L. A., & R. H. Trigg (1993). Artificial intelligence as craftwork. In S. Chaiklin & J. Lave, Eds., *Understanding practice: Perspectives on activity and context* (pp. 144–178). New York: Cambridge University Press.

Super, D. E. (1957). *The psychology of careers.* New York: Harper and Row.

Sweitzer, H. F., & M. A. King (1999). *The successful internship: Transformation and empowerment.* Pacific Grove, CA: Brooks/Cole Publishing.

Thomas, J. W. (2000). *A review of research on project-based learning.* San Rafael, CA: The Autodesk Foundation.

Tyler, R. W. (1949). *Basic principles of curriculum and instruction.* Chicago: University of Chicago Press.

Urquiola, M., D. Stern, I. Horn, C. Dornsife, B. Chi, L. Williams, D. Merritt, K. L. Hughes, & T. R. Bailey (1997, November). *School to work, college and career: A review of policy, practice, and results 1993–1997.* Berkeley: National Center for Research in Vocational Education, University of California at Berkeley.

U.S. Department of Education, National Center for Education Statistics (1999). *The condition of education 2000.* (NCES 1999–022). Washington, D.C.: U.S. Government Printing Office.

——— (2000a). *The condition of education 2000.* (NCES 2000–602). Washington, D.C.: U.S. Government Printing Office.

——— (2000b). *Vocational education in the United States: Toward the year 2000.* (NCES 2000–029). Washington, D.C.: U.S. Government Printing Office.

——— (2000c). *NAEP 1998 civics: Report card highlights.* (NCES 2000–460). Washington, D.C.: U.S. Government Printing Office.

U.S. 103d Congress. (1994). *The School-to-Work Opportunities Act.* Washington, D.C.: Author.

Vallas, S. P. (1990). The concept of skill: A critical review. *Work and Occupations, 17*(4), 379–398.

Vickers, M. (1995). Employer participation in school-to-work programs: The changing situation in Europe. In T. R. Bailey, Ed., *Learning to work: Employer involvement in school-to-work transition programs* (pp. 26–44). Washington, D.C.: The Brookings Institution.

Vo, C. D. (1997, January). Not for my child. *Techniques, 71*(9), 20–23.

Vygotsky, L. S. (1978). *Mind in society: The development of higher psychological processes.* (M. Cole, V. John-Steiner, S. Scribner, & E. Souberman, Eds.) Cambridge: Harvard University Press.

Wallace, A. F. B. (1970). *Culture and personality.* New York: Random House.

Walsh, W. B., & S. H. Osipow, Eds. (1988). *Career decision making.* Hillsdale, NJ: Lawrence Erlbaum Associates.

Watson, J. B. (1998). *Behaviorism.* New York: Transaction Publications.

Wenger, E. (1998). *Communities of practice: Learning, meaning and identity.* New York: Cambridge University Press.

Wertsch, J. V. (1981). *The concept of activity in Soviet psychology.* Armonk, NY: M. E. Sharpe.

——— (1985). *Vygotsky and the social formation of mind.* Cambridge: Harvard University Press.

Westchester Institute for Human Services Research, Inc. (1997, December). *New York State school-to-work opportunities system interim evaluation report: Lessons learned.* New York: Author.

Wieler, S. S., & T. R. Bailey (1997). Going to scale: Employer participation in school-to-work programs at LaGuardia Community College. *Educational Evaluation and Policy Analysis, 19*(2), 123–140.

William T. Grant Foundation on Work, Family, and Citizenship (1988, November). *The forgotten half: Pathways to success for America's youth and young families.* Washington, D.C.: Author.

Zeldin, S., & I. Charner (1996). *School-to-work opportunities through the lens of youth development.* Washington, D.C.: National Institute for Work and Learning, Academy for Educational Development.

Zemsky, R. (1994). *What employers want: Employer perspectives on youth, the youth labor market, and prospects for a national system of youth apprenticeships.* Philadelphia: National Center on the Educational Quality of the Workforce, University of Pennsylvania.

Index

245

Lightning Source UK Ltd.
Milton Keynes UK
UKOW03f0019100517

300758UK00002B/88/P